Praise for *The P*

"This timely book takes on ....nd
the influence of its false m.............................y (not only on
or coming from an isolated group of Christians, nor solely under the influence of Donald Trump). For anyone concerned with building a social
justice movement rooted in moral and constitutional values of equality,
truth, peace, and abundance for all, Cooper-White's diagnosis of and
prescription for such religious nationalism—rooted in psychology, history, and Christian understandings—is a must-read!"

—Liz Theoharis, director, Kairos Center for Religions,
Rights, and Social Justice, New York, and cochair, Poor
People's Campaign: A National Call for Moral Revival

"This brilliant and courageous book is the best treatment we have of the
complex psychological dynamics of the dangerous Christian nationalist
movement in America. Without losing sight of the humanity of even the
most racist and sexist of our fellow citizens, Pamela Cooper-White has
given us a powerful and needed text on just how close we are to losing
our democratic experiment."

—Cornel West, Union Theological Seminary

"In *The Psychology of Christian Nationalism: Why People Are Drawn In and
How to Talk Across the Divide*, Pamela Cooper-White turns our attention
to one of the greatest tasks facing the United States—how to stop the
tide of 'Christian' nationalism in this country. Hers is a nuanced analysis
of the rise of Christian nationalism and its relationship to white supremacy. Cooper-White's contribution to these concerns is her adeptness at
navigating the psychological, conscious, and unconscious motivations
that lead many to identify with sociopolitical groups that, on the face of
it, contradict their religious and moral values. A practical theologian to
the core, Cooper-White brings a tempered hope while arguing that the
way forward is the simultaneous pursuit of justice and love."

—Phillis Isabella Sheppard, E. Rhodes and Leona B. Carpenter
Associate Professor of Religion, Psychology, and Culture,
Vanderbilt Divinity School, and director of the James Lawson
Institute for the Research and Study of Nonviolent Movements

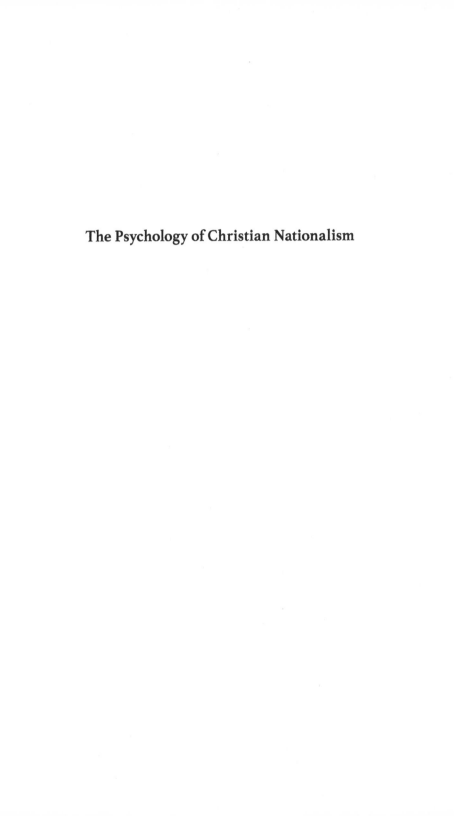

The Psychology of Christian Nationalism

Pamela Cooper-White

The Psychology
of
Christian
Nationalism

Why People Are Drawn In and
How to Talk Across the Divide

Fortress Press
Minneapolis

Contents

Introduction

On January 6, 2021, a violent mob attacked the US Capitol in a shocking effort to stop the certification of the election of Joe Biden as the next president of the United States. Members of the crowd, many heavily armed and wearing military fatigues, broke through the inadequately guarded barricades, scaled the walls of Congress like commando fighters, and shattered doors and windows to enter the Capitol building. The marauders paraded into the building, destroying property that many Americans revere as sacred symbols of democracy; threatened the lives of members of Congress, their staff members, and journalists; and killed and severely injured members of a poorly equipped and overwhelmed Capitol police force.

Horrifying video footage shows the extreme violence against a Washington, DC, Metropolitan police officer who was crushed in a doorway.[1] One zealous insurgent, Ashli Babbitt, an Air Force veteran, was shot and killed by a guard as she attempted to climb through a broken glass-paneled door into the Capitol where members of Congress were being evacuated.[2] Months later, Donald Trump called her "an innocent, wonderful, incredible woman, a military woman" on Fox News, leading to a right-wing upswell of outrage and sympathy for Babbitt as a martyr.[3] Three other people died in the mayhem that day, including a Georgia woman who was crushed to death during the rampage, two men who died of a heart attack and a stroke, and a police officer who was beaten and attacked with mace. Thus far, four police officers have ended their own lives since January 6, 2021, due to the trauma of the attack. One hundred fifty were injured.[4]

This mob was made up of disparate but equally enraged groups who coalesced around a false belief that Donald Trump had actually won reelection as US president and that the election of Joe Biden, which Congress was about to certify that day, was the result of widespread electoral fraud and manipulation of the "facts" by the liberal media and the machinations of an elite left-wing "deep state." They were spurred on by a rally near the

White House where Trump told the crowd, "We fight like hell and if you don't fight like hell, you're not going to have a country anymore."[5] He exhorted the crowd to take matters into their own hands and "stop the steal," instigating the violent insurrection.

Vice President Mike Pence and members of Congress pleaded with the president to send in the National Guard, but it was hours before they were deployed. Trump was observed pacing his quarters in the White House, appearing to take pleasure in the rioting as it unfolded. Pence became a special target of the mob after he refused to stop the routine certification of Biden's election. "Hang Mike Pence!" became a war cry among the insurgents as Secret Service agents hustled him and his family into hiding. Despite Pence's loyalty throughout Trump's term in office, the former president did nothing to defend his own vice president.

Even as investigations continue probing the many causal factors, organizers, and funders of the insurrection, there is no doubt this antidemocratic protest was planned and fueled by Trump and his minions across the country. The mob's size and fever testify to the impact of conservative social media, such as the right-wing site Parler, and other platforms then or still operating openly or underground.

Despite warnings received weeks in advance, national security and local police forces did not take nearly adequate precautions. Many commentators concluded that this was because the expected protest crowd would be largely white and was therefore perceived as posing minimal threat. By contrast, massive police presence and violent "crowd-control" measures were unleashed against mostly peaceful participants in earlier Black Lives Matter protests.

The Jericho March

Deep in the midst of this preplanning and the violence on the day itself was a loose-knit band of religiously motivated individuals who see themselves as devout Christians. Some of the most disturbing images on display among the crowds during the attack on the Capitol were the numerous flags and signs with Jesus Saves in bold letters and other Christian symbols proudly displayed alongside numerous blatantly racist ones. Those included a Confederate flag paraded through the halls of Congress and a noose hanging from a makeshift scaffold on the Capitol grounds. A photo that went viral showed a group of men before a seven- or eight-foot-high cross—one with his forehead pressed against it in apparent fervent prayer. One group among the mob called themselves a Jericho March called by God to bring down the walls of government.

Most surprising for many of us was Trump's appeal for millions of Christians whose stated values of honesty, fidelity in marriage, humility, charitable speech about others, and a general spirit of dignity are the exact opposite of all that the former president represents. That appeal goes far beyond certain conservative policies (about abortion, immigration, welfare, etc.) that Trump championed, which are congruent with the convictions of a broad swath of Christianity often called "evangelical." He tapped into a deep and broad reservoir that has been accumulating for decades, a large pool of Christians who feel they are being persecuted and are called by God to rise up and defend themselves against their enemies. And not only must they regain equal footing with others in society, many believe, but they must dominate and be in control—and all this in the blessed name of Jesus. This growing movement of desperate would-be Christian conquerors is referred to as *Christian nationalism.*

These beliefs, and a movement that includes a large segment of the population, will not go away just because there is now a different US president. A large percentage of Republicans—about two-thirds—continue to believe in the myth of widespread fraud in the 2020 election (as do about one-third of all Americans), and "14% of the American public say they will never accept Biden as president, including 3 in 10 (29%) Republicans and Republican-leaners."[6]

Lest we conclude this is a fringe movement involving only a small percentage of American Christians, statistics show that nearly two-thirds of mainline Protestants[7]—members of the supposedly "liberal" Christian denominations—and two-thirds of all Christians taken together[8] agree with many of the sentiments, if not the actions, of the thousands who marched on the Capitol on January 6.

Many of us have neighbors, friends, and family members who agree at least with the beliefs underlying that violent insurgence. Based on the best research to date, approximately half (52%) of Americans either fully embrace or lean toward the main tenets of Christian nationalism.[9] While this percentage decreased slightly between 2007 and 2017, Christian nationalists have become more visible and vocal since Trump's election in 2016. The 2001 attack on the World Trade Center (9/11) caused an upsurge in nationalistic fervor and a parallel rise in Islamophobia. A rise in anti-immigrant sentiment was stimulated by Trump's false "birther" accusations against President Obama during the 2008 and 2012 election cycles and subsequent rants against Mexicans as rapists and drug dealers in his own election campaign in 2015.[10]

A Pivotal Moment

I believe we are at a pivotal moment in the American experiment of democracy and also in the very character of American Christianity. As the research for this book will demonstrate, the very term *Christian nationalism* really means white nationalism and stands opposed to virtually everything Jesus taught, as embodied in the gospel vision of justice and compassion. Grim prognosticators have spun out scenarios in which the insurrection on January 6 was just the beginning of an attempt to undermine the core of democracy—the will of the people—and have forecast further attempts at a right-wing coup. Christians, both mainline and evangelical, have begun to sound the alarm about the dangers of Christian nationalism and its corrosive effects on Christian faith from within the church. Which way the nation will go depends on the answers to several questions.

Among those who got caught up in the fervor of the January 6 insurrection, and those who chose to overlook the extremes of the Trump presidency for the sake of particular conservative goals, many may now be asking themselves (at least in private), How do I know whom to believe after all? And many more people, especially those who were not on the side of the insurgents on that day (and were never swayed by the right wing's allegations of rampant fraud), are asking, How can people—even those we consider to be good people—get caught up in such a web of lies? Moreover, how can Christians who claim to believe in Jesus's Abba-God of love, mercy, justice, and truth participate in a movement that is founded in lies fueled by white supremacy and masculinism—and even far-fetched conspiracy theories—and remain inured to its fundamental propensity toward violence?

It is beyond the scope of this book to answer all these questions definitively. But as a pastoral psychotherapist and a historian of psychoanalysis and religion, it is my hope that insights from the study of group psychology might provide some, at least partial answer by illuminating both the conscious and unconscious allure of such mass movements as Christian nationalism and how people can become convinced of false and even delusional beliefs—especially under the influence of a charismatic, high-profile leader. Moreover, by understanding some of these dynamics, how might it be possible (if ever) to talk with people who have gone down the rabbit hole of brainwashing and irrational groupthink? Can dialogue help draw them back out? If so, how? Is it ever possible to "talk sense" into someone who has come to believe dangerous untruths that, if not addressed, can harm us all? Does reasoned argumentation ever convince someone to change extreme views implanted by a magnetic leader of an emotionally driven movement, especially one saturated with religious rhetoric and reinforced daily by the peer pressure of fellow adherents? When—and how and in what context—might dialogue be fruitful, and when does it simply raise the other person's closely guarded defenses and reinforce polarization?

As I have taught and written for many years, persons are internally complex and multiple. As humans, we have many conflicting ideas and impulses, both conscious and unconscious, which come to the fore in different contexts and relationships.[11] Each of us is comprised of a unique mixture of personal history, sense of identity, personality, emotions, moral impulses, and perceptions of reality. Our attempts to engage in serious efforts to change hearts and minds will therefore also be many and varied, depending on whom we are addressing at any moment, and will always begin with our own efforts to clarify our own values.

The goal of this book is to understand who comprises the Christian nationalist movement and what they believe, to examine how people get drawn into this movement and the overlapping groups that made up the stew of insurrectionists on January 6 (and before and after), and to offer some recommendations for how to "triage" when it is possible to have a meaningful conversation with Christian nationalist-leaning people (including our own neighbors, friends, and family members), when to go slow, and when not to attempt dialogue but to turn our energy and focus on wider efforts at social justice reform and education.

The Chapters

Chapter 1 lays the groundwork by exploring the following questions: What is Christian nationalism, and where does it fit in the larger picture of both white nationalism and Christian evangelicalism? What are the central tenets of this movement, and who are the Americans who subscribe to Christian nationalist beliefs? In what ways have certain segments of American Christianity become captivated by right-wing extremism and the role of both overt (violent) and covert (in denial, quietly complicit, or cynically expedient) white supremacy, xenophobia, antisemitism, sexism, and heterosexism in bringing disparate hate groups together in the last decade under a banner of "Jesus and Trump"? The best sociological research makes it clear that white supremacy and patriarchy are at the root of Christian nationalism and that white evangelical Christians are disproportionately responsible for perpetuating it—although many other Christians bear significant accountability as well.

Chapter 2 examines why and how people get hooked by demagogues and conspiracy theories. This chapter will explore the psychology behind people's vulnerability to being captivated by false teachings (both religious and political) and their personal investment in maintaining these beliefs. The chapter will include both conscious and unconscious motives for following Christian nationalism. Historian Richard Hofstadter's observations on the paranoid style in American politics[12] and the corrosive impact of economic inequality, class resentment, defensive masculinity, and "white rage" as America becomes increasingly multiracial and multicultural will be examined as conscious motivations. Unconscious motivations to be explored include the unconscious pull of group psychology (going back to Sigmund Freud's prescient analysis of groups in 1921) and parallels between Christian nationalism and cultlike groups and their leaders in their power to make and amplify false claims (including the role of both mainstream and social media).

Taking all of this into consideration, chapter 3 will directly address the question of how to talk across the extreme religious and political divide that has emerged from these trends in white, right-wing Christian nationalism. Is it even possible, and if so, how? And if not, what to do instead? Relative power and privilege and the importance of context and timing are important considerations. The purpose of this chapter is by no means to create a false "peace" forged by mainstream appeals to "unity," which effectively deny racism and other forms of oppression, and silence movements for justice and social change. A "triage" approach is recommended to discern when fruitful conversation might be possible and when it should not be attempted. When dialogue is not possible, engagement in education and activism is recommended. When fruitful conversation may be possible, how do we "put a toe in the water?" And when it does seem possible, some recommendations are offered, beginning with relationship building and including some specific approaches to respectful listening and responding that will keep the door open to genuine exchange and (perhaps even) changing minds.

A brief conclusion at the end of chapter 3 will encourage readers to take the long view, recognizing that the work of bringing people together and drawing people away from toxic Christian nationalist ideas—ever mindful of the necessity of the work of antiracism, immigration reform, interreligious openness, and true gender equality—is multigenerational work. It will take patience, persistence, self-reflection, and a willingness to listen—without either "cancelling" others or sacrificing core principles of justice by simply bypassing difficult conversations.

Acknowledgments

This book would not have been written without the invitation from Will Bergkamp at Fortress Press after attending a panel discussion of the Psychology, Culture and Religion (PCR) program unit of the American Academy of Religion, where I discussed the role of unconscious group dynamics in relation to the 2016 election presidential election. My colleagues in PCR, the Society for Pastoral Theology (SPT), and the International Association for Spiritual Care (IASC) and so many students past and present have been my constant inspiration and intellectual dialogue partners over more than three decades!

I am also deeply indebted to my faculty and staff colleagues and my brilliant students at Union Theological Seminary in New York for their thoughtful and challenging writings and conversations about theology, race, politics, and the role of religion in the work of social justice. I cannot name everyone on this long list, but I especially want to thank Timothy Adkins-Jones, Mary Boys, Eileen Campbell-Reed, Cláudio Carvalhaes, the late James Cone, Fred Davie, Gary Dorrien, Kelly Brown Douglas, Vanessa Hutchinson, Serene Jones, Daisy Machado, Sandra Montes, Su Yon Pak, Jerusha Rhodes, Kosen Greg Snyder, Mychal Springer, John Thatamanil, Lisa Thompson, and Cornel West for inspiring me and "calling me in"[13] when needed and the entire academic office team who are my Union "family." I would not be the same person I am today without these and many more in the Union community who encourage me to bring my best self every day. Special thanks to Nicole Mirando, my right-hand sounding board, astute endnote editor, and work partner every day. Gratitude is also due to the leaders and congregation at the Cathedral of St. John the Divine in New York City, who have been a source of collegiality, hope, and encouragement throughout the writing of this book.

Most of all, I am deeply indebted to my two very best research colleagues and companions—my spouse Rev. Michael Cooper-White, DD, and our daughter Dr. Macrina Cooper Dieffenbach. Chapter 1 was especially strengthened by Michael's reporting for the *Gettysburg Times* (in our colleague Bill Moyer's words, "one of the last great dailies in the US") on Pennsylvania State Senator Doug Mastriano and the January 6 Capitol insurrection and his close reading and insightful suggestions throughout several rounds of editing; chapter 3 was much enhanced by Macrina's award-winning doctoral research in the UCLA Department of Social Psychology on the neuropsychology of dialogue across polarized partisan attitudes and her work as a researcher at the nonprofit organization OpenMind.[14]

Finally, special appreciation also goes to my colleagues at the Rossing Center for Education and Dialogue in Jerusalem—especially Sarah Bernstein, Ruchama Weiss, and Ophir Yarden—for demonstrating that dialogue for peace and reconciliation is still possible even in the most violently polarized contexts and for expanding my imagination about how to talk even across a very great religious and political divide.

I

Unholy Alliances

Christian Nationalism, White Supremacy, and the Pursuit of Power

On January 6, 2021, in Washington, DC, the mob that grew in intensity over the day was really an amalgamation of various groups, their rage stoked just hours earlier by then president Trump's incendiary words at a rally near the White House. Many took the president's encouragement to fight ("if you don't fight like hell, you're not going to have a country anymore"[1]) as the direct order they had been awaiting. Before he even finished his speech, they began pouring along Constitution Avenue and the National Mall toward the Capitol building. Militant right-wing white-supremacist groups—the Proud Boys, the Three Percenters, and the Oath Keepers—mingled with the QAnon conspiracy followers and their bare-chested, fur-and-Viking-horn-clad "Shaman," Jacob Chansley. The mostly white crowd wore Trump's signature red MAGA (Make America Great Again) baseball caps and carried signs that read Stop the Steal along with overtly racist symbols, including a makeshift scaffold with a noose (eventually targeted at Vice President Mike Pence for his refusal to stop the certification of the election) and a prominent display of Confederate flags.

This insurrection was not a spontaneous igniting of outrage among right-wing Trump supporters (much less a "normal tourist visit"[2]) or a peaceful crowd full of love, as Trump later described it.[3] Nor was it a riot inspired by Antifa, as right-wing Republicans later tried to assert.[4] The multiple groups that made up the mass of protesters on the National Mall and at the Capitol had organized on mainstream and right-wing social media[5] and in local meetings and rallies since even before the 2020 presidential election, when Trump predicted that if he lost, it could only be due to widespread electoral fraud and the machinations of a left-wing elitist "deep state."[6] The insurrection, while it might have picked up additional participants as the day went on, was no impulsive uprising. It had been carefully planned.

Throughout this motley mob, Christian symbols were ever present on flags that read "Trump Is My President / Jesus Is My Savior"[7] and "God, Guns, and Guts Made America—Let's Keep All Three."[8] There were hand-written signs with quotes from scripture, a cross fastened atop an American flag,[9] and most striking of all, an at least eight- or nine-foot wooden cross. In a now viral Getty image,[10] one man presses his head to the cross, while another with a bowed head puts his hand on the first man's shoulder in a posture of fervent prayer. Standing close behind them are a white woman and someone wearing a cap emblazoned with "President Trump." A blurred figure of another man wearing a green camo cap raises his arms toward the cross with a look of prayerful reverence. The people in this photo were likely members of the self-named Jericho March, a subgroup of Christian nationalists.[11] This too was carefully organized in advance. As Emma Green wrote just two days after the event for the *Atlantic*, the Jericho March was "a gathering of Christians to 'pray, march, fast, and rally for election integrity.' After calling on God to 'save the republic' during rallies at state capitals and in D.C. over the past two months, the marchers returned to Washington with flourish. On the National Mall, one man waved the flag of Israel above a sign begging passersby to SAY YES TO JESUS. 'Shout if you love Jesus' someone yelled, and the crowd cheered. 'Shout if you love Trump!' The crowd cheered louder."[12]

Green cites the Jericho March's website,[13] which draws an analogy between the group's perceived corruption within the US government and the biblical story of corruption in the city of Jericho, brought down by Joshua's triumphal march around the city's walls. These marchers, a subset of Christian nationalists in the crowd more generally, imitated Joshua and his priests by blowing shofars[14] and decrying "the darkness of election fraud."[15] As Green describes it, "Defiant masses literally broke down the walls of government, some believing they were marching under Jesus' banner to implement God's will to keep Trump in the White House."[16] At the sound of a shofar on January 6, one woman sang, "Peace in the name of Jesus. The blood of Jesus covering this place."[17] Once in the Capitol building, one man shouted, "Jesus Christ, we invoke your name!"[18] In the Senate chamber, Jacob Chansley sat in the vice president's chair and prayed at length through a bullhorn, thanking a "divine, omniscient, omnipotent and omnipresent creator God" for "filling this chamber with patriots that love you and that love Christ . . . to exercise our rights, to allow us to send a message to all the tyrants, the communists and the globalists that this is our nation, not theirs."[19]

Throughout the crowd were banners proclaiming "Jesus saves," and in one photo, a smiling woman holds a large poster showing Warner Sallman's famous (and blond) "Head of Christ"[20] wearing a MAGA hat.[21] She stands with three additional protesters, two white women in Trump caps, and a Black man in a MAGA hat with a flag reading "Patriot vs. . . . ybody." Another woman in the same photo holds a banner with the QAnon slogan "Trust the Plan." Elsewhere, people were brandishing Christian flags alongside American flags and banners with more insider meanings such as the Israeli flag (signaling the Christian "dispensationalist" belief that the End of Times cannot arrive until the state of Israel is securely established with Jerusalem as the place prepared for Jesus to return to begin his reign);[22] a lone pine tree with the motto "An Appeal to Heaven,"[23] and the coiled rattlesnake on a yellow field with the motto "Don't Tread on Me" (adopted from the American Revolution by right-wing activists).[24] White supremacists wore T-shirts displaying a red Crusader cross.[25] Throughout the Capitol that day, the most deeply irrational and violent impulses of Christian nationalism were on full display, with ample amounts of paranoia, rage, and apocalyptic fervor.

"Colonel on the Call": An Example from Middle America

Early the same day, back in central Pennsylvania, a previously little known but highly ambitious state senator and military veteran, Doug Mastriano, and his wife, Rebecca, a Christian lay minister,[26] were rounding up "Mastriano's army"[27] to board buses and join the Jericho March as part of the pro-Trump rally in DC, where Mastriano was slated to be a speaker.[28] Mastriano, who frequently touts his military service, appears regularly on a right-wing talk radio program called "Colonel on the Call."

The January 6 event was posted on Mastriano's Facebook page, "Doug Mastriano Fighting for Freedom," and the trip was financed by unused contributions to his state senate campaign.[29] This gathering of Mastriano's faithful was preceded on November 25 by an unofficial "hearing" where Trump's former attorney and staunch ally Rudy Giuliani was a featured speaker, and Trump himself made a virtual appearance on screen before citizens were invited to "testify" before a nine-member all-white panel of state senators regarding their personal accounts of alleged electoral fraud in Pennsylvania.[30] Previously, Mastriano had posed for photo ops on the steps of the Pennsylvania State Capitol with white men in Hawai'ian shirts (the dress code of the Boogaloo Bois militia) and others in military fatigues carrying automatic weapons. He has promoted legislation to mandate teaching the Bible in public schools and allow adoption agencies to reject same-sex couples as parents.[31]

Throughout this time period, he continued to rally his faithful most evenings with rambling "fireside chats" on Facebook, in which he promoted his motto (lifted out of context from the Gospel of John), "Walk as Free People." Citing Covid-19 as a "fake crisis" and protective mandates as governmental overreach and an incursion on personal freedom—with particular animus reserved for Democratic Governor Tom Wolf and his publicly transgender health secretary, Rachel Levine[32]—Mastriano echoed Trump's downplaying of the pandemic. He openly encouraged people to refuse to wear masks or abide by other preventive mandates (this in spite of his own Covid-19 infection, detected during a White House visit in November). He claimed to have talked by phone with Trump "at least a dozen times" prior to January 6 and to have his special confidence.[33]

Mastriano's participation in the Capitol riot was met with predictably polarized responses in his home state. Several state legislators, appalled that he had participated in the mass gathering, called for his resignation from office.[34] Mastriano shrugged off these demands, saying (in spite of photographs to the contrary), "As soon as I saw that things were getting weird, I left." And, "When it was apparent that this was no longer a peaceful protest, my wife and I left the area." But he later stated in an interview that he witnessed the first assaults on the Capitol.[35] He has an ardent following of alt-right Republicans in central Pennsylvania and on January 8, 2022, announced his statewide campaign for the 2022 gubernatorial election, claiming that Trump encouraged him to run. He remains defiant and denies revelations about his role in trying to subvert the 2020 presidential election and a call by the US Senate Judiciary Committee to investigate his role in the January 6 insurrection.[36]

Mastriano is just one figure among many who fused political ambition with a ceaseless spewing of right-wing rhetoric in the months and weeks leading up to January 6. But he represents a style of Christian nationalist oratory common among such political figures—employing charismatic, cunning, self-styled (pseudo-) historical and theological expertise, and a virtually paranoid populist fearmongering, all laced with a sermonic evangelical fervor.

How Pervasive Is Christian Nationalism?

What exactly is "Christian nationalism"? And where does it fit within the broader picture of Christian faith in America and within the American nationalist movement? What are the core beliefs that characterize it, and what are some of the other overlapping belief systems to which many Christian nationalists also adhere?

In the most comprehensive research study conducted to date, sociologists of religion Andrew Whitehead and Samuel Perry mined two large-scale statistical studies of social attitudes and beliefs (together comprising over 16,000 respondents).[37] They conducted follow-up interviews and site observations to arrive at the following definition: "Simply put, *Christian nationalism is a cultural framework—a collection of myths, traditions, symbols, narratives and value systems—that idealizes and advocates a fusion of Christianity with American civic life*."[38] Elaborating in their conclusion, they write that Christian nationalism

> paradoxically holds America as sacred in God's sight while viewing its future as tenuous and bleak. It valorizes conquests in America's name and blood shed in its defense. It idealizes relations marked by clear (metaphorical or physical) boundaries and hierarchies both in the private and public realms. It baptizes authoritarian rule. It justifies the preservation of order with righteous violence, whether that be carried out by police against deserving (minority) criminals, by border agents against presumptively dangerous (minority) immigrants, or by citizen "good guys" with guns against rampaging "bad guys" with guns. And it glorifies the patriarchal, heterosexual family as not only God's biblical standard, but the cornerstone of all thriving civilizations.[39]

These authors created a "Christian nationalism scale"[40] to measure respondents' attitudes toward six statements on a scale of "strongly agree" to "strongly disagree":[41]

1. "The federal government should declare the United States a Christian nation."

2. "The federal government should advocate Christian values."
3. "The federal government should enforce strict separation of church and state." (reverse coded[42]—i.e., counting percentages who "disagree" rather than "agree.")
4. "The federal government should allow the display of religious symbols in public spaces."
5. "The success of the United States is part of God's plan."
6. "The federal government should allow prayer in public schools."

As noted in the introduction, their findings overall were that slightly more than half (52%) of *all* Americans agree with all or most of these statements. The vast majority of these (88%) are white evangelical Protestants, and *among* white evangelical Protestants, nearly 80% agree.[43] Non-Christians (including Jews, members of other religious traditions, and those with no affiliation) made up three-quarters of those Americans who disagree with Christian nationalist statements.[44]

Further breaking Christian nationalist–leaning Americans into two categories named by Whitehead and Perry—the "ambassadors" (those I would call the "True Believers," who *wholly* agreed with the six statements) and the "accommodators" (those I would call "soft" Christian nationalists, who leaned toward agreeing with the statements but were unsure or disagreed with some items[45])—reveals more about geographical and denominational trends.

Over half (55%) of "ambassadors"—the True Believers who want to spread Christian nationalist ideas—identify as evangelical Protestants (versus 19% of Catholics, 11% of mainline Protestants, and 10% of Black Protestants). Half live in the South, with one-third living in rural areas.[46] Slightly more than half are women, and 70% are white.[47] They are the oldest group surveyed (mid-50s on average, a good 10 years older on average than those who disagreed with Christian nationalist ideas).

Among the "accommodators" or "soft" Christian nationalists, white evangelical Protestants and Roman Catholics take the lead about equally (roughly one-third each), versus about 13% of mainline Protestants and about 9% of Black Church Protestants. Again, women slightly outnumber men. Found mostly in towns and suburbs, this group is slightly more diverse but still significantly white at almost two-thirds.[48] Similar to the True Believers, over one-third live in the South, but a large proportion also lives in the Midwest (comprising almost another one-third).

Regarding the Christian-ness of Christian nationalism, those who wholly endorse Christian nationalist ideas "overwhelmingly believe in God without any doubts at all and hold the Bible in high esteem" (94%, irrespective of actual church attendance [to be discussed further later],[49] and more than three-quarters of "soft" Christian nationalists[50])—over twice those who mostly resist Christian nationalism, and seven times more than those who reject it entirely.[51] Well over two-thirds of Christian nationalists endorse a literalist interpretation of the Bible, versus only about 5% of those who oppose Christian nationalist ideas; 85% believe the Bible to be the inspired word of God (over twice the number of those in opposition).[52]

The authors are careful to point out that "evangelicalism" and "white conservative Protestantism" are not synonymous with Christian nationalism. All these statistics can be somewhat confusing. To clarify, these percentages represent the proportions of Americans who agree or disagree with Christian nationalism and the breakdown of those Americans into various demographic and geographical groups. When we flip the analysis to look instead at the percentages of Christian nationalists *within* each of the faith groups, fully two-thirds of *all Christian groups taken together* agree with Christian nationalist ideas.[53] This includes nearly 80% of evangelical Christians (81% of whom also voted for Donald Trump in the 2016 presidential election)[54] followed by over two-thirds of Black Protestants (a perhaps surprising figure that will be nuanced later), almost two-thirds of mainline Protestants, and slightly over half of all Catholics.[55]

How Christian *Is Christian Nationalism?*

It should be noted that the statistics cited represent survey respondents who *self*-identify as belonging to certain Christian traditions. But this does not necessarily reflect their theologies or frequencies of formal religious observance. More is at work here than merely religious affiliation. As Whitehead and Perry summarize, "The 'Christianity' of Christian nationalism represents something more than religion. . . . It includes assumptions of nativism,[56] white supremacy, patriarchy, and heteronormativity, along with divine sanction for authoritarian control and militarism. It is as ethnic and political as it is religious. Understood in this light, Christian nationalism contends that America has been and should always be distinctively 'Christian' . . . from top to bottom—in its self-identity, interpretations of its own history, sacred symbols, cherished values, and public policies—and it aims to keep it that way."[57]

In my own perusing of books and articles by prominent pastors identified with Christian nationalism and videos of sermons and patriotic Christian revivals (e.g., on the Trinity Broadcasting Network [TBN]),[58] it has become clear that, as Whitehead and Perry also observe, "Christian nationalism is rarely concerned with instituting explicitly 'Christ-like' policies, or even policies reflecting New Testament ethics at all."[59]

A central theological belief running through numerous sermons and speeches is that America has fallen away from its original special blessing from God because of its decline into sinful beliefs and ways of living. Perceived contributors to this decline include the hot-button political issues of atheism, "socialism" (interpreted as too-big liberal government that espouses a "welfare state" and overruns individual freedom and self-governance), full and equal authority for women both in the workplace and in the home (including the #MeToo movement against sexual harassment and the fight for abortion rights), and equal rights for LGBTQ persons. Assaults on women's human rights, cloaked in biblical language, are intended to stave off perceived threats to a "proper" (i.e., heteronormative) gender hierarchy. As historian Kristin Kobes Du Mez writes in her book *Jesus and John Wayne*, "Today, what it means to be a 'conservative evangelical' is as much about culture as it is about theology. . . . The evangelical political resurgence of the 1970s coalesced around a potent mix of 'family values' politics, but family values were always intertwined with ideas about sex, power, race, and nation. . . . The reassertion of white patriarchy was central to the new 'family values' politics, and by the end of the 1970s, the defense of patriarchal power had emerged as an evangelical distinctive."[60]

While there are many examples of this culture war, one of the most insidious examples—because it is couched so carefully in terms of Christian child-rearing and the sanctity of family—is James Dobson's decades-long, widespread campaign to maintain and promote the traditional patriarchal family as the core of Christian values. Dobson's organization Focus on the Family has become the go-to resource for evangelical Christian couples and families, with guidance on "tough love" in marriage, strict parenting, and "God-honoring" sex (always within marriage).[61] Its online newspaper, Daily Citizen, is designed to be Christians' "most trustworthy news source . . . giving you timely and relevant analysis of current events and cultural trends—all from a biblical worldview." "Daily

Citizen features regular stories on the intersection of religion, patriotism, and family life."[62] As part of its cultural arm, the Focus on the Family website also features numerous posts proclaiming a strong "pro-life" stance against abortion.[63]

The antiabortion movement received a boost when Donald Trump flip-flopped his own position from "pro-choice" to "pro-life" and appointed the "born-again evangelical Catholic"[64] Mike Pence as his vice-presidential running mate. Many decided at that time to back Trump despite his personal immorality, comparing him to the biblical King Cyrus as restorer of the nation's religious freedom.[65] In particular, they recognized that Trump, with Pence's encouragement, would appoint like-minded justices to the Supreme Court (and many other judges to lower federal courts as well[66])—a prediction that proved true during Trump's administration and is beginning to show its impact as states press the courts to rule on ever more draconian antiabortion legislation.[67]

Called to Redeem God's Chosen Nation

A common belief among Christian nationalists that there has been a woeful decline of America's standing in the world because of growing degeneracy motivates their urgent call to restore the nation to its original godliness. Convinced that God has withdrawn "His" blessing from America because, like the ancient Israelites, "she" has fallen into profligacy and a violation of God's laws, Christian nationalists are desperate to redeem the times. Imitating the Old Testament prophets, Christian nationalist preachers exhort the faithful in sermons and song to "take this nation back"—even by force if required.[68]

The United States was founded, according to this group, by evangelical Christians—a belief based on a misreading of the more complex history of the framing of the Constitution.[69] Dominionism, which gained prominence in the 1970s, '80s, and '90s, is a belief that, given the growing secularism of America, Christians are commanded by God and the Bible to take over the government of the United States.[70] *A Christian Manifesto* was published in 1981 by Francis Schaeffer, one of the founders of the conservative splinter denomination the Presbyterian Church in America. The book was a best seller among evangelical Christians (with over 65 million copies sold, and read by as many as one in every five Americans[71]). It strongly influenced subsequent dominionist thinkers, including Tim

LaHaye—known best as the author of the Left Behind series.[72] LaHaye began his political activism in the John Birch Society[73] and later became a founding board member of the Moral Majority[74] and cofounder and first president of the more secretive behind-the-scenes right-wing Republican organization the Council for National Policy.[75]

Previously, most evangelicals were "*post*millennialists," believing that a 1,000-year reign of Christ would only begin after the apocalypse and that until then, humanity is living in an interim time awaiting this day of salvation. Dominionists, on the other hand, are "*pre*millennialists," who believe fervently that it is their Christian duty to "take dominion" in order *bring about* this Second Coming of Christ—essentially by establishing the United States as a Christian theocracy.[76] Dominionists do not all agree on specific strategies or theological fine points, but one group in particular, called Christian Reconstructionists, took as their manual a 1973 book by R. J. Rushdoony, *The Institutes of Biblical Law* (claiming status as a direct heir to the reformer John Calvin by alluding to Calvin's *Institutes of Christian Religion*). Rushdoony advocated for the establishment of Old Testament Law to guide all aspects of American life—including the execution of a whole range of sinners ranging from blasphemers and heretics to females guilty of "unchastity before marriage" and homosexuals (the favorite target of the Christian right). Adulterers would be publicly stoned.[77]

In 1987, the prolific extremist author George Grant, who, like Rushdoony, endorses capital punishment for homosexuality,[78] wrote the book *The Changing of the Guard: Biblical Principles for Political Action.* Grant stated plainly, "It is dominion we are after. Not just a voice . . . Not just influence . . . Not just equal time . . . World conquest. That's what Christ has commissioned us to accomplish. We must win the world with the power of the Gospel. And we must never settle for anything less. . . . Thus, Christian politics has as its primary intent the conquest of the land—of men, families, institutions, bureaucracies, courts, and governments for the Kingdom of Christ."[79]

Four years later, Pat Robertson, the founder of the Christian Coalition, published the book *The New World Order.*[80] This conspiracy-filled screed echoes much of the early 20th century *Protocols of the Elders of Zion*—a fraudulent, supposedly ancient document distributed widely by the Nazis that purported to reveal secret plans of Jews to take over the world.[81] Robertson's presidential run in 1988 brought dominionism to the national political stage. American historian Garry Wills wrote of Robertson and his movement, "'Dominion theologians,' as they are called, lay great emphasis on Genesis 1:26–27, where God tells Adam to assume dominion over the animate and inanimate world. When man fell, his control over creation was forfeited; but the saved, who are restored by baptism, can claim again the rights given Adam. Thus the true inheritors and custodians of this world are Christians who can 'name it and claim it' by divine right."[82]

While this extreme version of Christian theocracy thankfully seems to have declined from its heyday in the 1990s, its premillennialist and *theonomic* character (i.e., a desire for Christian rules for morality—as dominionists define them—to govern American society) has trickled down into Christian nationalist ideology and is still popular in many white evangelical circles. Katherine Stewart, a journalist who has long studied the religious right in America, reports, "Gary North [an influential Reconstructionist at the time of Reagan's ascendency] . . . observed that 'the ideas of the Reconstructionists have penetrated into Protestant circles that for the most part are unaware of the original sources of the theological ideas that are beginning to transform them. Then again, perhaps some of those circles are aware of the sources and their ideas after all. 'Though we hide their books under the bed, we read them just the same,' as one person put it."[83]

Several Christian-identified law schools' curricula are now explicitly designed to produce an ever-increasing cadre of graduates to strengthen the influence of conservative Christian beliefs on the practice of law, the judiciary, and the national government. As one example, "Liberty University School of Law exists to equip future leaders in law with a superior legal education in fidelity to the Christian faith expressed through the Holy Scriptures."[84] The university's Center for Law and Government has as its mission, "To influence public policy in America and to celebrate and spread conservative ideals."[85] While such schools carefully avoid extremist statements in their public advertising, the influence of Christian dominionism is clearly present in their mission statements and curricula.

Fanatical Beliefs and Antidemocratic Rhetoric

Although it has faded somewhat from public discourse in the last decade or so, the aims of dominionism are not so different from the views of a majority of Christian nationalists today. As sociologist Rebecca

Barrett-Fox has observed, by providing the most radical example, dominionism gives Christian nationalists a certain kind of cover.[86] It allows more mainstream-appearing conservative Christians the ability to claim that their own views are not extreme but belong to a traditionally conservative, even moderate, position in American political life. The gradual infiltration of premillennialist ideas also helps explain a number of ancillary beliefs and practices that are common among Christian nationalists.

First, there is the commendation of evangelicals for President Trump's strong alliance with Israeli Prime Minister Benjamin Netanyahu and the relocation of the US embassy on May 14, 2018, to the ancient and heavily symbolic city of Jerusalem from the more secular city of Tel Aviv.[87] Religion scholar Diana Butler Bass wrote that day that this action not only was a political maneuver but also was throwing a bone to his evangelical Christian base, "reminding them that he, Donald J. Trump, is pressing biblical history forward to its conclusion and that he is God's man in the unfolding of these last days."[88]

For conservative Christians (including then vice president Mike Pence), the United States' staunchly maintained support for the nation of Israel has very little to do with a sense of common cause with Jews (antisemitism, in fact, is rife among Christian nationalists[89]). In fact, "Zionist Christians" expect that Jews will be "left behind" at the time of the Rapture unless they accept the messiahship of Jesus.[90] The affinity with Israel is, rather, a combination of patriotic desire for a stronghold against Arab (i.e., Muslim) nations in the Middle East and access to their oil, together with a conviction based on a literalist reading of the Old Testament that the Second Coming of Christ cannot occur until the Jews are restored to their land and the second temple is rebuilt in Jerusalem.[91]

A second consequence of this emphasis on an imminent day of reckoning—even as soon as the year 2050[92] (not coincidentally the date the US Census Bureau first predicted the end of a white majority in the United States![93])—is that the need to address climate change and global warming is essentially moot[94] because the planet as we now know it will be consumed in a fiery day of God's punishment, ushering in a glorious new reign of Christ over a "new heaven and a new earth" (Rev 21:1; Isa 65:17).

Most ominous for the future of American democracy are dominionists' and many other Christian nationalists' convictions that God is uniquely on their side. A secretive Christian right legislative campaign, "Project Blitz," sponsored by the Congressional Prayer Caucus and other right-wing Christian groups since 2017, has pushed its "model bills" through state legislatures and has an annual "Playbook" for dominionist legislative strategy.[95] As the events of January 6, 2021, made evident, some will stop at nothing, including violence, to exert their partisan political will. Subsequent events—including widespread Republican efforts to curtail voting rights and stage ludicrous "election audits" in Arizona and Pennsylvania—confirm the antidemocratic impulses of True Believers, who deeply resist conceding defeats of the candidates or legislative initiatives they fervently support on the grounds of electoral fraud (regardless of the actual evidence of such).

Dissenting Evangelicals and Black Church Protestants

One important caveat is that not all those who agree with just some Christian nationalist sentiments should be painted with the same brush. As noted earlier, Christian nationalism is not synonymous with evangelical Protestantism[96] and certainly not with Black Church Protestants or with Christianity as a whole. Regarding self-identified evangelical Christians, although more than three-quarters *do* agree (wholly or in large part) with Christian nationalist ideas, this means that nearly a quarter do not. This significant minority swims against the tide, often at considerable personal cost.

Ron Sider, professor emeritus at Palmer Theological Seminary and founder of Evangelicals for Social Action, published an edited volume during the summer before the 2020 presidential election entitled *The Spiritual Danger of Donald Trump: 30 Evangelical Christians on Justice, Truth, and Moral Integrity*, challenging Christian nationalism and white evangelical support for Trump's political agenda.[97] Shortly after the January 6 insurrection, the Baptist Joint Committee joined together with an ecumenical group of faith leaders to issue a statement entitled "Christians against Christian Nationalism." The online multidenominational statement, signed by over 2,300 leaders who are theologically both conservative and liberal, begins,

> As Christians, our faith teaches us everyone is created in God's image and commands us to love one another. As Americans, we value our system of government and the good that can be accomplished in our constitutional democracy. Today, we are concerned about a persistent threat to both our religious communities and our

democracy—Christian nationalism. Christian nationalism seeks to merge Christian and American identities, distorting both the Christian faith and America's constitutional democracy. Christian nationalism demands Christianity be privileged by the State and implies that to be a good American, one must be Christian. It often overlaps with and provides cover for white supremacy and racial subjugation. We reject this damaging political ideology and invite our Christian brothers and sisters to join us in opposing this threat to our faith and to our nation.[98]

The same group has now created a free three-part curriculum, "Responding to Christian Nationalism,"[99] for use by churches and small groups who want "to take a deeper dive into the dangers of this ideology." The curriculum was launched with a webinar entitled "Democracy and Faith under Siege: Responding to Christian Nationalism" in July 2021.[100] The National Council of Churches also published a policy statement, "The Dangers of Christian Nationalism in the United States."[101]

Another public statement, "Say 'No' to Christian Nationalism: Condemning Christian Nationalism's Role in the January 6 Insurrection," was signed by over 1,000 clergy, religious educators, and others, including Jim Wallis, founder of Sojourners; Ron Sider; Jacqui Lewis, senior pastor of Middle Collegiate Church in New York City; and renowned biblical scholar Walter Brueggemann, professor emeritus at Columbia Theological Seminary. Their letter states, "We recognize the damage done by radicalized Christian Nationalism in the world, the church, and in the lives of individuals and communities. . . . We urge faith leaders to engage pastorally with those who support or sympathize with these groups, and make it clear that our churches are not neutral about these matters: we are on the side of democracy, equality for all people, antiracism, and the common good of all people."[102]

Regarding members of the Black Church, one surprising finding from Whitehead and Perry's research is that over two-thirds of Black Protestants scored positively on some aspects of the Christian nationalist scale (although less than half were *wholly* in agreement).[103] To keep this in perspective, when weighing the relative numbers of white evangelicals and Black Protestants, the Black Church accounts for only a little over 10% of *all* Christian nationalist supporters.[104] Only 13% of all African American respondents (and one-third of all persons of color combined, including

Blacks, Asian Americans, Latinx, and others), versus fully two-thirds of whites, support Christian nationalist ideas.[105]

Moreover, the *meaning* Black Protestants make of Christian nationalism stands in stark contrast to the goals of white Christian nationalists. Whitehead and Perry caution, "In some instances being a member of a racial minority group and holding certain Christian nationalist views is associated with having a stronger *racial justice orientation*, the exact opposite of what we see in white Americans. In this sense it is the *intersection* of race and Christian nationalism that matters."[106] Du Mez likewise observes, "Although white evangelicals and black Protestants share similar views on a number of theological and moral issues, the black Protestant tradition was suffused with a prophetic theology that clashed with white evangelicals' Christian nationalism."[107] Nor does agreeing with certain Christian nationalist statements on a large-scale survey mean that African Americans align with conservative white evangelicalism. In Du Mez's words, "Black Christians have long resisted embracing the evangelical label because it is clear to them that there is more to evangelicalism than straightforward statements of belief. Survey data indicate that *on nearly every social and political issue, black Protestants apply their faith in ways that run counter to white evangelicalism.* The differences may be rooted not just in experience but in the faith itself; in practice, the seemingly neutral 'evangelical distinctives' turn out to be culturally and racially specific. . . . To many black Christians [after the 2016 election], evangelicalism had become a 'white religious brand.'"[108]

Black Christians are also more willing than whites to openly acknowledge the political implications and potential impact of their beliefs. Black clergy and congregations were at the forefront of the civil rights movement in the 1960s and continue to be leaders in fighting for equal rights for people of color and the poor today.[109] Rev. Freddy Haynes, pastor of Friendship West, a Black megachurch in Dallas, said to journalist Kamau Bell on CNN, "Honestly, I think it's kind of fake to say you're *not* political because you can't even go to the bathroom without it being political. So then why not have some kind of influence that is, you know, *righteous*? For me, it's like I can't help but be involved in politics because I'm pushing for justice."[110]

Today, one of the leading prophetic movements for justice is the Poor People's Campaign (deliberately named to carry on the work of Martin Luther King Jr.'s call for a "revolution of values" in America), co-led by

Rev. Dr. William J. Barber II[111] and Rev. Dr. Liz Theoharis.[112] The group has as its mission to "confront the interlocking evils of systemic racism, poverty, ecological devastation, militarism and the war economy, and the distorted moral narrative of religious nationalism."[113] The campaign has staged nationwide vigils and nonviolent "moral marches," worked on voting rights and legislative initiatives, testified before the Congressional Budget Committee, released a "Poor People's Moral Budget," and disseminated carefully researched public information to dispel myths about poverty and racism.[114]

For prophetic evangelicals like Barber, such public critique of the status quo comes with a price. Journalist and Lutheran pastor Angela Denker notes that "Barber's presence [as a speaker at the 2016 Democratic National Convention] limits his influence within evangelical Christianity. Merely because he is tied to Democratic politicians and causes, many on the right in Evangelicalism refuse to work with him or join forces."[115]

To summarize, then, how Christian is (predominantly white) Christian nationalism? At the end of the day, it is scarcely Christian in any theological or practical sense of the term. It is not primarily characterized not by devotion to the gospel mandates of love, care, and justice as found in the teachings of Jesus but rather by a social and political goal of restoring the United States to a fictional origin as a "Christian nation" and a not-at-all-fictional origin in white, masculinist supremacy. A number of scholars have pointed out that it is right-wing politicians who have gradually hijacked evangelical Christianity, drawing it away from the gospel and substituting an aggressive, patriarchal, and white-supremacist narrative based on a few highly selective passages of scripture emphasizing a wrathful God and a final Day of Judgment. But many conservative Christians, especially evangelicals, also welcomed them in with open arms, recognizing the potential this alliance would have for increasing their power over American government and society.

Stewart has written, "For too long now America's Christian nationalist movement has been misunderstood and underestimated. Most Americans continue to see it as a cultural movement centered on a set of social issues such as abortion and same-sex marriage, preoccupied with symbolic conflicts over monuments and prayers. But the religious right has become more focused and powerful even as it is arguably less representative. It is not a social or cultural movement. It is a political movement, and its ultimate goal is power."[116]

Rather than faithful witness to the Christian gospel, predominantly white Christian nationalism is, therefore, a highly and often explicitly political movement that aligns itself with conservative—mostly right-wing and racist—convictions, social attitudes, and legislative objectives. Cloaked in a narrow interpretation of a misrepresented Bible and "Judeo-Christian" tradition (*Judeo-Christian* itself being a misnomer and an example of viewing Judaism and Jewish scripture exclusively through a Christian lens[117]), it misuses Christianity rather than being shaped by it.

The Nationalism in Christian Nationalism

What is *nationalism* per se, and how does it differ from patriotism? Patriotism, simply stated, is love for one's country, while nationalism is the identification of that country with a historically dominant ethnic, cultural, and/or religious group and a fierce loyalty to protecting that national identity.

Rev. Elizabeth Eaton, presiding bishop of the mainline Evangelical Lutheran Church in America (ELCA),[118] stated in a panel shortly after the Capitol insurrection that it is "very important to understand we are not condemning being patriotic."[119] Rev. Walter Kim, president of the National Association of Evangelicals, stated, "Certainly I love our country, and as the son of immigrant parents I am deeply grateful for the hope this nation represents. But as a Christian, my highest allegiance is to Christ."[120] Baptist pastor Dean Inserra, a member of the Ethics and Religious Liberty Commission of the Southern Baptist Convention and a critic of Donald Trump on social media, told Denker in an interview, "In this linking of nationalism and Christianity, we are forgetting about the message of Jesus. . . . When we do that, we have a gospel distortion. . . . We have to be Christian first. If you are American first, Jesus will be at odds with you. Patriotism is not a fruit of the Spirit. It's idolatry on the Fourth of July."[121] Russell Moore, former leader of the Southern Baptist Convention's public policy division (who left the denomination in early 2021, accusing it of ignoring sexual abuse in its ranks),[122] said on the same panel noted earlier that he was enraged by the sight of a Jesus Saves sign at the riot, calling it "not only dangerous and *unpatriotic* but also blasphemous, presenting a picture of the gospel of Jesus Christ that isn't the gospel and is instead its reverse."[123]

Historian Hans Kohn notes that nationalism is an ideology that emphasizes loyalty to the nation above all other "individual or group interests."[124]

For many centuries, as Kohn describes, this was not the case. People gave their loyalty to other entities, such as "the city-state, the feudal fief and its lord, the dynastic state, the religious group, or the sect. The nation-state was nonexistent during the greater part of history, and for a very long time it was not even regarded as an ideal. In the first 15 centuries of the Common Era, the idea was the universal world-state, not loyalty to any separate political entity."

Kohn cites the multiregional and multicultural example of the ancient Roman Empire, which was not ethnic in identity but organized under the umbrella of imperial rule. Historians know that religion was often used by emperors as a unifying force to bind individual nations together under their authority, as in the examples of the 1,000-year Roman rule, Constantine's embrace of Christianity in the 4th century, Charlemagne's adoption of Christianity in the 9th, and the Habsburgs' imposition of Catholicism over much of Europe from the 13th to the early 20th century. According to Kohn, it was in the 18th century, propelled by revolutionary movements with their emphasis on individual rights, that nationality came to be entwined with particular "peoples" as opposed to a collection of ethnically diverse subjects living under one imperial rule. Individuals came to define themselves by their ethnic and cultural traditions, language, food, dress, and other distinguishing beliefs and practices; attachment to a particular geography; and religion.

Nationalism, thus, as opposed to basic affection for one's native land, became unwavering and uncritical loyalty to a particular ethnic, cultural, and often religious group, identified with the nation as a sacred "homeland" (over and above other groups' claims to the same geography). In this way, nationalism becomes indistinguishable over time from xenophobia (literally, "fear of the stranger," "the foreigner," "the other," or simply, "fear of the strange"). Yale University sociologist of religion Philip Gorski describes how "Christian nationalism is heavily connected to the idea of blood, both as a sign of ethno-national purity (thus the connection between Christian nationalism, racism, and xenophobia) but also in terms of bloody conquest and sacrifice in war."[125] It means promoting exclusive rights to govern and to enforce conservative white Christians' values and beliefs over all "others'," even to the point of violence, both internally (as in relation to other ethnic groups) and externally in the form of limiting the rights of immigrants—even the right of entry to refugees and asylum seekers fleeing persecution under international law.

Wars have continually broken out in modern times across the globe over territorial and political disputes among feuding ethnic groups and tribes.[126] In the United States and much of Europe and the (post-Brexit) United Kingdom, nationalism continues to express itself in xenophobic assertions of white Protestant or Catholic "culture." The emotional appeal to one's native land as sacred ground for a particular group of people has been used by nationalist groups throughout the 20th and 21st centuries to stir up isolationism, protectionism, and wars of conquest (as in the case of Hitler and his genocidal appeal to the "true" Germans of the "*Heimat*" ["homeland"]). The language of "homeland"—as in George W. Bush's introduction of a new federal agency after 9/11, the Department of Homeland Security—can often be understood as supporting a xenophobic agenda.

Historically, populist, anti-immigration, and nativist sentiments have also been strongest in rural regions of many nations (as is the case in the United States). At least in part, this is because of a populist distrust of urban, more formally educated, and wealthy "elites" who are seen to be threatening "ordinary people's" power to define who is a true American—this despite the fact that the vast majority of such "ruling elites" in government and business are also white and Protestant. Here class differences come strongly into play alongside racism—and as Isabel Wilkerson has persuasively argued, race and class in America are closely intertwined.[127]

In terms of formal education, the vast majority (83%) of Whitehead and Perry's "ambassadors"—the fully convinced Christian nationalists—have not graduated from college. Annually, they earn the least among all Americans, with a majority at $50,000 per household or less and many below the poverty line.[128] Accommodators, or "soft" Christian nationalists, have somewhat higher rates of formal education (about one-third have college degrees or beyond), but slightly over half still earn only $50,000 or less, with almost a quarter below $20,000—which in most cases also amounts to living in poverty.[129]

Christian Nationalism and White Supremacy Go Hand in Glove

As Wilkerson describes in her book *Caste*, one of the animating racist beliefs among poorer whites is their place above African Americans in the social hierarchy,[130] sometimes expressed by the saying, "Well, I may be poor, but at least I'm not Black."[131] Given the lower income level of most Christian nationalists, this observation leads directly to the intersection between Christian nationalism and white supremacy. White supremacy and racism are by no means confined to low-income citizens, however. To be clear, I am using the term *white supremacy* here not only to refer to organized white extremist hate groups often referred to as *white supremacists*, including by their own self-definition.[132] Rather, I adhere to a broader definition that encompasses both conscious and unconscious assumptions ingrained in American society that white people are superior to all other people. This obviously impacts whites and persons of color differently, manifesting as unearned (and often denied) privilege for whites and internalized feelings of lowered self-esteem for persons of color.

Although "race" is itself a pseudoscientific construct developed in the 19th century in Europe to justify racist categorization of human beings and who gets to "pass," or be considered white, is somewhat fluid over time, race still functions as a potent *social* reality, resulting in ongoing systemic oppression of people of color throughout society. It is "a political, economic and cultural system in which whites overwhelmingly control power and material resources, conscious and unconscious ideas of white superiority and entitlement are widespread, and relations of white dominance and non-white subordination are daily reenacted across a broad array of institutions and social settings."[133]

In the United States, the main threat to a white Protestant national identity has shifted demographically with waves of immigration over time. Discriminatory and exclusionary attitudes and policies targeted the Irish, southern and eastern Europeans,[134] and all non-Protestants (including Catholics,[135] Italians,[136] Greeks,[137] and Jews[138]) throughout the 19th and 20th centuries, some of which—especially antisemitism[139]—persist and have increased since the Trump presidency. One of the January 6 insurrectionists was photographed wearing a "Camp Auschwitz" sweatshirt.[140] A worldwide fight against communism (which also carried the specter of atheism), from postwar McCarthyism through the Republican presidencies of Richard Nixon, Ronald Reagan, and George Bush Sr. (as well as Democrats John F. Kennedy Jr. and Lyndon B. Johnson!), shaped foreign policy well into the 1980s and beyond, perpetuating Americans' fear and hatred of Soviets, Chinese, North Koreans, Cubans, and many others in Central and South America, as well as Jews, who historically continued to be linked with socialism and communism throughout the 20th century. Some of the focus of white Christian dread shifted after 9/11 to Islamophobia and the false equation of all Muslims and Arabs with terrorists bent on destroying democracy and the United States and Israel in particular.[141] Anti-immigrant fears and anti-Muslim profiling often swept up many Christian Arabs in the same net during the so-called Muslim travel ban established by the Trump administration.

Underlying the xenophobia directed toward immigrants stand America's original sins: First was the subjugation and murder of the Native Americans on whose land the United States was first established by invasion, theft, and genocide—both literally and culturally (to "kill the Indian, save the man").[142] As white settlers/invaders moved westward, the term *Manifest Destiny* was another use of religious rhetoric (and misuse of scripture) to justify territorial conquest of Native American lands. Along with white settlers came the violence of chattel slavery, also justified by biblical references and later, the brutal exploitation of Asian immigrants. These traumatic and ongoing legacies of racial violence continue to this day throughout the United States, undergirded by the still ingrained and prevalent (even if denied) belief in white supremacy.

Southern Christian nationalists in particular frequently conflate a (defensive) pride in Southern antebellum white "culture" with evangelical Christianity. Nostalgia for the "Old South" and the myth (or even "the Religion"[143]) of the "Lost Cause" of the Confederacy—promoted by clergy immediately after the end of the Civil War[144]—remains strong to this day. In the words of historian W. Scott Poole, the Lost Cause was a racist "aesthetic . . . steeped in romanticism and evangelicalism" that "replaced slavery as the cohesive narrative of the south."[145] It also perpetuated a cultural myth of the pure and innocent Southern white woman, coupled with a belief in Black inferiority and propensity for male sexual violence, which obligates white Christian gentlemen to defend the women's honor—taking the law into their own hands when necessary.

This Lost Cause mythology undergirded white opposition to Reconstruction[146]—including the rise of the Ku Klux Klan and the wave of lynchings and cross burnings that terrorized Southern Blacks well into the 20th century (and still haunt people of color to this day). It gave rise to Jim Crow and its traumatic legacy today of mass incarceration[147] and police shootings of unarmed Black men. It lives on as a doctrine of racial inferiority that underpins white supremacy and anti-Black violence carried forward—covertly and overtly—by Christian nationalists today. As journalist Clint Smith wrote just months after the January 6 insurrection,

> The myth was an attempt to recast the Confederacy as something predicated on family and heritage rather than what it was: a traitorous effort to extend the bondage of millions of Black people. The myth asserts that the Civil War was fought by honorable men protecting their communities, and not about slavery at all. . . . For so many [Confederate sympathizers], history isn't the story of what actually happened; it is just the story they want to believe. It is not a public story we all share, but an intimate one, passed down like an heirloom. . . . Confederate history is family history, history as eulogy, in which loyalty takes precedence over truth.[148]

To this day, devotees of the Confederate battle flag literally "whitewash" its meaning by saying it symbolizes Southern "heritage, not hate."[149] Similar arguments are made against removing Confederate statues and monuments as a protest against "erasing history."[150]

Shortly after the deadly 2015 mass shooting at Bethel African Methodist Episcopal Church in Charleston, South Carolina, by white supremacist Dylann Roof (who not incidentally drew a figure of a white Jesus in his journal),[151] there were numerous calls for the removal of Confederate flags and monuments across the South. In a number of cases, they have succeeded, notably the removal of a statue of Robert E. Lee from the North Carolina State House lawn. The recent removal of the statue of Robert E. Lee in Richmond, Virginia, the former Confederate capitol, was a victory for antiracist activists and an emotional moment for African Americans in that city and beyond.[152]

Living part-time for over two decades in Gettysburg, Pennsylvania, I have witnessed these arguments firsthand. Following the horrific "Mother Bethel" shooting, the Gettysburg Lutheran Seminary[153] announced a policy that it would no longer allow the Confederate battle flag to be displayed, including in Gettysburg battle reenactments on its campus—only in the Seminary Ridge Museum as a historical artifact.[154] In the wake of this decision, hate mail poured in against seminary leaders, including a vicious curse in a letter from an irate woman: "If you do this, may your children get sick and die!"[155]

Denominational Resolutions Often Lack Teeth

In response to overt challenges to their ethos of white supremacy, many Christian denominations have voted for resolutions and public pronouncements that they believe will undo their historic complicity with slavery and quell accusations of continuing racism. As a case example, take the Southern Baptist Convention's (SBC) 1995 resolution repenting for its own history of racism and acknowledgment of its role in slavery.[156] At a gathering for the 150th anniversary of the predominantly white (85%[157]) denomination's founding, the resolution passed by a show of hands and received a standing ovation from the 20,000 delegates, called "messengers."[158]

A Black pastor, Gary Frost, elected to second vice president, responded, "On behalf of my black brothers and sisters, we accept your apology, and we extend to you our forgiveness in the name of our Lord and savior, Jesus Christ." Robert Jones, the founding director of the Public Religion Research Institute (PRRI), describes this resolution as "a piece of contrived cultural theater that seemed to imply that a kind of magical reconciliation had instantaneously occurred." As Jones puts it, "Enthusiastic applause erupted from the overwhelmingly white delegates. In less than fifteen minutes, 150 years of Southern Baptist white supremacy was seemingly absolved."[159]

The moment received laudatory media attention, but many Black Church leaders were not convinced. Jones cites Rev. Arlee Griffin Jr., pastor of a Brooklyn megachurch, who took a wait-and-see attitude, telling the religion reporter of the *New York Times*, Gustav Niebuhr, "It is only when one's request for forgiveness is reflected in a change of attitude and actions that the victim can then believe that the request for forgiveness is authentic." Griffin, himself a member of the more liberal Progressive National Baptist denomination and its official historian, called for the SBC to put its money where its mouth was by "substantially racially integrat[ing] its leadership, agency staffs, and seminary faculties." Southern Baptists, he said, "have a long history and legacy to overcome."[160]

Anthea Butler, in her book *White Evangelical Racism*, notes the SBC's acknowledgment of its founding during the Civil War as a schismatic church that endorsed slavery on biblical grounds. But reading more deeply, she also critiques the statement for its failure to examine "the theologies that were constructed around slaveholding or the perpetuation of those beliefs in the denomination. It does a great job at apologizing, but it does not address restitution for the structural racism within the denomination."[161]

The Baptists' focus on individual faith and freedom is reflective of a broader key theme for both Christian nationalists and conservative politicians. Religious freedom has begun to be used as a seemingly patriotic cover for the freedom to discriminate in the name of religion.[162] This element of Christian nationalism is undergirded by a selective "originalist" reading of the US Constitution that attempts to discern the founders' "original" intent. It uses this interpretive lens, for example, to emphasize individuals' freedom to own guns, to limit the rights of LGBTQ persons, to refuse to receive a Covid-19 vaccine, and in general, to keep white, at least nominally Protestant men in charge of both the nation and the social order. It aligns with political conservatism in that its strategy is to maximize personal rights and states' rights over the federal government's role (an echo and a whitewashing of the Confederate agenda during the Civil War). This claim of God-given freedom to justify refusing to wear masks during the Covid-19 pandemic rings hollow, however, in light of recent draconian state laws aimed to abolish abortion and the precedent of *Roe v. Wade*.

Sociologists Michael Emerson and Christian Smith have pinpointed that this emphasis on personal freedoms is reinforced by evangelical Christian theology's focus on individual sin and salvation, personal piety, the importance of the individual's decision to accept Christ as Lord and Savior, and the ethical focus on proper personal relationships rather than larger systemic or structural issues.[163] They write, "Individualism is very American, but the type of individualism and the ferocity with which it is held distinguishes white evangelicals from others. . . . Unlike progressives, for them individuals exist independent of structures and institutions, have freewill, and are individually accountable for their own actions. . . . The roots of this individualist tradition run deep, dating back to shortly after the sixteenth-century Reformation, extending to much of the Free Church tradition, flowering in America's frontier awakenings and revivals, and maturing in spiritual pietism and anti-Social Gospel fundamentalism."[164]

Jones further notes that a theology of individual responsibility for salvation by accepting Jesus as Lord and Savior and an emphasis on personal racial reconciliation rather than societal justice have allowed generations of white evangelical Christians—especially as led by the SBC—to evade responsibility for institutional and systemic racism (and other social injustices in general).[165] This emphasis on individual sin and confession conforms well with political conservatism, including right-wing extremism, in that it reserves these individual rights primarily for white men of at least moderate economic status and is threatened by liberal-to-progressive calls for empowerment and equal rights for the poor, women, LGBTQ persons, and all people of color.

Anthea Butler amplifies, "Sin for evangelicals is always personal, not corporate, and God is always available to forgive deserving individuals, especially, it seems, if the sinner is a white man. The sin of racism, too, can be swept away with an event or a confession. Rarely do evangelicals admit to a need for restitution."[166]

The SBC attempted to update its initial pronouncement on racism at subsequent conventions. Nevertheless, the evangelical focus on individual sin—and wariness to acknowledge systemic racism—persists in more recent official statements. Although in 2012 Rev. Fred Luter was elected first Black president of the SBC (whether as a genuine gesture of diversity or a token move), there has been little change in the tone of SBC declarations. Efforts to introduce tougher resolutions in 2017 (which explicitly decried "nationalism") and 2019 (which held up critical race theory [CRT] as worthy of exploration) were suppressed by SBC authorities. The most conservative wing of the SBC denounced CRT as contradicting the primacy of scripture as the "first, last, and sufficient authority with regard to how the Church seeks to redress social ills."[167]

The 2019 Convention erupted into controversy, and the resulting resolution was "refined" by a resolutions committee made up of "very conservative men and women . . . who made all kinds of qualifications in their address of CRT . . . not embracing CRT but simply carving out a safe lane for someone—not in the pulpit, not in the elementary school or high school, but in the safety of a college or similar classroom—to help build cultural competencies in future pastors and church leaders that there are some things that can be systemic racism."[168] It passed, mainly by incorporating both opposing points of view in an almost line-by-line oscillation. Its original author, Pastor Stephen Feinstein, told a Religious News Service reporter that he regretted having proposed it at all, given the ensuing conflict that erupted.[169] The resolution does not define CRT or note its origins in legal scholarship (just as many of its most vocal opponents cannot do so either). It merely notes, almost as an aside, that "evangelical scholars who affirm the authority and sufficiency of Scripture have employed *selective insights* from critical race theory and intersectionality to understand multifaceted social dynamics."[170]

Despite its insipid doublespeak, just that much of a nod toward CRT elicited loud disapproval. In the following year, the council of the six Southern Baptist seminary presidents issued a full-throated dissent, declaring that while they condemn "racism in any form . . . affirmation of Critical Race Theory, Intersectionality, and any version of Critical Theory is incompatible with the Baptist Faith and Message."[171] The statement was initiated by Al Mohler,[172] who years earlier led a fight to restore the most conservative stance of the SBC (including rescinding the ordination of women to the ministry).[173] Pointing to the "2000 Baptist Faith and Message" document as their guide, the presidents continued with a statement that CRT and intersectionality are "antithetical to the Bible and the only Gospel that can save."[174]

Four Black pastors immediately and publicly announced their departure from the Southern Baptist Convention, raising questions for many African Americans within the SBC about whether they could continue in the denomination.[175] Pastor Seth Martin of Minneapolis was outraged that the SBC should have even had this debate so soon after the murder of George Floyd (two blocks from where he himself lives) and in the face of the resulting racial protest movement.[176] Rev. William Dwight McKissic, author of the original, much stronger 2017 resolution draft, said that while he was still considering whether to leave, "the reaction has been like a bomb exploded."[177]

The SBC had gained significant numbers of Black member churches in the past two decades—a 43% increase by their own reckoning—although the vast majority of African American Christians belong to historically Black churches.[178] Some Black pastors who had joined the SBC to take advantage of its financial resources, including pension funds and missionary support, are now reconsidering their affiliation. The denomination's response to confronting racism, tepid at best and overtly racist at worst, is threatening to erode that gain in membership as a matter of integrity for Black members and for many white members—especially younger ones[179]—as well. The SBC's membership peaked in 2006 (16.3 million) and as of May 2021 had declined by 2.3 million—although the denomination also gained 588 congregations.[180] It remains the largest Protestant denomination in the United States today.

Further wrangling at the 2021 SBC convention produced yet another resolution, which in essence rolled back the stance of the SBC on racism to its tepid apology in 1995 and renounced critical race theory altogether, stating, "We reject any theory or worldview that finds the ultimate identity of human beings in ethnicity or in any other group dynamic, and . . . we reject any theory or worldview that sees the primary problem of humanity as anything other than sin against God and the ultimate solution as anything other than redemption found in Jesus Christ, and . . . we, therefore reject any theory or worldview that denies that racism, oppression, or discrimination is rooted, ultimately, in anything other than sin."[181]

This Baptist walk-back fits a pattern Jones has called "the white Christian shuffle—a subtle two-steps-forward-one-step-back pattern of lamenting past sins in great detail, even admitting that they have had pernicious effects, but then ultimately denying that their legacy requires reparative or costly actions in the present."[182] The protracted negotiating and hand-wringing that produced both the SBC's 2019 and 2021 resolutions on critical race theory perfectly fit his description of this "sophisticated rhetorical strategy that emphasizes lament and apology, expects absolution and reconciliation, but gives scant attention to questions of justice, repair, or accountability."[183] Any effort to confront racism as something structural and embedded in church and society—rather than a matter of individual sin—was effectively quashed.

None of this description of the SBC's conflicts should be taken to let other predominantly white denominations, including the more liberal mainline denominations, off the hook. Other conservative churches also fell in line with the alt-right, from the 1980s and beyond. *All* majority white churches must confront racism and their own racist histories and practices, both internally and through advocacy in the wider society. Predominantly white denominations need to move beyond anodyne resolutions to meaningful action in the public arena. And as Jones has observed, the more liberal, even progressive attitudes and resolutions voted by mainline Christian leadership are not necessarily "an accurate barometer of the influence of white supremacy among white Christians sitting in the pews."[184] But to the extent that the SBC, as the largest white Christian evangelical denomination in the United States, is a bellwether of conservative Christians' failure to confront racism in any meaningful way, it is clear that evangelical Christianity still has a long way to go—and right-wing forces still wield considerable power in tamping down more justice-oriented initiatives from within.

Conclusion: Christian Nationalism, White Supremacy, and Power Politics

Whitehead and Perry found in their study that "far and away the strongest predictor of Christian nationalism is identifying oneself with *political conservatism*," with the next three predictors being variations on being "Bible-believing."[185] Summing up the political power agenda that underlies the Christian nationalist movement, they write, "Christian nationalism is significant because calls to 'take America back for God' are not primarily about mobilizing the faithful toward religious ends. Some social scientists have argued that when evangelicals appeal to the religious heritage of the United States or work toward privileging Christianity in the public sphere they are focused on encouraging greater religious devotion. We disagree. They are instead seeking to retain or gain power in the public sphere—whether political, social, or religious. Christian nationalism, is therefore, ultimately about privilege."[186] Citing Gorski, they declare Christian nationalism to be "a political idolatry dressed up as religious orthodoxy."[187]

If roughly one-half of all Americans, two-thirds of all *Christian* Americans, and nearly 80% of evangelical Christians align at least in part with the beliefs associated most strongly with Christian nationalism, then it is not surprising that right-wing conservative views have gained such traction among white Christians and among white evangelical Christians in particular, especially in the regions where Christian nationalists are most prominent—the South and, to a lesser extent, the Midwest.

As historians and journalists have pointed out, this trend did not just emerge as a backlash to the election of the first Black president, Barack Obama, although Donald Trump, in his rise as a provocative national figure (riding on the wave of popularity of his TV show *The Apprentice*), had already planted the false "birther" suspicion that Obama was not an American citizen. As a candidate in 2015 and eventually as sitting president, Trump's rhetoric, with his overt racist comments and more covert "dog whistles" aimed at his alt-right base, gave permission to his followers to let festering hate speech back out into the open. Charles Yu, author of *Interior Chinatown*,[188] describes the situation as follows:

> Trump did not initiate the fiction in which so many Americans have been living these past four years. He inherited the script. But Trump . . . rebooted the series, freshening it up for the social-media age. In doing

so, he gave the narrative a new reach. Trump was both a co-writer and the main character, mouthpiece and vessel, at times the generator of the story, at other times the perfect avatar for enacting his audience's fantasies. In the process, Trump has conjured what all worldbuilders desire: audience participation. At some crucial tipping point, the best fictional worlds become collaborative acts. By way of collective effort and belief, a fantasy achieves a kind of mental sovereignty . . . a universe that people never have to leave, one they prefer to reality.[189]

There had been a steady creep of hate and divisiveness for decades before Trump exploited and gained benefit from the rise in numbers of right-wing Christian nationalists. The ground had been prepared by waves of nationalism going back to the 1970s, fertilized under Ronald Reagan's feel-good Americanism and that vision of the "shining city on a hill." It has been cultivated by extreme right-wing political operatives ever since.[190] The shock of the 9/11 attacks did not cause but became the excuse for more overt expressions of hate, officially sanctioned torture, and ongoing violations of civil rights (such as the continued imprisonment of 39 suspected Muslim terrorists at Guantánamo without trial as of this writing[191]).

As noted earlier, the US Census Bureau predicted in 2004 that by the year 2050, the United States would no longer be majority white, and in 2008, they revised this estimate downward to the year 2042.[192] This demographic shift is deeply threatening to 21st-century nationalists, for whom it represents not only a possible leveling of economic status and governing power but an assault on their own "American way of life," which is equated with white Protestant values, norms, and cultural traditions.

At times, this is couched in the seemingly gentler terms of "family values" rather than admitting to the racism of white Christianity directly. But as Du Mez writes, even though "evangelical opposition to government-mandated racial integration predated anti-abortion activism by several years,"[193] the language of family values is often simply a cover for white supremacy: "For evangelicals, family values politics were deeply intertwined with racial politics, and both were connected to evangelicals' understanding of the nation and its role on the global stage."[194]

As John McCain's vice-presidential running mate, Sarah Palin, put it most blatantly in an October 2008 speech attacking Obama: "I'm afraid if he wins, the Blacks will take over. He's not a Christian! This is a Christian nation!"[195] Although they lost the election to Barack Obama and Joe

Biden, McCain and Palin won 74% of the white evangelical vote in 2008.[196] Anthea Butler's words should awaken us all: "Why have evangelicals and their leadership made choices over and over again to embrace racism? Because it is what has allowed them to attain and hold political power. . . . Evangelicals hold old resentments about being shut out of the power-broker positions mainline Protestants traditionally held in America. . . . What evangelicals did have was whiteness, and whiteness eventually gave them power, social and political."[197]

Butler documents the backlash from Christian evangelicals after 9/11 intensified by the Democrats' choice of Barack Obama as the first Black presidential candidate. Sarah Palin embodied the rise of a new, explicitly racist, populist Christian nationalism. Butler quotes Palin's rant in an October 2008 campaign speech: "[Barack Obama] is not a man who sees America as you and I see it. We see an America of exceptionalism." Butler continues, "The response was electric. . . . Her reference to Obama not seeing America as 'you and I do' tapped into a deep well of nationalistic racial pride. . . . Palin began to make a populist racialized turn—one that brought out the pitchforks."[198]

Evangelical Christians piled on, further encouraged by the appearance of the Tea Party on the political scene with its agenda of cutting social safety nets and its rhetoric of "real Americans and patriots,"[199] alongside the continuing popularity of James Dobson's conservative pseudopsychological parenting advice through Focus on the Family and his Family Research Council and, perhaps above all, the rise of Fox News in the cable TV arena with its lead conspiracy theorist Glenn Beck.[200] Butler summarizes, "Both Palin and Beck, in their roles as America's evangelists of the right, promoted a pseudo-religion of guns, God, and flag that closely resembled dominionism."[201] The movement they and other such prophets of the right pursued during Obama's two terms as president was mirrored by an obstructionist right-wing Republican agenda in Congress. It fueled the wave of pent-up right-wing backlash that swept Donald Trump into the White House in 2016, supported heavily by white evangelical Christians and the Christian nationalism that had become such a dominant feature of the conservative Christian landscape.

Donald Trump's seemingly irrational and unshakable sway over Christian nationalists is completely understandable when his slogan "Make America Great Again" is heard by a large swath of Americans as *Make America White Again.*

2

Why Are People Drawn In by Extremist Beliefs?

Conscious Needs and Unconscious Lures

In chapter 1, we began with the observation that on January 6, 2021, there was a mob made up of various groups, all hypnotized to some degree by the charismatic power of Donald Trump and his repeated claims not only that the 2020 presidential election was a sham but that true patriots needed to fight to win back the country. We cannot draw a perfect Venn diagram of how all these movements intersect with one another or know the exact proportion of Christian nationalists within the Capitol mob on that day. But by examining what motivates Christian nationalists to believe as they do, it may become clearer how they overlap with, and may even join together with, other right-wing and white-supremacist groups and at times, as seen on January 6, become indistinguishable from them.

Up to this point, we have looked at sociological research and public surveys to understand the scope and place of Christian nationalism in the American population overall and what Christian nationalists believe. Large-scale surveys count and compare people's attitudes. The data collected, especially when the surveys reach a large and comprehensive enough "sample" of respondents, can tell us a lot about what people are thinking, who and how many share certain attitudes versus others, and trends in public opinion over time and across various demographic, religious, and political groups.

Such statistical studies can tell us quite a lot in and of themselves. By ranking people's agreement with statements representing political, social, and religious views, social scientists are able to quantify and even predict how many individuals fall into certain groups. They can then even reveal how responses to some sets of questions predict alignment of attitudes between groups. In chapter 1, drawing from sociologists' research, we saw strong correspondences between white evangelical Christianity, conservative (even right-wing) nationalism, patriarchal "family values," and above all, white supremacy.

As I have often told my students, this type of statistical research is very good at telling the *who* and the *what* of a given social issue—demographics, attitudes, behaviors, and the correlations among them. But a different kind of research is needed to explore *how* and *why* people believe and act as they do. For this reason, social scientists today also frequently use "qualitative" as well as "quantitative" (statistical) methods. Qualitative researchers employ processes such as interviewing, convening focus groups, and attending various organizational gatherings and events as "participant observers."[1] The goal is to listen to individuals share in their own words why they believe as they do, what they think they should do as a result of their beliefs, and the contexts in which they have formed their opinions.

Quantitative research *measures* the attitudes and opinions people hold and to what degree; qualitative research seeks to uncover the *personal meanings* behind these beliefs, within the contexts of people's lives. Quantitative data consists of numbers that represent how much and how many there are of whatever is being studied. Qualitative research depends on oral and written narratives, often elicited more relationally through conversation and dialogue[2] or open-ended "essay" questions on surveys. Allowing participants to put their thoughts in their own words rather than conducting an interview with pre-set questions, and going back to participants a second or even third time to clarify responses or get further feedback on what other respondents have shared, are ways that go beyond statistics to better understand empathically—to the degree possible—the participants' beliefs and feelings from their own points of view.

Careful social research today thus very often incorporates both statistical *and* narrative methods (sometimes called "mixed methods" research) to understand more deeply the *who, what, when, how,* and *why* of a given social reality. Whereas chapter 1 focused on the *who, what,* and *when* of Christian nationalism, drawing from the research of others, as well as my own experience, this chapter explores those deeper questions of the *how* and *why.* We understand from multiple sources that Christian nationalists are more nationalist than Christian and that slightly over half of all Americans agree wholly or in part with their convictions. Christian evangelicalism has come to exist in a symbiotic relationship with right-wing political operatives. Both sides of this unholy alliance promote white supremacy, patriarchy, and a conservative theonomy that serves their interests. They are united around common targets: critical race theory, feminism, LGBTQ rights, communism, Islam, and more open immigration policies (even to the extent of opposing asylum for persecuted refugees).

Their goals are big. It is not a stretch to understand that, from different starting points, they really seek nothing less than world domination ("winning the world for Christianity"—as they define it—and maintaining the role of a Christian United States as the world's number-one economic and military superpower). These are the stated aims of the leadership of both Christian nationalists and right-wing politicians, promulgated under a triple banner of personal salvation, individual freedom/rights, and what they perceive to be American-style democracy.

But what motivates the rank and file, ordinary citizens, to join this movement? What are the more personal, emotional factors that draw so many mainstream Christians into the apocalyptic fervor of Christian nationalism? In this chapter, we will first examine the feelings that Christian nationalists themselves express and then explore even deeper dynamics underlying what draws people to extreme social movements—particularly the magnetic pull of charismatic leaders and the unconscious needs they appear to fulfill in their followers.

Conscious Motivations

There are many conscious or at least close-to-the-surface feelings that people can describe about themselves—sometimes quite publicly—to explain why they adhere to Christian nationalist ideas. Prominent among these feelings, which are mutually conducive and mutually reinforcing, are

- evangelization and the need for belonging and a sense of purpose;
- fear of loss of white social status, resentment, and a desire for power;
- fear of loss of patriarchal authority; and
- the irrational allure of conspiracy theories.

The Need for Belonging and Purpose: Surround-Sound Evangelization

The need for belonging is a deep-seated human desire and certainly not unique to Christian nationalists as a group. Nevertheless, it is one of the motivating factors underlying people's attraction to Christian nationalism as a movement. In addition to providing this social connection, which is a basic human need, the movement combines two features that can initially draw people in and then hold them tight: first, a strong sense of spiritual purpose and, second, a means of acting on that sense of purpose by engaging in a battle—even a cosmic battle between good and evil.

In her careful analysis of the rise of Christian nationalism, journalist Michelle Goldberg links this directly to the need so-called megachurches (generally, nondenominational 2,000+ member congregations with an informal, nonliturgical worship format) fulfill for many people. While less than 3% of American churches have over 1,000 members (and less than 0.5% have over 2,000—the standard definition of a "megachurch"), almost a quarter of American Christians belong to churches of 1,000 or more.[3] And nearly three-quarters of US megachurches are growing in attendance today. Although since 2005, megachurches have become *slightly* more multiracial[4] and more diverse politically (about two-thirds of these churches' leaders say there are political differences, and almost as many now avoid discussing politics as a result[5]), a 2019 study shows that churches of 1,000+ members were about nine times more likely to be *theologically* conservative than liberal and one-third again more likely to be conservative than "right in the middle" theologically.[6] In the same study, the small sample of 1,000+ member churches were seven times more likely to be *politically* conservative than liberal, and were also about as likely to self-identify as "right in the middle." Not unlike the demographics described in chapter 1, these large churches are twice as likely to be located in the South, together with Mountain and Pacific regions, than in the Northeast or northern Midwest.[7]

Historically, the influence of the megachurches has been outsized in terms of fostering Christian nationalism, and while there may be more political diversity today, Goldberg's description is still relevant and points to the way in which the human need for belonging can be exploited for political aims: "The rootlessness and disconnection of the exurbs is a large part of what makes the spread of Christian nationalism's fictitious reality possible, because there is very little to conflict with it. If the only public forums are the mall and the megachurch, then the range of views to which most people are likely to be exposed are very small. Those who want other perspectives can easily find them, but reality doesn't intrude on the movement's lies unless it's actively sought out."[8] Regarding Christian nationalism, journalist Katherine Stewart also observes,

The rank and file come to the movement with a variety of concerns, including questions about life's deeper meaning, a love and appreciation of God and Scripture, ethnic and family solidarity, the hope of community and friendship, and a desire to mark life's most significant passages or express feelings of joy or sorrow. They also come with a longing for certainty in an uncertain world. Against a backdrop of escalating economic inequality, industrialization, rapid technological change, and climate instability, many people, on all points of the economic spectrum, feel that the world has entered a state of disorder. The movement gives them confidence, an identity, and the feeling that their position in the world is safe. Yet the price of certainty is often surrendering one's political will to those who claim to offer refuge from the tempest of modern life.[9]

From my own observations, most people who become supporters of Christian nationalism do not begin as right-wing political activists first (although political leaders may cynically exploit Christian nationalists for their own white nationalist power campaigns). On the contrary, Christian nationalists start out as Christian first. Especially in the evangelical church realm, they are drawn into community by highly motivated evangelists who use such activities as food pantries to engage people in conversation, turn the conversation toward the ways in which people are hurting, and then in a confiding, personal statement, share how coming to faith transformed their own lives. An invitation follows to come and see what the church is all about: "No pressure, just come and check us out." And many people do.

Leaders who aspired to create megachurches in the 1980s and '90s realized that the next step after getting people in the door was to offer high-octane worship geared toward "seekers." Many smaller, often struggling churches, both evangelical and mainline Protestant, also began to learn from and emulate their approach. Once in the door, people might find themselves "love bombed" by enthusiastic welcomers or emotionally captivated by the highly professional, theatrical quality of the worship production itself. (More will be said later about megachurches' emotionally engulfing style of worship.) Surrounded by others with closed eyes and uplifted arms, it is difficult for a newcomer to resist the pull of communal ecstasy and to avoid feeling like part of something much bigger than oneself—something overpowering, warm, and wonderful.

Experts on evangelism also recognize the importance of forming personal relationships as soon as possible. Follow-up phone calls—especially by lay members, not by clergy—plant seeds of friendship and a sense of personal welcome. A 2016 Pew Research Center study determined that having friends or family in the congregation is a key factor in becoming and remaining a member for 45% of older adults and 62% of millennials.[10] This is accomplished by enrolling them into one or a myriad of small groups—many of which have the flavor of self-help groups. Other small groups focus on Bible study or on some form of "discipleship" (i.e., a ministry in the community). Many groups incorporate some combination of all three of these elements.[11] Small-group participation, with its carefully chosen Bible studies and informational curricula, becomes the next step into an inner circle of like-minded friends and is the glue that will keep them coming. In this way, visiting "seekers" become inside "believers."

"Bringing others to salvation" is the preeminent value within evangelical Christianity,[12] in response to Jesus's command, "Go into all the world and proclaim the good news to the whole creation" (Mark 16:15). Evangelization is reinforced by Jesus's commissioning to his followers at the end of the Gospel of Matthew: "Go therefore and make disciples of all nations, baptizing them in the name of the Father and of the Son and of the Holy Spirit, and teaching them to obey everything that I have commanded you" (Matt 28:19–20a).

While evangelism (which means spreading the "good news" or *euangelion*—"gospel" in English) is considered a firm directive within all Christian denominations (even if it causes many liberal mainline Christians to squirm[13]), it is front and center among evangelicals. Converting non-Christians is imperative to save their souls from hell or damnation—especially urgent when combined with a belief in an imminent Day of Judgment. The passage in Matthew 28 itself ends with an apocalyptic reference: "And remember, I am with you always, *to the end of the age*" (Matt 28:20b; emphasis added).

Historically, this commandment was of little concern to the first white "settlers" in America, all of whom were Christian. Their primary concern was *which* branch of transplanted European Christianity would dominate in each region or colony and how much religious tolerance would be allowed, eventually giving rise to American denominationalism.[14] But by the early 19th century, the two Great Awakenings had taken evangelization to new heights.[15] Evangelists believed that being a Christian was not just subscribing nominally and socially to the religion of one's birth but making a conscious decision to invite Jesus into one's heart and to feel a resulting emotional and moral transformation and the promise of personal eternal life—to be *saved*.

This was a new breed of American Christian with a fervor to evangelize. The preachers were passionate and inspired emotional responses in their hearers. Men shouted and women swooned. Revivalism and Pentecostal experiences—such as being slain in the spirit, speaking in tongues, and even snake handling in some remote mountain communities—created a divide with more staid Congregationalists, Presbyterians, Lutherans, and Episcopalians with their attachment to scripture, tradition, and reason. Traditional or "mainline" Christians looked on these revivalist practices with disdain if not horror, while hotly burning evangelists wanted to save their tepid souls from the fires of hell—often with the zeal of the newly converted.

In the 20th century, revivals grew in popularity again, in tune with various political trends. American revivalism was influenced by international movements and blossomed especially in reaction to the perceived ungodliness of the social upheavals of the 1960s. While crusades and large rallies like those made famous by Billy Graham continue in some places, today's evangelists have become increasingly sophisticated with their use of social media and online educational platforms. Evangelical seminaries were early adopters of online learning. There was less hand-wringing about "incarnational presence" and what might be lost in face-to-face education in many evangelical schools, which makes a certain kind of sense—if one must receive information about the faith to make a personal decision for Christ, then "informational technology" is a perfect tool for disseminating it.

Alongside extravagant worship and intense small-group fellowship, among evangelicals, there is also all the "merch." LifeWay and other Christian stores and online outlets do a brisk business in book sales (both nonfiction and romance novels), videos and movies, "Christian music," and online media—even clothing and home decor.[16] As historian Kristin Kobes Du Mez points out, the merchandise creates an all-embracing white patriarchal culture.[17] Devotional and nonfiction books tend to present a conservative Christian viewpoint using teacherly rhetorical appeals to logic, biblical scholarship, and factual or factual-sounding knowledge. Evangelicals promote their own versions of the Bible in order to ensure followers are exposed to the "true word of God."

There is the *American Patriot's Bible: The Word of God and the Shaping of America* (New King James Version), published in 2009 by the well-known Bible publisher Nelson and advertised as "the one Bible that shows how 'a light from above' shaped our nation."[18] Zondervan Publishing, which owns the rights to the New International Version of the Bible, was set to release a new *God Bless America Bible* that would also include the US Constitution, the Bill of Rights, the Declaration of Independence, and the Pledge of Allegiance, as well as the lyrics to Lee Greenwood's song "God Bless the USA," just in time for the 20th anniversary of 9/11 in September 2021. But after receiving petitions opposing its publication, the parent company HarperCollins withdrew the Bible from its list.[19]

Today, televangelists and live revivalists employ expensive production techniques, with sophisticated light and projection technology and fervently emotional singers. Productions geared toward an older generation (Christian nationalists' core supporters) typically feature praise music performed by (mostly blond) women in sparkly dresses and dramatic makeup and stout, middle-aged men in suit jackets and ties, along with some sedate (i.e., whitened) renditions of Black gospel music performed by their one Black male or female vocalist. This ensemble is completed by a late-night-talk-show- or Lawrence Welk–style backup band (mostly white and middle-aged). Productions for a younger generation (perhaps in their 30s and 40s) feature younger, sexier-looking men in tight jeans and short-sleeved button-down "muscle fit" shirts and women in casual-chic clothes and (again) dramatic makeup who sing accompanied by folk and rock bands amplified by the baddest, loudest speaker systems imaginable.[20] At the center of it all, regardless of the targeted audience's generation, preachers pace the stage, modulating their voices from confidential whispers to impassioned yelling. They repeat simple appeals to come to Jesus, interlaced with idiosyncratic interpretations of biblical passages, exhortation to conservative moral values, and populist political provocation.

By the 1980s,[21] revival-style worship could be consumed any Sunday morning (and many Saturdays) in megachurches around the country. Promoted by the so-called church growth movement, it had trickled into some smaller evangelical and even mainline churches as well. Praise bands and large projection screens are to be found in congregations of most denominations throughout the land. For children, there are Dobson-approved Sunday school curricula with carefully produced media resources, summer vacation Bible schools, and the ever-popular and engaging VeggieTales videos (many authored by none other than the extremist Eric Metaxas[22]) for home viewing—with all their charming silliness.

All of this works psychologically to provide spiritual thrills that, with enough repetition, create a vibrant sense of community, a feeling of belonging to something special that transcends everyday life. The extent to which the people in the pews are actually inspired to become evangelists on their own is probably fairly limited. But the leaders know that by repeating essentially the same emotionally charged message week after week, amped up by the carefully planned rise and fall and rise again of excitement throughout the service, just getting people in the door a few times is already more than half the battle. For many, consuming Sunday productions, occasional revivals, and/or televangelist programming is enough to keep the fires for Jesus and the political right burning.

Cultlike Recruiting

Although it may seem shocking, the steps involved in this gradual induction into the community are not so different from those of actual cults, with varying degrees of similarity depending on the extent to which the particular church expects to control individual members' and families' behaviors and thoughts. Psychologist and cult expert Margaret Singer identified several steps and tactics that might or might not pertain to any one church or local organization:[23]

- invitation—including finding something in common, showing caring interest, and showing how coming to an event would benefit the recruit's interests
- encouragement to attend an event right away—not giving the recruit time to mull it over
- benign first contact with an idealistic group that functions as a front for the leaders' more hidden self-serving purposes
- love bombing—overwhelming the guest with welcome and expressions of care
- gradual exposure to classes, events, and/or experiences that begin to separate the new member from their previous life and contacts, gradually changing them without their realizing it (and in the case of younger recruits, exploiting normal ambivalence toward parents to alienate them)

- sleep deprivation and control of access to information (mostly for residential groups)
- manipulation and deception—for example, leaders telling compelling personal stories that turn out to be fabrications and exploiting coincidences to reinforce the idea that what the group is doing has been foreordained
- restricting food and modes of dress, assigning purity or badness to certain choices
- inducing guilt—drawing clear lines between "good" and "bad" and alternating love bombing with condemnation and humiliation, further isolating them from "bad" people outside
- inducing trance states through guided imagery and repetition of phrases, evoking a feeling of universality, and introducing contradictory statements that induce cognitive dissonance and a distancing from reality
- "indirect directives"—a tactic of a leader suggesting something might be good without actually ordering it, rewarding compliance and punishing noncompliance (by withdrawing love and attention, or more actively humiliating or hurting the member)
- trickery—using deceptive techniques to gain knowledge about a person and then appearing to be omniscient by revealing that knowledge
- revision of personal history—expecting members to give testimony of how before joining, their lives were miserable, but since joining, everything is so much better (Versions of this are of course regularly found in both 12-step groups and in evangelical churches as the practice of witnessing, or testifying.)
- peer pressure and modeling—once in a tight-knit group, people quite unconsciously begin to imitate the behaviors of the other group members in order to strengthen a sense of belonging
- emotional manipulation and therapeutic pretensions—for example, eliciting and using previously private "deep" (and I would add shame-inducing) revelations of pain in the past in order to strengthen the attachment to the group and the leader

To this list, psychoanalyst Daniel Shaw adds "purification of ego" (encouraging individuals to let go of their own subjectivity—including healthy self-regard and critical thinking—in order to become "pure"), demanding perfection (as defined by the leader, so that no one can avoid abusive criticism), incessant urgency (emphasizing the need to crush enemies), violation of boundaries as a norm (satisfying the leader's needs in order to regain a scrap of recognition), rooting out internal deviance (initially by punishing deviations from the established norm, eventually internalized by members so they will punish themselves), and defending the leader "no matter what." In the end, "by remaining loyal to the leader, the followers persuade themselves that their own existence is given meaning and validity by their support of the leader's mission."[24]

Shaw further suggests that in the induction process, there is a "bait and switch" in which cult leaders encourage recruits to "surrender" in a healthy way—"as a letting go of defenses, and an opening to the possibility of the sublime, both as an internal state and as interpersonal experience." But all too soon, the authoritarian leader turns this (by use of many of the same tactics Singer enumerated) into "submission"—"the bait being surrender, the switch being masochistic submission to a cruel and controlling, yet idealized, leader."[25]

Let me be clear: I am not saying that all church evangelism is insidious or evil. Many liberal churches have adopted similar methods for church growth, motivated by a genuine love for the gospel, appreciation for the fellowship they have found through their congregational life, and a desire to bring others in to share it. It is the *content* of worship, and the articulation of theology and mission in these more mainstream congregations, that distinguishes them from churches that consistently alloy personal salvation through belief in Jesus as savior with a panoply of conservative social values that gradually turn to right-wing political activism.

More socially progressive churches engage in political activism as part of their faith convictions. The Black Church historically has always tied the struggle for empowerment, justice, and advocacy for the poor to its reading of the Bible (including on-the-ground economic efforts such as low-income housing, low-interest loans, and grassroots community organizing).[26] Ebenezer Baptist Church in Atlanta, Georgia, to cite a well-known example, does not simply rest on its historic legacy as the church where Martin Luther King Jr. and Sr. both preached. Rather, it is a model today of community renewal and urban Black empowerment, under the leadership of Rev. Dr. Raphael Warnock, who was also elected a US senator in 2020. The goals of this kind of activism are distinct from exclusionary right-wing churches' and leaders' agendas. At their best, churches that focus on a mission of empowerment and care—rather than on the ego of the minister—are expansive and inclusive, aimed to lift up "the least of these." But "seekers" should beware: the same strategies for "church growth" can also be used by conservative church leaders to channel newcomers toward a right-wing agenda that may initially be disguised by the emphasis on fellowship, outreach, and the love of Jesus.

Once invited and welcomed into fellowship in a conservative white church, the chances are great that a person will slowly but surely be immersed not only in praise for Jesus but also in praise for the United States—in sermons, symbol, and song. Baptist pastor Dean Inserra, cited in chapter 1 as an evangelical opponent of Christian nationalism, said regarding this brand of evangelism, "What you win them with is what you win them *to*," suggesting, according to Angela Denker, that "because Southern Baptist pastors and churches rely so heavily on patriotism and 'God, guns, and country' to get people into their churches, they've constructed a mass of people for whom faith in Jesus is nothing more than a blind allegiance to America, nostalgia, guns, and support for the military. In the absence of preaching that challenges GOP politics, an entire generation of Southern Baptists became susceptible to a populist nationalist [Donald Trump] who claims to be supporting Christians."[27]

Once drawn in, a "seeker" who has become a "believer" and has become involved in one or more small groups and outreach ministries is usually firmly held in the embrace of the church. This is the point at which evangelism can also become hard core political indoctrination. Moreover, once a person has become embedded in the church, and made the journey from "seeker" to "believer," it is extremely difficult to leave.[28] To repudiate the ideas held by the group, or even to think critically or ask too many questions, means risking losing the friendships, losing the feeling of spiritual clarity and purpose, and being cast out again from the circle of belonging into aloneness and uncertainty in an inhospitable world.

Singer enumerates six "compliance principles" that bind members to cults and make it psychologically difficult to leave (summarized in my own words as follows): reluctance to break a commitment, feeling indebted, seeing others behaving as if there is nothing wrong, ingrained loyalty toward the authority of the leader, still feeling wanted and loved by many, and fear of missing out on what the group has promised to offer.[29]

From my own work with intimate partner violence, I can see a similarity to the ways in which batterers slowly induce dependency and a fear of leaving in their victims—tactics one domestic violence expert compared to the experiences imposed on prisoners of war.[30] Also, as with many victims of battering in an intimate relationship, it is not weakness but strength and a personal sense of responsibility that may hold a person in a relationship[31]—or a group. What would it mean to give up on the relationship? And what would leaving imply about what one believed to be true while in the relationship? Is it important to stay for the sake of caring for others (the batterer / other members of the group / even the leader, who is not always bad)? As Singer has summarized, "Because of the powerful combination of belief, loyalty, dependency, guilt, fear, peer pressure, lack of information, and fatigue, all of which probably have equal psychological weight, members do not readily leave cults. Decent, honorable people do not easily give up on commitments, and the cult environment is such that it makes leaving practically impossible."[32]

It is not coincidental that the rise of megachurches and smaller congregations with this same style of evangelization arose just as sociologist Robert Putnam was writing poignantly of the demise of American community life in his book *Bowling Alone*.[33] Putnam used the example of dwindling bowling leagues to describe a late 20th-century decline in Americans' involvement in civic and social activities—from the PTA to clubs (Rotary Club, the Masons) to churches and local political organizations. This decline, he argued, was responsible for an overall sense of diminished life satisfaction as people became more isolated and disconnected from the social bonds that create "social capital" (i.e., the collective value of networks among people and the reciprocity they foster).[34] In his revised edition, he further explores the ways in which social media can connect people but also serve to further alienate them from the fabric of American society.[35]

Sin and Salvation: Personal Not Corporate

A key element in the evangelism agenda, of course, is the need to guard against sin and to save others from damnation as well. There is some contradiction here theologically—if one is saved by accepting Jesus as Lord and Savior, as most Protestants would assert, then one is at that moment personally freed from the bondage of sin. However, the temptation to sin, planted in the Christian mind by the ever-present and crafty devil, is a theme as old as Christianity itself and has been prominent in every version of American Christianity from Puritanism to the Great Awakenings.

While many mainline Christian theologians tend to emphasize the corporate and communal nature of sin (as in structural racism and the economic exploitation of people in the Global South), evangelical Christianity focuses on salvation of individuals from damnation caused by personal sin.[36] In the sermons of adept politically conservative preachers, it is an easy step to make from talking about sin to blaming the rise of secularism in America on ever-increasing corruption that draws good people toward bad behavior. It is then a short step to link the traditional sins (including some of the seven deadlies) to whatever controversial social issue is the current target on the Christian nationalist agenda (be it trans athletes, who should use what bathrooms, abortion, evolution,[37] the removal of the Ten Commandments from courthouse walls, or the latest focus of right-wing ire—critical race theory—as discussed in chapter 1).

Conservative Christian leaders have long understood that to infuse Christian values into American society, those values must be inculcated in children. Accordingly, many of the most contested issues converge around the education of children and what should or should not be taught (or prayed) in public schools. For many, this has meant fighting for each of these agenda items, and more, all the way from local government to state and federal courts on up to the Supreme Court.

Beginning in the late 1980s, activists who were brought together under the banner of the Christian Coalition also began to run for public office—including local school boards.[38] For some others, the desire to integrate conservative Christian values and beliefs with primary and secondary education has meant removing their children from public school altogether and enrolling them in evangelical-run schools or homeschooling them (another arena where Focus on the Family is ready to provide advice, sell curricula, and hold homeschooling conventions for Christian parents). Similar to the Jericho March on the US Capitol in 2021, Michael Farris, a leader of the Christian homeschooling movement (and another protégé of Tim LaHaye), had already envisioned two decades ago raising up an entire "Generation Joshua" "to conquer corrupt culture" and "restore American values."[39] Generation Joshua's director, Ned Ryun, predicted, "Homeschoolers will be inordinately represented in the highest levels of leadership and power in the next generation. . . . You're starting to see them all around the Hill, as staffers on Capitol Hill."[40]

In all these ways, Christian nationalist church leaders are highly skilled in a range of programmatic initiatives from evangelism to education, using sophisticated methods of recruitment and retention to win souls for (their) Jesus and win psyches for the political right wing.

Fear of Loss of White Social Status, Resentment, and a Desire for Power

Another significant conscious factor behind white Christian nationalism is *fear* motivated by a recognition that one's position at the top of the race hierarchy is being eroded. This occurs among all social classes, of course, and in institutions mostly inhabited by those with more wealth, education, and political power, the fear is managed by the now-familiar practice of hiring token persons of color to appear diverse without changing the balance of power too much. This is also true regarding women. Pay inequities, poor family leave benefits, and inertia with regard to meaningfully addressing realities of sexual harassment and racial aggression (macro or micro) further discourage employees of color and women from staying in an organization, or even in the professional workforce at all.

Whistleblowers who challenge overt racism or sexism are often gaslighted. If the proportion of professionals of color becomes too great for white leadership to tolerate, other tactics may be employed, such as expecting those employees to take on extra work because the organization "needs their point of view" (i.e., a person of color) on every project or committee, or setting them up for failure with tasks that are unachievable. Add to this what some people of color have called "the Black tax": "The psychological weight or stressor that Black people experience from consciously or unconsciously thinking about how White Americans perceive the social construct of Blackness. Blackness in America is often portrayed through a deficit lens and is associated with racial stereotypes. The cognizance of how Blackness is defined by the dominant culture, coupled with the unjust treatment Black people have endured, and continue to be subjected to, due to racism, results in a psychological burden known as the Black Tax."[41]

The vast majority of white professionals are unaware of (and don't want to know about) these daily stressors faced by their colleagues of color, and due to unconscious bias, they may assume they earned their own status just by their own merit and superior ability. They perceive a slight pendulum swing toward a more diverse working environment as greater progress toward a true place of social and economic equality—and also therefore a greater implicit threat to their positions—than is actually the case. Their previously assumed white (mostly male) privilege is far from gone. But even the slight shift toward a more level playing field sets off tremors, often accompanied by backpedaling, dithering on action to increase diversity, saying the right thing but doing nothing to promote real change, and turning a blind eye or circling the wagons in more overt instances of racial and sexual harassment. And all this occurs in spite of having policies to the contrary (as in the struggles of the Southern Baptist Convention in its first baby steps toward becoming a more diverse church described in chapter 1).

Many of these professionals consider themselves to be liberal or at least moderate politically, and they would even consider white Christian nationalists to be a completely different kind of people (lower education, lower class, different *taste* in virtually all matters[42]). Yet much racism is perpetuated by "nice," even self-avowed progressive white people,[43] in both their professional and family lives. Ta-Nehisi Coates has pointed out that attributing Trump's 2016 electoral victory mainly to the economically disadvantaged, as many commentators did in the weeks following his election, fails to take into account that Trump supporters generally had a higher mean household income ($81,898) than those who did not vote for him ($77,046). Coates excoriates white journalists, pundits, and liberals in general for focusing on the plight and resentment of lower-income white men while ignoring the overwhelming dominance of the white vote for Trump across all other demographic categories: "The focus on one sub-sector of Trump voters—the white working class—is puzzling, given the breadth of his white coalition. Indeed, there is a kind of theater at work in which Trump's presidency is pawned off as a product of the white working class as opposed to a product of an entire whiteness that includes the very authors doing the pawning."[44] Protectionism and the fear of erosion of white privilege cuts across all education and class levels—and with it, a tolerance (if not enthusiasm) for a conservative political agenda among higher-earning whites, both men and women, when it promises personal economic or social benefit.

The majority of white Christian nationalists do not, however, belong to the highly paid, more formally educated demographic, as we saw in chapter 1, and do not share their economic or social advantages. For average middle-class, working-class, and poor whites, the basic statement "they are taking our jobs" is a common refrain. It originates in, and reinforces, both racism against American-born people of color and anti-immigration xenophobia. While in professional and upper-class settings, anxiety about "letting in too many of *them*" is often cloaked in smooth, obfuscating rhetoric, or accomplished through behind-the-scenes networking, such subtle channels of influence are mostly inaccessible in the lives of average working Americans. Straight talk is what is valued, as is more overt aggression. This was one major reason white Christian nationalists overwhelmingly voted for Trump in 2016. His supporters often said, "He tells it like it is," and many applaud his most overtly violent (supposedly side) comments.

Hillary Clinton's unscripted hot mic comment about "deplorables" simply clinched the suspicion of many white Trump supporters that the "liberal elite" not only disregarded them but actually had contempt for them. Dee Davis, founder of the Center for Rural Strategies in Whitesburg, Kentucky, told one *Politico* commentator, "We think people are talking down to us. What ends up happening is that we don't focus on the policy—we focus on the tones, the references, the culture."[45] (Some have proudly flipped the "deplorable" epithet into a badge of defiance, like a woman I encountered early in the Covid-19 pandemic while grocery shopping one day, defiantly maskless against the store's policy and wearing a T-shirt that read, "Adorable Deplorable.")

Economically, for millions of white working-class and poor individuals and families, the "American dream" feels like a bait and switch. Hard work and physical labor no longer elevate large swaths of the population (if they ever did). The transformation of a labor economy to a technology and service economy further punctured the idea that one can, like Horatio Alger, work one's way up the ladder to success (at least as defined by having enough money to enjoy life as more than a daily grind). The taste of the American dream has soured in the mouths of the working poor, especially those whose ancestors swallowed the myth that, as long as they were white, they still had someone else to look down on (people of color and the "indigent"). Their sense of personal dignity was built on the widely promoted myth of personal willpower and perseverance opening up opportunity for all. And there were just enough examples of people who made it from "rags to riches" to make the dream seem attainable.[46]

This sense of futility is another reason so many poor and working-class people continue to idolize Donald Trump.[47] Ignoring the fact of his privileged upbringing, many believe (erroneously) his carefully constructed image as the kind of rough-talking, self-made man they aspire to be.[48] "He's one of us," they conclude—even though he isn't. The reality is that for any one individual, the odds of leaping up the economic ladder are not much better than winning the lottery. According to the Pew Research Center, "the wealth gap between America's richest and poorer families more than doubled from 1989 to 2016."[49] According to the US Census Bureau, "By 2018, the [top] 20 percent was earning fully 52 percent of all U.S. income, while the bottom 20 percent, by contrast, only earned 3.1 percent."[50] The harsh and enduring truth for most working-class and poor whites is that white privilege mostly applies to wealthy whites already in power and not to those who subsist much lower in the economic pecking order.

This contributes to a feeling among many whites, even in the middle class, that the issue of "white privilege" is a myth fabricated by liberal elites. They do not *feel* privileged but rather see themselves as under siege. A number of economists and social scientists attribute the rural drug crisis, rising alcoholism, severe health disparities, and escalating suicide rates among poor and lower-educated Americans to the despair caused by the transformation of the US economy into "an engine of inequality and suffering."[51] From their own point of view, many Trump supporters were not voting against their own self-interest, as so many liberals misunderstood.[52] They were voting for the promises Trump repeated about returning jobs to American farms and factories, convinced he would make good on them because they mistook his bluntness and bombast for honesty and business acumen.

Since the 17th century, when white slave holders began to separate European slaves from Africans, allowing white indentured servants to work off their debt but leaving African slaves in a state of permanent hereditary subjugation,[53] many poor and working-class whites have tried to prop up a sense of dignity over and against Blacks.[54] As time went on, what white working-class people also failed to see throughout the decades of Jim Crow and postwar prosperity—or didn't want to see—is that whatever upward climb they could achieve was on the backs of people of color.

Because of systematic educational, housing, and employment discrimination, Blacks, Asians, Latinx, and Indigenous people have had to keep doing the jobs upwardly mobile white achievers no longer wanted to do. The biggest lie, or bait and switch, is not that white people were sold a bill of goods; it is rather that the story of upward mobility is supposedly for everyone, native-born, immigrant, and people of color alike. But for some, the ladder has always been broken or nonexistent (with the exception of a few granted honorary "white" status as tokens to fill ethnic quotas or jazz up a company's image and expand its market). For others—a majority of people of color and the indigent poor—there has never been a ladder at all.

Underlying the loud denunciation of secularism and its supposed destruction of traditional Christian values (and a traditionally white middle-class lifestyle) is the awareness that both Christianity and whiteness are statistically on the decline in America. There is no question that at least numerically, white people—including white Christians—are declining as a percentage of the overall American population. As noted in chapter 1, the US Census Bureau revised its prediction of a majority nonwhite population downward from 2050 to the year 2042.[55] The most recent US Census report shows that as of 2020, there is no majority racial group among persons under age 18, and whites declined (from 53.5% to 47.3% over the last decade) for the first time since the Census began.[56] Latinx and Asian populations grew the most, and the number of people identifying as mixed race more than tripled (from 9 to 33.8 million in 10 years) and now make up 10% of the US population overall.[57] People of color now outnumber "non-Hispanic whites" in California, Hawaii, New Mexico, and the District of Columbia. And rural areas, where white Christian nationalism is strongest, are experiencing the greatest decline in total population, with over 86% of Americans now living in metropolitan areas.[58]

The tide is turning as the United States becomes more multicultural, and those who cling to white identity are seeing a gradual, natural change as if it were a tsunami threatening to drown them. Even before his presidential campaign, Trump understood and was able to tap into this vein of fear, for example, when he set in motion the big, persistent "birther" lie (the controversy that Barack Obama was not really an American and was probably a Muslim because of his middle name "Hussein").[59]

There is no more blatantly racist effort currently than the campaign by right-wing politicians and Christian nationalists to discredit and abolish critical race theory (CRT) in education—not only in the church (as described regarding the Southern Baptist fight in chapter 1) but also in public schools. Already, there have been numerous efforts to pass state laws also lamented blance of CRT, reminiscent of the vocal campaign to stop teaching evolution or to teach it alongside creationism.

Since the 1970s and '80s, white mainline Protestant churches have also lamented the loss of the post–World War II "glory days" of high church attendance and large Sunday schools. Sociologists Robert Putnam and David Campbell observed in 2012 that since that postwar boom time in mainline churches, "roughly one-third of the people raised in one of the mainline Protestant denominations has left the faith, mostly to become evangelical or none . . . [and] another 20 percent of mainline offspring have stopped coming to church, while remaining nominally in the faith."[60] White evangelicals, by contrast, after a lull in the 1940s and '50s, grew in their capacity to retain successive generations to almost 80% in the 1990s[61] during what the authors called a "the heyday of neo-evangelicalism" beginning in the 1970s and '80s.[62]

Religious affiliation has begun to shift again in the 2000s. Putnam and Campbell note that the retention of the younger generation by evangelical Protestants declined again to about 62% after the turn of the 21st century.[63] The latest study by the Public Religion Research Institute (PRRI) in 2020 also shows white evangelical Protestants declining since 2006 from 23.3% of the US population to 14.5% and white Catholics declining from 16% to 11.7%.[64] White mainline Protestants, representing 16.4% of all Americans as of 2020, have lost only about 1% since 2006 (rebounding after a decline and low point in 2016).[65]

Meanwhile, most threatening to conservative Christians, the percentage of *unaffiliated* white Americans rose from 16% in the same time frame to about one-quarter of the American population in 2020.[66] Slightly over two-thirds of Republicans identify as white and Christian, with 29% identifying as white evangelicals, 22% white mainline Protestants, and 15% white Catholics. About 40% of Democrats identify as white and Christian, with 16% identifying as white mainline Protestants, 13% as white Catholics, and only 9% as white evangelicals.[67] Religiously unaffiliated Americans have gained numbers in both political parties.[68]

To summarize, the growing perception among white Christian nationalists that they are "losing the battle" in terms of societal and even religious dominance is not incorrect. The sheer demographic reality has aroused an ever-escalating desperation to hold onto power and put down the rising tide of persons of color and of non-Christians in the American populace. We see this desperation manifested currently in Republican-led voter suppression efforts, which disproportionately and quite transparently target people of color.

No Rules, Just Rights: Defending Patriarchal Authority

Emerging alongside the civil rights movement of the 1960s was a feminist reawakening in the country and, with it, a notable backlash among conservatives, in both evangelical and mainline churches. Growing anxiety about the rise of "uppity women" fuels a sense of threat among many Christian nationalists convinced that a man is the "head of the household" and must be the "leader" in any arena.

Lewis, one of Angela Denker's interviewees, stated, "[Trump's] commitment to America First—we liked that. And he cannot be bullied. He is unafraid. He is unbulliable."[69] Denker notes that "what is most appealing about Trump to Lewis and other Red State Christians . . . is not his faith but his strength, a sign they see that God is behind Trump's presidency."[70] Authoritarian male leaders commonly boast of their virility—some quite explicitly bragging of their many sexual conquests. Especially when "strongman" rhetoric is interspersed with shows of emotion (as Trump does in his comments about "love"), these displays of masculinity are attractive to some women followers—and also to men who are made to "feel better about their own transgressions" by transforming envy into identification with the leader.[71] Like the motto for Outback Steakhouse, these men promote a utopian masculinist vision of "No Rules, Just Rights," echoed in State Senator Mastriano's own motto (as described in chapter 1), "Walk as Free People"—that is, free to do whatever I want with no one to tell me I can't. Historian Ruth Ben-Ghiat, who has studied strongman leaders, states, "The strongman's rogue nature also draws people to him. He proclaims law-and-order rule, yet enables lawlessness. . . . The special psychological climate that strongmen create among their people—the thrill of transgression mixed with the comfort of submitting to his power—endows life with energy, purpose, and drama."[72]

As we have seen, the current Christian nationalist movement has many of its roots in the conservative backlash to the cultural upheavals of the 1960s. In the decades following World War II, it seemed that evangelicals' growing push to gain the upper hand in society was succeeding. Historian Kristin Kobes Du Mez writes that in this period, "evangelicals had become more and more confident that they had a providential role to play in strengthening American defenses and upholding American faithfulness."[73]

This confidence was soon to be challenged, however. Increasingly coming under fire from several directions, Christian nationalism has become a reactive movement, a defensive mobilization aroused by a feeling of backs against a wall. Beginning in the late 1960s, the war for America's soul (i.e., white patriarchy) has been fought simultaneously on two home fronts—the political (the masculine halls of Congress, the White House, and the Supreme Court), and the domestic (the feminine sphere of raising

Christian children and keeping a Christian home). Du Mez writes compellingly of how fear has increasingly become the underlying driver of the Christian nationalist agenda:

> Fear had been at the heart of evangelical postwar politics—a fear of godless communism and a fear that immorality would leave Americans defenseless. . . . The events of the 1960's . . . and the realization that the larger culture seemed to scorn what they had to offer, undercut their newfound confidence. Among evangelicals, a rhetoric of fear would persist, though it would be aimed at internal threats as much as external ones. Instrumental to their efforts to reclaim power, the rhetoric of fear would continue to bolster the role of the heroic masculine protector. There might be a place for the softer virtues, but the perilous times necessitated ruthless power. In the words of Baptist scholar Alan Bean, "The unspoken mantra of post-war evangelicalism was simple: Jesus can save your soul; but John Wayne will save your ass."[74]

In an essay just prior to the 2016 election, Alan Bean, who directs Friends of Justice, a coalition for criminal justice reform,[75] answers the question asked about Donald Trump by so many liberals then and now: *How could Christians of any stripe support such a blatantly immoral man as a candidate for president?* Bean writes,

> Liberals can't understand how a follower of Jesus could be so enamored of an arrogant, ignorant, spiteful, vicious, unforgiving and brazen casino magnate like Donald Trump. Trump, by all appearances, is the antithesis of Jesus. . . . And yet the quintessential Baptist preacher [the Christian nationalist pastor Robert Jeffress] is working to get Trump elected. Why? No one was surprised when John Wayne's daughter,[76] standing at a podium in front of a wax statue of her sainted dad, endorsed Donald Trump for president. . . . How can Barack Hussein Obama personify idealized white masculinity? He can't. Hence the appeal of birtherism. Donald Trump markets himself as "the meanest, toughest, son of a you-know-what" in America—the John Wayne stand-in the Reverends Jeffress and Falwell were looking for. Which is why Donald Trump really could stand in the middle of Fifth Avenue and shoot somebody without surrendering support. This isn't about liking the man, or approving his lowdown ways; it's about the kind of salvation that really counts.[77]

As Du Mez has described, the need to be in continual fight mode against an enemy—be it Black civil rights and the demand by feminists for equal rights for women, or communism with its concomitant threat of an atheistic takeover, or more recently perceived societal threats to white male power ranging from Islamic terrorists to LGBTQ rights to critical race theory—prompted an entire movement among white evangelicals to masculinize Christianity. This muscle flexing is necessary in order to win the battle for souls (i.e., for the preservation of conservative white patriarchal values unleashed in America by rising liberalism and secularism). Victorian images of a beautiful, somewhat feminized blond Jesus holding a lamb and looking benevolently at a gaggle of white children at his feet (in itself a cultural distortion) would no longer do. Du Mez describes how evangelical leaders "worked for decades to replace the Jesus of the Gospels with an idol of rugged masculinity and Christian nationalism—or in the words of one modern chaplain, 'with a spiritual badass.'"[78]

To be sure, this is not a new movement within modern Christianity. Du Mez points to antecedents such as the "muscular Christianity" preached by Billy Sunday and others in reaction to a perceived "feminization" of Christianity during the Victorian era. As the United States joined World War I, Sunday declared, "In these days all are patriots or traitors, to your country and to the cause of Jesus Christ."[79] Citing an account titled "40,000 Cheer for War and Religion Mixed by Sunday" in the *New York Times* in 1917,[80] Du Mez writes, "Sunday was known to leap atop his pulpit waving the American flag."[81]

Beginning with World War II, Billy Graham took a leading role and carried the torch for masculine revivalist preaching and evangelical institution building in a socially and politically conservative key. Frequently a White House guest, regarded by many historians as unofficial chaplain to the nation, Graham's blend of evangelical fervor and American patriotism had an enormous impact on building the Christian nationalist movement. Throughout the postwar decades of the 1950s to the 1980s, evangelicalism was a stronghold of opposition to communism abroad, movements at home for civil rights, peace and disarmanent, and what conservative Christians regarded as the erosion of family values.

The Patriarchy Persists: Keeping Women in Their Proper Places

Patriarchy and heterosexism are still alive and well in evangelical churches and typically are linked together in images of what a Christian family should be, as portrayed in sermons, books, and online media. Dobson's Focus on the Family, for example, asserts the following as one of its foundational values: "We believe God created humans in His image, intentionally and immutably male and female, each bringing unique and complementary qualities to sexuality and relationships. Sexuality is a glorious gift from God to be offered back to Him either in marriage for procreation, union, and mutual delight or in celibacy for undivided devotion to Christ."[82]

Evangelical church teachings make a distinction between "egalitarianism," or equality between men and women—which they reject as an infiltration of secular feminist culture on biblical values—and "complementarianism," in which men and women are considered to have essentially different needs, characteristics, and roles in family, church, and society.[83] Male and female are equal before God, but it is men's role to be the heads of their families (emulating Christ and his bride, the church), and wives must submit trustingly to their husbands' leadership. Dobson's website offers the following rationale: "Biblical submission allows a wife to confidently follow her husband's lead. And Ephesians 5:23 makes it clear that a man does have responsibility for leadership in his home. But again, it's only as a *leader* that his wife submits to him—not as a *tyrant* or her *superior*. Unfortunately, 'male bashing' in our culture makes it too easy to forget about the importance of masculine leadership altogether. We can't swing so far one way trying to avoid male domination that we go to the other extreme and strip husbands of their authority."[84]

In the past decade, Dobson and other evangelical clergy and pastoral counselors, under some pressure from both within the evangelical church and the wider societal movement to end violence against women, have begun to qualify their assertions about husbands' headship by making a rather tortured distinction between headship and abuse. Maintaining "headship," however, does not address the underlying dynamic of intimate partner violence, which is maintaining power and control.[85] The Focus on the Family site continues,

> That said, leadership doesn't give a husband the right to rob his wife of being a unique individual. He doesn't get to disregard or mock her opinions and feelings. And he should never misuse leadership to get his own way. A husband must love and cherish his wife—to die for her if necessary—even as Christ loved the Church. He should include

her in important decisions and consider her perspectives carefully and respectfully. Day by day, he should become increasingly sensitive to leading with love because he'll ultimately answer to God for the way he treats his wife. Sadly, we know that's not always the case. . . . If a wife believes that her husband is misusing his role and won't listen to her concerns, we'd be the first to urge her to get help—especially if there's abuse. . . . In all things, a woman is responsible *first* to God. If she cares about her marriage, her family, her community, and her relationship with the Lord, she doesn't submit mindlessly to every decision her husband makes. Submission and obedience aren't necessarily the same thing.[86]

Nevertheless, the rule of male headship remains unquestioned in this statement.[87]

The same complementarianism is reflected in the gender hierarchy of many evangelical churches. Southern Baptists went through a painful schism in 2000 after over two decades of fighting for control between the "biblicists" (biblical literalists who wanted to impose a strict fundamentalist reading of the Bible throughout the denomination) and the "autonomists" (who wanted to preserve the Baptist tradition of local congregational control).[88] The first ordination of a woman pastor in a Southern Baptist church occurred in 1964 and was followed by many more in the 1970s and early '80s. By 1987, there were 500 ordained clergywomen in the SBC, although only 18 served as parish pastors.[89] The autonomy of congregations made such moves possible at the local level. However, the conservative wing within the SBC increasingly took power and moved to rescind the clerical status of women who had been ordained previously.

The beginning of the SBC schism occurred in 1979 with the rise of a biblicist, Adrian Rogers of Memphis, to the presidency. Sensing the shift in the winds toward literalism and biblical inerrancy, 33 Baptist women clergy formed a caucus in 1983, Southern Baptist Women in Ministry, or SBWIM.[90] Backlash was swift to follow. Conservative church leaders immediately pushed through a 1984 "Resolution on Ordination and the Role of Women in Ministry," stating that women should be honored for their "unique and significant contribution to the advancement of Christ's kingdom, and the building of godly homes," but "to preserve a submission God requires because man was first in creation and woman was first in the Edenic fall . . . we encourage the service of women in all aspects of church life and work other than pastoral functions and leadership roles entailing ordination."[91] This was codified in the 2000 revision of the church's official statement of faith, the "Baptist Faith and Message 2000" (BFM), and was a key tipping point in the schism of the SBC.[92]

Dissenting women—and men—split off to form the Cooperative Baptist Fellowship as early as 1990, as well as the Alliance of Baptists and other more liberal groups.[93] In 1998, SBC leaders wrote an addendum to the BFM, stating that a wife should "submit herself graciously" to her husband, upholding "the God-given responsibility to respect her husband and serve as his helper in managing the household and nurturing the next generation."[94] The 2000 revision of the BFM added the statement that "the office of pastor is limited to men as qualified by Scripture."[95] A popular Bible teacher, Beth Moore, finally left the SBC as she came to terms with both the prohibition of women's ordination and the (long overdue) public disclosure of sexual abuse within the denomination. She publicly stated in March 2021, "We were in the middle of the biggest sexual abuse scandal that has ever hit our denomination. And suddenly, the most important thing to talk about was whether a woman could stand at the pulpit and give a message."[96]

Two months later—and less than a month before the SBC was to convene its 2021 annual meeting—Saddleback Church, a megachurch founded by Rick Warren (bestselling author of The Purpose Driven Life[97] and related spinoff books), jubilantly announced on Facebook, "Yesterday was a historic night for Saddleback Church in many ways! We ordained our first three women pastors!"[98] Al Mohler,[99] among others within the most conservative wing of the SBC, immediately condemned Saddleback's action, calling for an investigation and blaming women clergy for the "feminization of liberal Protestantism" and the decline of American Christian churches: "Liberal theology is the kiss of death for any church or denomination. . . . Little remains but social justice activism and deferred maintenance."[100]

In a related 2019 action, further delineating the "proper" place of women in society at large, the SBC convention also approved a resolution "On Expanding the Selective Service to Include Women." They reasserted their conviction about gender complementarianism by opposing the inclusion of women in the draft: "Requiring women to register for the Selective Service alongside men would be to treat men and women interchangeably and to deny male and female differences clearly revealed in Scripture and in nature. . . . We honor women who wish to engage in military service as volunteers, however, we oppose efforts to force women into military service by government coercion."[101]

It is the issue of sexual abuse within the church, however, that has most challenged the SBC and other evangelical churches to face the consequences of their ingrained patriarchal attitudes toward women. Church leaders could attempt to block out the sound of the voices in the #MeToo movement[102] beyond their walls, dismissing them as part of secular feminism and socialism. But a tipping point finally came when former gymnast and attorney Rachael Denhollander (who had previously been the first to report sexual abuse perpetrated by sports physician Larry Nassar) disclosed repeated abuse at the age of seven by a college student during a weekly Bible study. Denhollander was given the podium at the SBC's 2019 annual meeting, along with Beth Moore and several other Southern Baptist women, to testify to the extent of unchecked sexual abuse in the church.

Many mainline churches had begun to grapple with the issue of sexual abuse of both minors and adult congregants over two decades ago, and the Catholic Church has been embroiled in an ever-deepening series of public revelations of abuse. But most conservative Protestant churches have tended to try to keep things under wraps, perpetuating traditional patterns of protecting church leaders, blaming victims, failing to implement meaningful discipline, and keeping abuse secret from public authorities.

In response to the revelations of sexual abuse within the church in 2019, the SBC passed a resolution "On the Evil of Sexual Abuse," condemning "all sexually abusive behavior as unquestionably sinful and under the just condemnation of our Holy God" and calling for church leaders to "fulfill their obligation to implement policies and practices that protect against and confront any form of abuse in the future."[103]

Demanding the reversal of a long-standing pattern of secrecy and protection of offenders, the resolution also called for perpetrators to "confess their crimes to civil authorities" and for all persons to report to civil authorities and to exercise "appropriate church discipline." While the Baptists' move can be seen as a step forward, as with their actions on racism, it continues to define sexual abuse in terms of "sexual immorality" and individual sin. Here too there is an unwillingness to examine the institutional and structural power imbalance and reassertion of male authority over women and children that have perpetuated such abuse.

Moreover, the resolution did not prompt any meaningful reforms, as in the case of resolutions against racism[104]—on the contrary, it seems that it generated more strenuous patriarchal backlash, as revealed just before the SBC convened again in 2021, when two letters written by Russell Moore were leaked.[105] Moore, the now former president of the SBC's Ethics and Religious Liberty Commission (ERLC), exposed the ways in which the executive committee failed to investigate most allegations of abuse, engaged in a deliberate cover-up to please conservative male donors, and threatened the existence of the ERLC itself.

Meanwhile, the most conservative wing of the Southern Baptists, known as Founders Ministries, seeks to roll back any commitments to refer allegations of abuse to secular authorities or even independent investigators. Jared Longshore, the Founders' vice president, stated at a gathering one day before the SBC's June 2021 convention that such calls for outside reviews "do not fit biblical teaching. God 'has a word to say' about such reviews. . . . Disputes in the church should be settled internally."[106] The resistance to take sexual abuse seriously within the church mirrors the refusal to competently address and condemn the horrors perpetuated in the home by male "heads of households." In both instances, patriarchal privilege and lordship provide the foundation and the excuse for outright violence against women in the church, the home, and society.

Some Women Resist, Others Emulate Toxic Masculinity

The masculinity ingrained in modern evangelical Christianity is mainly—though certainly not entirely—promoted and defended by men and justified by church leaders who cling to selective, literalist readings of scripture. While patriarchy is still both a theological and structural given in evangelical churches, however, some women are beginning to resist. Some do this within the church by questioning the rules (together with male allies within the system), and others by defecting, adding to the decline in overall evangelical church membership, especially among young adults.

Patriarchy is still alive and well in both white evangelical and historically Black churches, and women are often denied positions of leadership in many Black congregations. Multiple studies show that the percentage of ordained women is still very low overall (and many denominations still do not ordain women). Breaking this down, about one-third of mainline congregations (a percentage that has doubled or tripled since 1994[107]) versus 9% or fewer evangelical churches have female clergy.[108] Women being ordained in evangelical churches are often ordained to very specific roles such as chaplains or youth or women's ministers and very rarely as senior pastors.[109] At the same time, women are beginning to be ordained or licensed to preach in the Methodist-oriented Black Church denominations and even elected bishop in a growing number of denominations.[110] There was widespread acclaim for the election in 2000 of Rev. Dr. Vashti Mackenzie as the first woman bishop in the African Methodist Episcopal (AME) Church. Similarly, in 2011, Rev. Dr. Teresa Snorton became a presiding bishop in the Christian Methodist Episcopal (CME) Church—and more Black women have been ordained in intervening years.

Some African American women who feel called to ministry are not waiting for their particular congregations or denominations to ordain them. Some are striking out as entrepreneurs, forming their own vibrant ministries, both in person and on social media. Stereotypical white femininity has never been a feature of women in the Black Church. But as Rev. Dr. Chanequa Walker-Barnes has so well described, to avoid burnout, African American women today must still battle the stereotype of the "Strong Black Woman" who should be able to take care of everyone and everything without faltering.[111]

Many white evangelical women also do not conform to the stereotypically feminine image promoted by Dobson and other white male church leaders, even though in contrast to their Black sisters, socially and politically they still tend to support Christian nationalism. Women evangelists and singers may create a rather uniform, traditionally feminine appearance—not unlike Trump's "type"—a Barbie doll figure, beautiful clothes and jewelry, a mane of blond hair, and false eyelashes. But a majority of women in the pew do not emulate this look or have time for this lifestyle.

Denker describes regional differences among women in the Southeast, in Southern California, and in the Rust Belt. She claims that evangelical women in the South are still to varying degrees conditioned by romanticized antebellum ideas of femininity, purity, fragility, and the need to be protected. Some of these women may under the surface be "steel magnolias" as portrayed in the popular film, but they conform outwardly to a stereotypically feminine appearance. Many Christian women in Orange County, California, as Denker describes them, also tend to strive for a more fashionable, perfectly coiffed, high-heeled appearance, befitting the glamour of such megachurch edifices as the (former) Crystal Cathedral.[112]

The difference between the Southern and West Coast women that Denker interviewed and many other Christian nationalist women is not merely regional or historical, however. It is also wrapped up in class differences. White working-class women in any part of the country have never had the time or money to spend on lavish wardrobes or expensive haircuts and makeup. They often have no choice but to work, unlike some wealthier evangelical women who may choose not to. Surrounded by other women in the same circumstances, they do not often consider a more glamorous lifestyle within reach—or even particularly desirable. Working women put on their jeans and T-shirts, or for a special occasion, a blouse or dress from Walmart, and get down to the business of keeping their families washed, fed, and perhaps able to achieve more in the next generation than they themselves could afford. They are tough, often because they have to be—they are the steel without the magnolia.

A woman of my acquaintance, "Shirley,"[113] is a good example of the complexity that characterizes many politically conservative white Christian women. Before her divorce after years of physical and emotional abuse, she was a stay-at-home mom who homeschooled her kids, kept chickens and a vegetable garden, dressed simply, and appeared to support her husband's role as breadwinner and head of the family. When her husband was severely injured in a truck accident, her kids went back to public school so that she could visit him in the hospital every day as he went through multiple surgeries, requiring a two-plus-hour round trip. She got work as a part-time home health aide and took on additional odd jobs. Since her divorce, she still keeps chickens, works part-time, drives a pickup, chops wood, and owns a rifle—and knows how to use it. Like many white women in rural middle America, she is not easily categorizable.

Both within and beyond evangelical Christianity, there is a shift away from the stereotypically feminine in women's self-image and self-portrayal. The stereotype of the fragile feminine woman has never washed with poor and working-class women, regardless of religion. And at least among those who show up at Christian nationalist rallies and revivals, regardless of class, women are now taking on more of the toughness that was once the exclusive domain of men.

At a biker rally I attended in the summer of 2021, hosted by State Senator Mastriano, the women were far from fragile. Although most rode behind their husbands on the motorcycles, their right-wing political T-shirts, jeans, and leather boots matched those of the men. The event also demonstrated how it's impossible to generalize on the basis of class, since the "dressed down" look belies the reality that many bikers are affluent enough to invest tens of thousands of dollars in luxury chrome and steel. Traditional markers of both gender and class break down at events like these. The common thread is a fierce nationalism undergirded by at least nominal Christian identity.

Sarah Palin's sudden appearance on the national scene as John McCain's running mate may well have redefined for many women—and men—what a Christian nationalist woman leader can be like. Du Mez writes that although evangelicals were concerned about Palin's violation of some traditional gender norms (which would seem to preclude a woman serving in such a public leadership role), there were more overriding fears—namely, the prospect of retaining in office a Black US president. Palin also possessed the right religious and class bona fides:

> Raised in nondenominational evangelicalism with a dose of Pentecostalism, Palin was a self-described "Bible-believing Christian," a down-to-earth candidate ("just your average hockey mom") who appealed to plain-folk evangelicals, to those tired of being disparaged by "liberal elites." She was also a creationist, she was staunchly pro-gun and anti-abortion, and she had just given birth to her fifth child, who had Down syndrome. But Palin didn't only, or even primarily project a maternal image. A former beauty queen, she embodied an ideal of feminine beauty that had been elevated to a new level of spiritual—and political—significance. She was the ultimate culture warrior, a Phyllis Schlafly for a new generation, a moose-hunting pit bull in lipstick who could give feminists a run for their money, without compromising her sex appeal. In this way, Palin embodied the conservative ideal that "their" women knew how to please men. And Palin delighted in undermining the masculinity of liberal men, especially Barack Obama. Many voters found Palin's unpredictability and general ignorance of world affairs disqualifying, but to many evangelicals, she was . . . "a rock star."[114]

In national politics today, there are a number of conservative white women who have adopted a similar persona. Like many Christian nationalists, they blend religion with politics in the same breath, mainly pointing to their Christianity to appeal to their evangelical base and to buttress their right-wing political conservatism, at its most extreme in some cases.[115] One *Washington Post* columnist noticed that so many Republican women candidates and elected politicians were being photographed wearing or carrying guns that it has become "a new political meme."[116]

Georgian Kelly Loeffler narrowly lost her ultraconservative campaign for reelection to a seat she had held in the US Senate as an appointee. Her challenger was Rev. Raphael Warnock, pastor of the historic Ebenezer Baptist Church in Atlanta. Loeffler, a wealthy businesswoman, owner of the WNBA women's basketball team The Dream, and longtime donor to Republican politicians, in some ways resembles the evangelical Christian look with her careful makeup and long blond hair. But she also frequently dons jeans and a USA baseball cap and generally displays a Sarah Palin–like, pretty-but-tough demeanor. In one campaign ad, Loeffler described herself as "more conservative than Attila the Hun."[117]

Declaring, "I'm a Christian, I'm a person of deep faith," Loeffler campaigned proudly on her "100% Trump voting record."[118] Her ads featured vicious attacks against Warnock and his faith, including taking statements from his sermons out of context and accusing him of "us[ing] the Bible to justify abortion and to attack our men and women in the military."[119] In the end, Warnock's long history of fighting for equality and social justice, following his sense of call as a Black pastor, and standing in the legacy of Martin Luther King Jr., whose church he now serves, convinced a plurality of voters that it was his brand of Christian conviction they wanted to see in the Senate—flipping a long-held Republican Senate seat blue.

Marjorie Taylor Greene, who won her bid for a seat in the US House of Representatives, represents perhaps the most extreme version of this blond, tough-talking, Trump-supporting Christian nationalist woman. In one campaign ad, "Marjorie Green: Save America, Stop Socialism," she appeared driving a Humvee onto a field where she took aim with an AR-15 and blasts away one tin can target after another, each with a caption: "gun control . . . open borders . . . the green new deal . . . and socialism."[120]

In another ad soon after winning a primary runoff election, Greene posted a cobbled-together image on Facebook showing herself dressed in a black jacket and white shirt, holding an AR-15 semiautomatic weapon aimed in the direction of a black-and-white montage of House Representatives Alexandria Ocasio-Cortez, Ilhan Omar, Ayanna Pressley, and Rashida Tlaib (all progressive women of color, two of them Muslim, dubbed collectively "The Squad"). The ad's caption was "The Squad's Worst Nightmare," and the text posted below it included an explicit shout-out to

Christian nationalists: "Hate American leftists want to take this country down . . . Politicians have failed this country. I'm tired of seeing weak, Establishment Republicans play defense. Our country is on the line. America needs fighters who speak the truth. We need strong conservative Christians to go on the offense against these socialists who want to rip our country apart. Americans must take this country back. SAVE AMERICA. STOP SOCIALISM. DEFEAT THE DEMOCRATS!—Marjorie"[121]

Omar and Tlaib responded quickly on Twitter, condemning the post as incitement to violence and noting that there were already death threats in response to the post. They, along with many others in Congress, including Speaker Nancy Pelosi, demanded that Facebook immediately take the post down. Facebook did remove the post the same day, but since nothing dies on the internet, the image is still readily searchable. In January 2019, Greene also "liked" a social media post saying that a "bullet to the head" would be the quickest way to remove Pelosi from the House speakership.[122]

"God, Guns, and Guts Made America—Let's Keep All Three"

All these threats to a way of life characterized by patriarchy and white supremacy also underlie conservative Christians' and other right-wing supporters' adamant insistence on unfettered gun ownership. A poll as of January 6, 2022 revealed that 30% of Republicans are convinced that "American patriots may have to resort to violence" to save the country.[123]

Recall the flag brandished by one Trump supporter at the January 6 insurrection: "God, Guns, and Guts Made America—Let's Keep All Three." In the gun culture that characterizes much of the geographical regions where Christian nationalists are most numerous, guns are looked upon not as frightening but rather as utilitarian and reassuring. Much of this traditionally has had to do with hunting—a food source as much as a sport in many rural areas. When my spouse Michael first became president of the Lutheran Theological Seminary in Gettysburg, he was promptly informed by staff that the opening of deer season was an unofficial but rigorously observed day off for much of the maintenance crew and other staff. When chatting with Shirley on one occasion, I heard rifle fire in the woods nearby and flinched. She said, "Oh, I don't worry about that. I've always lived around guns." On another occasion, when we were comparing notes about how we might thwart "Pokey," our resident groundhog, from devouring all our zucchini, she helpfully offered, "Next time you see him, just give me a call, and I'll come right over with my rifle."

Hunting has been eclipsed in recent years, however, by a desire for protection. Two-thirds of gun owners today say protection is their main reason for owning a gun, while over one-third list hunting, and close to another third cite sport shooting (target, trap, and skeet).[124] Denker quotes a Lutheran pastor and former US Marine who coleads a church in Appalachia with his wife. The pastor said he knows people carry guns to worship in his congregation, several among whom are law enforcement officers. He and most of his members have concealed-carry permits. He said, "To a certain extent it's a *fear thing and a control thing*. When you have [a gun] in the building, it's just one less thing to worry about." Guns are so much a part of his community that when a group of young women asked him to join a class with them one Sunday, he was expecting it to be on yoga "or maybe pottery," but "they wanted to do a concealed-carry class."[125] Another of Denker's interviewees, however—a pastor in northwest Iowa who grew up hunting as a regular part of his rural culture—noted his concern "that people want guns for power rather than for practical reasons and hunting for sport." He noted sadly that "a place that literally means safety does not have that vital purpose anymore. Sanctuary is not sanctuary anymore."[126]

Recent research on religion and gun ownership provides evidence from multiple data sources that evangelical Protestants own more guns than the general American population (41% to 30% according to a 2017 Pew study)[127] and are also significantly more likely to own guns than mainline Protestants or adherents to "other religions."[128] Multivariate analysis based on data from a 2012 PRRI report shows that "only among Evangelical Protestants do a majority of respondents report having a gun in the household (57%)," but this is followed closely by mainline Protestants at 49% and "adherents of other religions" at 45%. Based on the same PRRI study, "only 37% of those with no religion report having a gun, followed by 32% of Catholics and 30% of black Protestants."[129]

Black Protestants (at over three-fourths) are the most likely to support passing stricter gun control laws, followed by Catholics and "nones" (both at about two-thirds). Slightly less than half of mainline Protestants also favor stricter gun laws, while evangelical Protestants are the least in favor (at slightly over one-third). Evangelicals are most likely to favor *loosening* gun control laws (37% versus 23–28% of all other religious groups). Evangelical Protestants are most likely to support the concealed carry of guns in churches (but not by a large margin versus mainline Protestants—29% versus 24%, tapering to 21% in "other religions," 19% of "nones," and 14% of both Catholics and Black Protestants).[130]

New Yorker writer Eliza Griswold interviewed Shane Claiborne, an evangelical from the millennial generation who is trying to change what he sees as the alignment of evangelical Christianity with conservative politics. Claiborne has coauthored a book, *Beating Guns*,[131] aimed at persuading Christians to turn away from "gun culture" and follow the words of the prophet Isaiah to "beat their swords into plowshares, and their spears into pruning hooks" (Isa 2:4). Griswold writes,

> Claiborne believes that conservative culture often conflates Christianity and nationalism, placing, as he puts it, "the American flag above the cross." This has long involved aligning religion with American gun culture. Last year, Wayne LaPierre, the executive vice-president of the National Rifle Association, said, in a speech, that the Second Amendment was not a right "bestowed by man, but granted by God to all Americans as our American birthright." In 2017, after a shooting at a Southern Baptist church near San Antonio, Texas, left twenty-six people dead and twenty injured, some Christian leaders called for members of their church to arm themselves; Robert Jeffress, the pastor of the First Baptist Church in Dallas, said, on "Fox and Friends," that he felt more secure knowing that his congregants were carrying weapons. After the shooting in San Bernardino, California, in 2015, Jerry Falwell, Jr., the president of Liberty University, urged his students to procure gun permits. (Along with a year-round ski facility, Liberty's campus is home to a sprawling firing range.) "I've always thought that if more good people had concealed-carry permits, then we could end those Muslims before they walked in," he told students. Claiborne said, "The irony is that you can't have a beer at Liberty, but you can have a gun."[132]

Guns, of course, are also a multivalent symbol of masculine potency[133]—and are now enthusiastically carried by many women as well. The protester waving the "God, Guns, and Guts" flag on January 6 was a white woman. During a Black Lives Matter (BLM) demonstration my husband and I attended in the Gettysburg town square on Fourth of July weekend, two men showed up in a Jeep, dressed in full military camo and holding semiautomatic weapons. A similarly dressed small boy stood between them. A woman (dressed in civvies) also strolled amid the BLM protesters with an assault rifle slung casually over her shoulder. This self-appointed militia was a remnant from a right-wing mobilization on the Civil War battlefield just days before to "protect the Confederate monuments from Antifa." (There was no actual Antifa "invasion"; local police had advised prior to July 4 that this was a social media hoax.) These militia members were vastly outnumbered by the BLM protesters, but we kept a wary eye on them, while a few, refusing to be intimidated, tried engaging them in conversation (to little effect). While all this was occurring, a flatbed truck careened through the square with several men brandishing their own weapons and shouting "Second Amendment! Second Amendment!"

In the current supercharged political climate, the right to own and carry a gun is often conflated with antimask and antivaccination sentiments under the banner of "personal freedom." At the same time Doug Mastriano encourages school boards to defy a Pennsylvania mandatory masking policy, he has introduced legislation that would compel law enforcement in the Commonwealth to refuse to enforce any new federal gun control laws. Simultaneously, he has cosponsored proposed legislation that would remove even the current minimal law requiring a permit for concealed carry.

Following a spate of school shootings, some liberal churches responded to calls for gun control by publicly naming their sanctuaries "gun free zones," while many conservative congregations encouraged parishioners to carry weapons and even hosted "Bring Your Gun to Church" Sundays. The website www.concealedcarry.com advises its visitors that scripture supports Christians using deadly force in self-defense or defense of others and encourages pastors to recruit and train an armed security team. This section of the webpage features a photo of a pistol resting atop a Bible.[134] Conveniently, church leaders can also browse weaponry on the same website and view informational videos on gun owners' rights.

Denker interprets the enthusiasm of conservative Christians for guns as a response to all the ways in which they have perceived evidence of America's moral degeneration:

> They saw broken families and lamented the exodus of prayers in schools. They saw a loss of a certain American innocence. They saw young people lacking steady ground on which to stand. They blamed social media and the internet and birth control. The shootings were rooted in people who didn't speak English and too many refugees

and ISIS encroaching on American borders. For many Red State Christians, a world in which people felt cornered led to the Parkland shooting. The "American carnage" depicted by Trump in his inauguration speech came alive in the images of students running out of their schools, hands over their heads, terrified. In this scary, unfamiliar America, Red State Christians would never surrender their guns. They had to hold them tighter. In fact, they had to arm teachers. They had already lost so much that had previously kept them safe. Guns, in this view, were one final defense against the encroachment of an amoral, irreligious world.[135]

Revival-style worship reinforces the pervasive sense of fear and doom among evangelical Christians. The sensory immersion of this style of worship and preaching often whiplashes back and forth between warnings about not being pure and prepared enough to be raptured or salvaged from among the sinful on the Day of Judgment and warnings of the degradation of America today. As Denker describes, "The necessity of impending doom keeps the fear and defensiveness of many Red State Christians at a fever pitch, which keeps them a captive audience and emotional prey for pastors like Allen [whom she observed preaching at a heavily armed church in Tampa Bay, Florida] or presidents like Trump." The language of "spiritual warfare" further reinforces the militancy with which Christian nationalists push back against their fear of creeping secularism and loss of their way of life. It justifies taking (or at least considering) extreme measures to defeat the foe, which is variously described as Satan, the Left, or both in one breath.[136]

This feeling of being continually embattled bleeds into the prevalent belief that Christians are being persecuted not only in other nations (which in some contexts is horrifyingly true) but in America itself. Goldberg reports, "The refrain that Christians are under siege creates a sense of perpetual crisis among the movement's grass roots. Talk of persecution is common. I've heard well-spoken, kind believers—people who say they long for empathy and understanding to replace the harsh divisiveness in America—worry that one day in the future, the American government might start rounding up Christians and executing them."[137]

Finally, a chronic perception of oneself and one's group as downtrodden can lead to a perpetual low-level feeling of paranoia. Not long after the end of the McCarthy anticommunist witch hunts, historian Richard

Hofstadter observed that American politics has always had more than a faint trace of paranoia. As a nation born out of a revolution against an authoritarian monarchy just 250 years ago (which, in comparison to most countries' history, is a very short time), a certain suspicion against authority continues to be passed down the generations. It shapes a characteristic American embrace of individualism and personal freedoms and also returns over and over in different generations as a tendency to mistrust institutions and authorities. Hofstadter wrote, "American politics has often been an arena for angry minds. . . . I call it the paranoid style simply because no other word adequately evokes the sense of heated exaggeration, suspiciousness, and conspiratorial fantasy that I have in mind."[138] He noted a tendency toward obsessively seeking out "evidence to prove that the unbelievable is the only thing that can be believed"—not for the sake of honest debate but as "a means of warding off the profane intrusion of the secular political world. The paranoid seems to have little expectation of actually convincing a hostile world, but he can accumulate evidence in order to protect his cherished convictions from it."[139]

Paranoia, as opposed to realistic fear, is an irrational and all-encompassing belief that the world is evil and that threats are everywhere. Clinically paranoid individuals (as in paranoid schizophrenia) are afflicted with this belief to a delusional degree caused by an organic brain disorder.[140] But paranoia exists on a spectrum of mental health diagnoses, from frank psychosis to neurotic anxiety in otherwise rational people. Especially when reinforced by a steady diet of mis- or disinformation on social media or through other social contacts—including fears instilled by persuasive religious leaders—very unreasonable fears can seem at least plausible. And all too often, fear, especially when denied or repressed, can turn to hate.

Down the Rabbit Hole: The Irrational Allure of Conspiracy Theories

Paranoia—comprised of both fear and hate—provides a fertile, receptive ground for the seeds of conspiracy theories to take root and grow. Several years before Donald Trump's presidency, with its manifold increase in outright lies to the public, Goldberg wrote,

> America is full of good people, but something dark [sic] is loose. There's a free-floating anxiety that easily metastasizes into paranoid

and a hatred for the same enemies always targeted by authoritarian populist movements—homosexuals, urbanites, foreigners, intellectuals, and religious minorities. Rationality is losing its hold; empirical evidence is discounted as the product of a secular worldview or a scheming liberal elite. In such an atmosphere, most mainstream sources of information are assumed to be deceptive, so many people find ascertaining the true state of things very difficult. Thus trusted authorities—preachers, politicians, radio demagogues—hold enormous sway. All truth except biblical truth becomes relative, and biblical truth is entwined with American history and national destiny. Democracy suffocates in this atmosphere, and space opens up for something else to supplant it.[141]

She goes on to quote Hannah Arendt, who wrote in her post-Holocaust analysis of the Nazi terror, *The Origins of Totalitarianism*, "Before they seize power and establish a world according to their doctrines, totalitarian movements conjure up a lying world of consistency which is more adequate to the needs of the human mind than reality itself. . . . The force possessed by totalitarian propaganda—before the movements have the power to drop iron curtains to prevent anyone's disturbing, by the slightest reality, the gruesome quiet of an entirely imaginary world—lies in its ability to shut the masses off from the real world."[142]

In my own work, and in my personal life, I have tried to resist the notion of "two Americas" that has become a frequent phrase in political commentary in recent years.[143] My research for this book has changed my view. After attending a political biker rally, visiting a gun shop, and viewing televangelists on YouTube and television, I have had the disorienting experience of finding myself in a completely different world, surrounded by people living in an alternate reality. Christian nationalism is, indeed, as sociologists have described it, a political movement with religious symbols and trappings to justify it. But more than that, it is a completely immersive culture. If culture is defined by a combination of social, political, and religious beliefs with food, dress, artistic expression, and ethnicity, then Christian nationalism readily fits the definition. It excludes and derides those who do not fit in a majority of these categories, particularly in their beliefs but also in many of the other markers of cultural belonging. But its exclusivity also reflects a layer of dread—of losing this culture, being "replaced" by a liberal America that its members fear—and this fear leads to hate.

This fear, hate, and desire to "take back" the rest of America (to be like the America they live in and want to protect) can veer toward violent extremism. When that bridge is crossed, "good people," to use Trump's characterization, can end up picking up torches and joining together with activist white-supremacist hate groups such as the Proud Boys, the Boogaloo Bois, and others, as they did in Charlottesville, Virginia, in a Unite the Right march on August 11–12, 2017. David Duke, the head of the Ku Klux Klan (who also endorsed Trump for the presidency), was in attendance. Expressing the hate fueled by fear of losing white Christian supremacy, they chanted, "Jews will not replace us! You will not replace us!"

At this "Unite the Right" rally, organized to protest the removal of a Confederate statue, a right-wing demonstrator rammed his vehicle into a crowd of antihate counterprotesters, killing one woman, Heather Heyer, and injuring over a dozen others. Two state troopers also died in a helicopter crash while surveilling the scene. The Governor of Virginia declared a state of emergency, while Trump responded with a comment ambiguously condemning an "egregious display of hatred, bigotry and violence on many sides, *on many sides*," which most commentators understood to equate the counterprotesters' peaceful demonstration with the right-wing activists' violence, pandering to the alt-right members of his base.[144] White supremacists have committed at least 73 murders since Charlottesville,[145] as mass shootings and hate crimes have been on the rise.[146]

Christian nationalists are, as several writers have noted, "vulnerable" to right-wing conspiracy theories, ranging from antivaccine campaigns (even before Covid-19) to QAnon. All these distorted notions (once considered fringe but increasingly amplified by social media and right-wing radio talk shows and TV news) align well with one of the foundational sentiments of Christian nationalism—that their "way of life" is being undermined by a cabal of child-abusing liberal politicians and "anti-American" elites.

While statistics vary widely on what percentage of overlap may exist between Christian nationalists and groups organized around conspiracy theories, a survey by the American Enterprise Institute found that over a quarter (27%) of white evangelical Christians and almost a third (31%) of white evangelical Republicans agreed "mostly" or "completely" with "the core tenet of QAnon: 'Donald Trump has been secretly fighting a group of child sex traffickers that include prominent Democrats and Hollywood elites.'"[147] Another survey (of over 1,700 Americans) from Denison

University found that *50% of white evangelical Christians* "agreed" or "strongly agreed" with QAnon.[148] ABC news reporter Kaleigh Rogers writes, "Comparative surveys have also shown a correlation between Christian nationalism and conspiratorial thinking, specifically a belief in QAnon. And it's something members of the church have been sounding the alarm about for months."[149] However, it should be noted from a recent PRRI study that "a nontrivial 15%" of *all* Americans believe that the government, media, and finance are controlled by Satan-worshipping pedophiles and that American patriots may have to resort to violence to save the country, and a full 20% believe that "there is a storm coming soon that will sweep away the elites in power and restore the rightful leaders." In this PRRI study, white evangelicals lead other religious groups in believing QAnon theories (at 22%), followed closely by Hispanic Protestants and Mormons (both at 21%). Other Christians fall in a range from 17% to 12%, with unaffiliated Americans at 9% and Jews at just 2%.[150]

Marjorie Taylor Greene, described earlier, has made numerous public statements straight from the QAnon playbook, including the spread of conspiracy theories about the "deep state."[151] She ended a "MUST READ" blog post by writing, "The frightening fact that all of us must face is that these articles are not conspiracy theory. They are written with factual data backing them up. The MSM will avoid these real issues, but we must do our part to push them into light, and to force these evil things to stop and be brought to justice."[152] As a lawmaker, Greene may seem like an extreme example, but roughly 230,000 (or 75%) of voters in Georgia's majority white and Republican 14th District elected her to the US House of Representatives[153]—a telling result about the current disposition of the right-wing, white, Christian electorate considering that Greene was a candidate who campaigned on far-right Christian nationalism mixed together with a wholehearted embrace of QAnon and other conspiracies.

As another example of the intertwining of Christian nationalism and QAnon, Jacob Chansley—the horned and furred QAnon shaman at the January 6 break-in at the Capitol (as noted in Chapter 1)—took the vice president's seat in the Senate chamber and, while brandishing an American flag, shouted into a megaphone,

> Thank you, heavenly Father, for being the inspiration needed to these police officers to allow us into the building, to allow us to exercise our rights, to allow us to send a message to all the tyrants, the Communists,

and the globalists, that this is our nation, not theirs, that we will not allow the America, the American way of the United States of America, to go down.... Thank you, divine, omniscient, omnipotent, and omnipresent creator God for filling this chamber with your white light and love, your white light of harmony. Thank you for filling this chamber with patriots that love you and love Christ.[154]

It is interesting in light of QAnon's focus on child abuse and sex trafficking that evangelical Christians have for more than a decade elevated sex trafficking as their primary campaign against sexual violence, while work to end sexual and domestic violence and other forms of sexual abuse remains largely the domain of secular nonprofit organizations, with some notable faith-based exceptions.[155] There is no question that sex trafficking is a worldwide horror,[156] involving tens of thousands of women and girls;[157] Covid-19 pandemic lockdowns have exacerbated the problem for the victims.[158] But emphasizing this one form of sexual violence (mostly targeting women and girls) while often ignoring other issues such as sexual abuse and exploitation in the church itself (as noted earlier) carries the missionary whiff of white saviors helping victims from the Global South escape evil predators (who themselves may be from the Global South). This single-minded zeal for victims of trafficking sidesteps the vast extent of violence against women, girls, and LGBTQ persons perpetrated by and against Americans. Meanwhile, "nice" white Christian American men—whose own wives may be fundraising to end human trafficking—head from their suburban homes at night to certain desolate urban locations, directed there by social media sites, to purchase sexual "services" from enslaved girls and women.

Child abduction and abuse is, of course, a powerful emotional issue, and QAnon goes straight for the maternal jugular when it comes to recruiting highly protective white suburban moms. Journalist Seyward Darby points to the impact of the Covid-19 pandemic on women due to the lockdown and isolation: "Stuck at home, fragile, malleable, and absorbing bad ideas that make sense to them."[159] Women are made to feel empowered by the message that they can protect children while staying at home caring for their own families and participating in a movement on social media. Susan Shaw, citing Darby, also writes,

> Women no longer have to be part of an organized extremist group to participate; they just have to believe the extremist messages and stand up for them through posting online, going to a rally, or protesting. In

fact, as Darby notes, many of these women who have been radicalized wouldn't even see it that way. After all these ideas have been articulated by the president [Trump] and repeated over and over on media outlets. Often these extremist ideas get softened as they move from organized hate into the mainstream. What is overtly racist language in hate groups becomes coded language about immigration, crime and making America great again.[160]

This flow from the fringe to the mainstream goes both ways. The fringe, according to Darby, "is just a manifestation of central ideas in US culture. Extremist groups magnify these ideas, and then the ideas come back into the culture in softer language that allows them to be mainstreamed."[161] And the messages are spread everywhere—even apparently sweet online affinity groups such as ones for knitters have been infiltrated, and normal-sounding gossip spreads lies and hate.[162]

All too often, then, people can get drawn in by conspiracy theories and political lies without even realizing they have gone down a slippery slope into an alternative universe. In the current media culture, it's easy to fall into a bubble or an echo chamber, where only certain ideas are allowed, and these ideas are amplified by repetition until they just *feel* like they must be true.[163] As Susan Shaw writes, "Extremist ideas have moved from the dark corners of the internet into mainstream thinking among many conservatives."[164] Some of this happens as unwitting participants repeat and amplify increasingly right-wing messages, but much of it is calculated through deliberate infiltration and reinforced by repetition.[165]

The bubble provides a social network and a feeling of belonging that is emotionally appealing. And the core beliefs of the group are held not lightly but with zeal. People become passionate and are cheered on by the others inside the group with "likes" and thumbs-ups on social media. Social media researchers have noticed a "soft" appeal, for example, to the QAnon conspiracy. Women influencers on social media comingle recipes for comfort food, makeup tips, and household advice with comments on child abuse and trafficking that would concern any good person, any good *mother*. And they ask things like, "I know it sounds crazy, but what if Q is right? What if there really *is* a child trafficking ring?" Sounds reasonable enough to be concerned and to ask to learn more—"What if we ignore this and it turns out to be true?" Then the next question continues down the slippery slope: "What if Q is right that the government is trying to cover it up because they're actually the ones *doing* evil things—there's a deep state they don't want us to know about!"

So when this seed of a "deep state" is planted in people's minds, wrapped in the natural concern for the safety of children, it is easy to take the next step down that slippery slope (reinforced by media platforms' algorithms that steer people toward ideas they have already "liked") and begin to follow threads on social media with the hashtags #qanon, #deepstate, or even the seemingly benign #savethechildren! When this antiauthoritarian passion is conjoined with another—the fervor of self-appointed, heavily armed militias, organizing under the banner of the constitutional rights to free speech and to bear arms—and with groups of white supremacists, both long-standing and new, a violence-prone mob mentality can break out. All kinds of long-simmering resentments and fears can come bubbling up when they are given approval by a strong leader, adding fuel to the fire.

When a charismatic public leader appears to give permission to this rhetoric of rebellion, even permission to hate,[166] it can be the final catalyst that brings the disparate antiauthoritarian groups together to form an armed rebellion. The FBI reported a 20% surge in hate crimes since Trump became president, with hate-related murders at their highest level in three decades and hate crimes generally the highest in a decade.[167] The storming of the Capitol on January 6, seen through *this* lens, should not have been a surprise. There was a fuse ready to be lit, and it exploded into violence.

Once conspiracy theories take root, they are also very difficult to dislodge. It is frustratingly difficult to prove the nonexistence of something, and there are always lingering questions in the face of all evidence to the contrary: "But what if QAnon is right about child abuse? If I ignore this, am I allowing more children to be harmed? What if the 'Stop the Steal' movement *is* true? The idea that there could be widespread fraud sounds so plausible in this day and age, when there is so much corruption in government." And how can a person just walk away when it feels so fulfilling to be involved in such a seemingly righteous, patriotic cause?

Unconscious Motivations

In the preceding pages, we have explored a range of feelings and motivations that draw people into Christian nationalism. While adherents may not readily articulate these factors that heavily influence them, to a large degree, they are on the level of consciousness. Unconscious motivations are, of course, more difficult to pin down, and by the very nature of the psychoanalytic theory that undergirds this line of inquiry, examining what emotional dynamics may lie beneath the surface of anyone's adherence to a particular group or ideology is a somewhat speculative exercise. Nevertheless, psychologists studied unconscious group dynamics even before the beginnings of psychoanalysis with Sigmund Freud and his own circle of followers.

Readers might be wondering, "Why refer to Sigmund Freud in this day and age—aren't his theories outdated?"[168] Of course, yes, many of Freud's ideas have been superseded by a century of further research and theorizing, particularly regarding women, homosexuality, and gender identity. But Freud's most basic insight is still relevant: that the mind comprises much more than what is held in conscious awareness, that unconscious drives and our early childhood experiences of caregivers often prompt us to think, react, and behave in ways that we ourselves find puzzling, even self-sabotaging.

Moreover, when it comes to group psychology, no one to this day has made more keen observations on the ways in which a group also has a kind of collective psyche that encompasses and in certain ways takes over the attitudes and actions of the group's individual members. Freud wrote his seminal book *Group Psychology and the Analysis of the Ego*[169] in 1921, just a few short years after the end of World War I. He had lived through fear for his sons' lives, both of whom had enlisted (they survived). He then lost a beloved daughter and grandson to the Spanish flu, which swept through an impoverished Europe in the aftermath of the war. And all of this was wrapped up in a lifelong experience of being the target of antisemitism—which was rising again in Vienna in overt political rhetoric and public acts of violence by the time he was writing the book.[170]

Having come to a feeling of deep disillusionment about patriotism and the leaders of nations—and pessimism about the human capacity for violence and aggression—Freud struggled to understand how seemingly rational people could come under the sway of a group to the point of participating in collective violence that they would never commit as individuals. Given the similar rise in unabashed hate speech and mob violence in the United States today, his observations on the unconscious dynamics of groups remain highly relevant and contribute another dimension to understanding how people can be drawn into groups that are destructive of the social fabric, even leading to violence.

The Magnetism of Groupthink

Freud himself was not the first psychologist to study groups and to recognize that when people join a group, they begin to participate in a social dynamic that transcends individuals' particular attitudes—even to the point of sacrificing their own personal morality and capacity for critical thinking. Freud drew heavily in his *Group Psychology* on the late 19th-century work of Gustave Le Bon (1841–1931), whose treatise *The Crowd: A Study of the Popular Mind*[171] laid the foundations for the study of groups, especially mass movements. Le Bon's work, like Freud's, was prompted by experiences of war (the Franco-Prussian War) and its devastating economic aftermath, including a short-lived antiauthoritarian revolt in Paris in the 1870s. Le Bon wrote, as quoted by Freud,

> The most striking peculiarity presented by a psychological group is the following. Whoever be the individuals that compose it, however like or unlike be their mode of life, their occupations, their character, or their intelligence, the fact that they have been transformed into a group puts them in possession of a sort of collective mind which makes them feel, think, and act in a manner quite different from that in which each individual of them would feel, think, and act were he in a state of isolation. There are certain ideas and feelings which do not come into being, or do not transform themselves into acts except in the case of individuals forming a group. The psychological group is a provisional being formed of heterogeneous elements, which for a moment are combined, exactly as the cells which constitute a living body form by their reunion a new being which displays characteristics very different from those possessed by each of the cells singly.[172]

Le Bon believed that under the pressure of a group, distinctive characteristics of individuals would come to be submerged in a larger group unconscious that tapped into a common human disposition—somewhat like Jung's later articulation of a "collective unconscious."[173] Freud approvingly quotes Le Bon again: "The individual forming part of a group acquires, solely from numerical considerations, a sentiment of invincible power which allows him to yield to instincts which, had he been alone, he would perforce have kept under restraint. He will be the less disposed to check himself, from the consideration that, a group being anonymous and in consequence irresponsible, the sentiment of responsibility which always controls individuals disappears entirely."[174]

Freud contends, citing Le Bon, that a form of contagion arises in groups, similar to hypnosis. This group contagion or suggestibility can induce individuals to take actions that they would not necessarily take as individuals. Freud also agrees with Le Bon that in groups, people regress—they lose touch with their most highly developed thinking capacity and begin to behave more in accordance with primal drives: "spontaneity, violence, ferocity, and also enthusiasm and heroism." He quotes the German poet Schiller: "Jeder, sieht man ihn einzeln, ist leidlich klug und verständig; Sind sie in corpore, gleich wird euch ein Dummkopf daraus." (Everyone, when viewed as an individual, is quite astute and mature; when in a group, they become stupid.)[175] Freud adds that a group is more likely to think, as young children do, in images rather than words and concepts, so "agreement with reality is never checked by any reasonable agency. The feelings of a group are always very simple and very exaggerated. So that a group knows neither doubt nor uncertainty."[176] It is easy to see how today social media can reinforce this, since it is a visual world of images including both photos and videos.

Freud goes on to set his pessimism aside momentarily and allows that groups can be guided by high ideals and not only the most animalistic impulses: "Under the influence of suggestion groups are also capable of high achievement in the shape of abnegation, unselfishness, and devotion to an ideal." Here the group may have a modifying effect on individuals' self-interests, and although Freud believed that the group dulls individuals' intellectual capacity, it may also raise their moral values. So group persuasion can move individuals in two extreme directions: a group's "ethical conduct may rise as high above [the individual's] as it may sink deep below it."

What is the differentiating factor that makes some groups constructive in their goals and others so destructive? This is where Freud's own contribution went beyond the observations of Le Bon, which focused mainly on emotional contagion within a group. Freud proposed that the character and aims of a group (altruistic or nefarious) also depend heavily on the character and aims of the leader.

The Unconscious Power of the Leader:
Identification, Idealization, and Narcissistic Leaders

Freud describes the relationship of followers to a leader as something more than simple admiration, or even the desire to have a relationship with that person. Two unconscious motivations come into play when group members begin not only to admire or like their leaders but to idolize them. The first is what Freud called "identification," and the second is idealization. Identification has come into general parlance to some extent—"I identify with the female characters in this book," "I identify with other introverts," "I can't identify with Jan's hyper work ethic," "I don't identify with their frustration about that," and so on. In psychoanalytic terms, it means unconsciously adopting another person's characteristics, beliefs, or ways of being as a form of psychic internalization. I take your attributes into myself, and they become a part of me, a part of my identity, my self-image. Unlike admiration or agreement, which are conscious, this is a process that largely happens without a person realizing it (although both admiration and identification can be going on at the same time).

In infancy, this is the first way in which a child forms an attachment to the parent (Freud thought literally the mother)—by taking her in (bodily, and then by forming internal representations of her in the mind). In normal development, the child begins to experience self and other as separate and can love the other as other (as well as a range of other feelings from positive to negative, depending on the nature of the relationship itself). A positive remnant of early identifications remains in the form of what has been taken in as good and idealized. Freud called this internal part of the self the "ego ideal," which can be a foundation for one's values, and the component of the ego related to conscience.[177]

For healthy individuals, identification with another person is an element in forming good relationships—an inner sense or intuition of having something in common that resonates with early positive experiences. But identification in adulthood, if it is too prominent, can also lead to a regression to a more dependent state of being, as in early childhood, in which the other person's traits, actions, and beliefs are internalized and unconsciously begin to shape and even alter identity. This regressive form of identification is often driven by an unconscious sense of lack and a compulsive need to make up for a loss or deficit in early childhood—such as a parent's chronic emotional misattunement, unreliability, frequent absence or abandonment, or outright abuse.

It is precisely this type of regression that Freud sees occurring in groups that become attached to a strong leader. The members of such a group have unconsciously substituted the charismatic figure of the leader for their individual ego ideals. The resulting bond creates both forceful emotional ties among the members of the group, who now all share a common ego ideal,[178] and a strong bond of loyalty with the leader (who is now a part of themselves). Some of Freud's more speculative, and many would say outdated, notions come into play in his theory here as well—that the leader is a psychological stand-in for the father and his authority. And since for Freud, these strong emotional ties are "libidinal" (i.e., coming from a primal sex drive), he also sees the attachment to this leader and to other members of the group as fulfilling a deep, instinctual wish (disguised in more socially acceptable form).

Freud does not account for—or even take into consideration—the possibility of similar attachments to women leaders. There are, of course, groups attached to leaders who are not "fathers" (although women leaders can also be unconsciously identified with as such). There is not space in this book to delve into the extensive debates about women's leadership, how it might or might not essentially differ from men's, or how Freud's views on paternal authority were limited by his own time and culture. There are certainly many examples of strong women leaders at all levels of society. But in our own time, we have not escaped the socialization to expect masculine and feminine models of leadership to be differentiated by an expectation of male *authority* versus female *care*. Most women leaders will admit, if only privately, that members of their organization will not automatically grant them the same authoritative style of leadership that would be expected, even admired in men, and that often it becomes strategically necessary to adopt "softer" ways of relating to the group in order to maintain a necessary amount of authority for group cohesion and effectiveness.

Many feminist writers and thinkers have advocated for a more egalitarian style of leadership, not only as more befitting what is supposedly women's innately maternal care for the group, but as a healthier model of organization for people of all genders. Any sort of egalitarian model is vanishingly rare in Christian nationalist circles. Freud's *Group Psychology* is as relevant a description today as it was in his own time regarding the psychologically symbiotic bond between followers and their idealized patriarchal leaders, a symbiosis that psychologists have variously called "mass hypnosis," "mutual intoxication," and "the spell cast by persons—the nexus of unfreedom."[179]

One final element in Freud's observations about this type of leader is the element of *narcissism*. Freud understood that the psychology of individual members of a group and the psychology of the father figure leader were symmetrical, not identical. The individual still longed for emotional ties with others, but "the father, chief, or leader . . . had few libidinal ties; he loved no one but himself, or other people only in so far as they served his needs. . . . Even today the members of a group stand in need of the illusion that they are equally and justly loved by their leader; but the leader himself need love no one else, he may be of a masterful nature, absolutely narcissistic, self-confident, and independent."[180] Love, said Freud, "puts a check on narcissism"[181] and as such is crucial to civilization. But the narcissistic leader loves only himself and exploits the love and devotion of his followers only and always for his own benefit (as he sees it, according to his whims).

Heinz Kohut, a psychoanalyst in the generation after Freud and founder of a later psychoanalytic movement called self psychology, extended Freud's theories on narcissism.[182] Kohut distinguished between pathological narcissism and the healthy narcissism in adulthood that is probably a requirement for successful leaders (e.g., possessing reality-based self-confidence and a willingness to be decisive and authoritative when needed—but not authoritarian). Primary narcissism (Freud's term for the normal self-orientation of infants and toddlers) becomes problematic in Kohut's view when the very young child does not receive the "mirroring" needed at the appropriate time—admiration, applause, the "gleam in the parent's eye" when the baby achieves a developmental step like walking or talking, and most of all, empathy for who the child actually is, as opposed to who the parents want or unconsciously need the child to be. Neglect, disregard, or narcissistic parenting—in which the parent views the growing child as an extension of the parent's identity and needs rather than promoting the child's own natural personality, interests, and abilities—can result in a depressive sense of emptiness and lack that can persist into adulthood.

Professor of psychiatry and former CIA profiler Jerrold Post perceives that the narcissism of charismatic leaders has its origin in this developmental deficit in early childhood—what he calls, citing Kohut, a "mirror-hungry personality."[183] Relevant to Christian nationalists, Post notes regarding narcissistic leaders' use of religious rhetoric,

> The invocation of divine guidance and use of Biblical references are surely the currency of American political rhetoric, and no politician worth his salt would ignore them. What is the difference between the politician whose use of such rhetoric rings false, as hollow posturing, and the politician whose religious words inspire? . . . The narcissistic individual who does indeed consciously believe that he has special leadership gifts and accordingly has a special role to play may utilize religious rhetoric much more convincingly. . . . While the ability to convey belief is an important asset, real belief is most convincing. This is also true of the polarization of good and evil, we versus them. Again, while it is a common political tactic to attempt to unify the populace against an outside enemy, the rhetoric of polarization is most effective when, as in the case of Hitler, they are absolutely believed to be the source of the problem, they are evil, and to eliminate them is to eliminate our problems. . . . In order to be effectively charismatic it is a great asset to possess paranoid conviction.[184]

Post believes this "mirror-hungry" character of the narcissistic leader attracts a particular type of personality as followers—drawing on the other main deficit Kohut identified as a primary infantile need—that of "idealization."[185] Kohut believed that in addition to a need to be applauded for age-appropriate achievements and just being who the child really is turning out to be, there is a second "pole" of development, which is a need to have a person—normally a parent or other caregiving figure in early childhood—who can be idealized, someone they "want to grow up to be like." Kohut believed that the needs for mirroring and idealizing are lifelong needs that are modulated in intensity by healthy development.[186] However, adults can also become "ideal-hungry," in Post's wording, becoming especially susceptible to the hypnotic appeal of a charismatic leader: "Leaders such as Trump, who convey this sense of grandiose omnipotence, are attractive to individuals seeking idealized sources of strength; they convey a sense of conviction and certainty to those who are consumed by doubt and uncertainty. . . . Trump's motto 'Make America Great Again' had a strong resonance."[187]

This may sound a bit like blaming the victim—a criticism also leveled at times toward researchers of cults and their recruits.[188] Post hastens to add that in times of overwhelming stress, adults who normally would not be vulnerable to following a narcissistic leader may also be drawn in. He points out that especially "at moments of societal crisis, otherwise mature and psychologically healthy individuals may temporarily come to feel overwhelmed and in need of a strong and self-assured leader. But when the historical moment passes, so too does the need. . . . Indeed, the process of idealization carries within it the seeds of disillusion."[189]

Cult expert Margaret Singer further asserts that *anyone* under the right circumstances can be drawn in by a highly manipulative narcissistic leader: "When we hear of . . . individuals' being controlled and influenced by others, we instinctively try to separate ourselves from those persons. . . . Just as most soldiers believe bullets will hit only others, most people tend to believe that their own minds and thought processes are invulnerable."[190] Singer calls this the "not me myth," going on to write that "it has become clear over the years that everyone is susceptible to the lure of these master manipulators."[191]

Based on her research, about two-thirds of cult members "came from normal, functioning families and were demonstrating age-appropriate behavior around the same time," while about one-third "had diagnosable depressions related to personal loss . . . or were struggling with age-related sexual and career dilemmas."[192] Countering social researchers who assign blame, for example, to "strictly pathological types,"[193] Singer writes, "We are all being influenced all the time. And we all are potentially vulnerable . . . especially as our society becomes more and more commercialized, violent and alienating, dishonest and corrupt, polarized and without structure."[194]

Since at least 2015, much ink has been spilled and considerable radio and TV airtime has been spent describing Donald Trump and his blindly obedient adherents in just such terms. Throughout his campaign, and increasingly during and after his term as president, Trump has exhibited the exact traits of Singer's "master manipulators" and even reveled in them. He has an insatiable need to be cheered by adoring crowds and to ensure absolute loyalty (beyond all reason) from those who worked for him directly. Trump, like other strongmen before him, is still viewed by many right-wing Christians as the divinely ordained leader of the country. Sarah Huckabee Sanders (daughter of Baptist pastor and former Arkansas governor Mike Huckabee) said, while serving as Trump's press secretary, "God wanted Donald Trump to become President."[195] This prophecy was one of the elements fueling the January 6 insurrection[196] and has not been abandoned by Christian nationalist True Believers as of this writing. A billboard depicting Trump as the son of God (using a misquote from scripture, attributing "unto us a son is given, and the government shall be upon his shoulders" to "joint heirs Romans 8:17") appeared as recently as September 2021 in Fort Oglethorpe, Georgia. It was subsequently taken down after numerous protests.[197]

It is important to remember, however, that Christian nationalism preceded Donald Trump. At present, even out of office, he continues to wield enormous authority over white churchgoers, the church leaders who have hitched their own wagons to his power, and political leaders who fear retaliation if they defect. But he is not the only charismatic leader in Christian nationalist circles. There is a hierarchy that runs broad and deep, from those "spiritual advisors" closest to him, such as the prosperity gospel preacher Paula White, to those in the leadership of the Southern Baptist Convention, some of the megachurches, and other large conservative church organizations, down to the leaders of smaller congregations and church-related agencies and institutions. On a parallel track are the right-wing Christian-identified politicians, from Trump's inner circle of Republicans in national government positions, to governors, to state and local officials such as Doug Mastriano. On both these parallel tracks, leaders take their own marching orders from the leaders above them, on up the ladder.[198]

A number of commentators have referred to such religiously tinged political groups as a kind of cult. As noted already, while there are many conservative churches and political organizations that do not fall within the definition of a cult, there are many cultlike dynamics within the whole range of Christian nationalism. The further out on the spectrum of extremism and conspiracy thinking one goes, the more cultlike the ethos will be.

Robert Lifton, one of the preeminent scholars of cults for several decades, has identified the following criteria for a group to be a cult: "First, a shift in worship from broad spiritual ideas to the person of a charismatic guru [sic][199]; second, the active pursuit of a thought reform-like process that frequently stresses some kind of merger with the guru; and third, extensive exploitation from above (by the guru and leading disciples)—whether economic, sexual, or psychological—of the idealism of ordinary followers from below."[200] He also observes that a "sense of apocalypse turns out to be present in extremist political movements no less than in extremist religious cults," motivated by a "strong emotional commitment to apocalyptic world purification."[201] The leader increasingly imposes an alternate, paranoid worldview, which encourages the group to act with some urgency to fight against a creeping "defilement" of the world (or nation) in order to restore an imagined ancient purity. While from a certain postmodern or "constructionist" perspective, we might say that *all* "reality" is in some way socially constructed,[202] facts and evidence still delineate parameters of what is true versus delusional. Cult leaders, or "mental predators" as Lifton calls them, "are concerned not only with individual minds but with the ownership of reality itself."[203]

Mystical fabulations, rigid religious rules for behavior, and outright political lies, when repeated often enough, can become normalized to the point where reality and fiction blend together. At a certain point, especially when input is missing from other sources, this creates an alternate reality. The group becomes bonded even more closely together under the mantle of the leader, not only in an "us versus them" designation of certain enemies, but now in an "insider versus outsider" version of reality itself.

Cults are distinguishable from healthy groups not merely by their recruiting strategies (some of which are shared by any group keen on membership growth, as described earlier) but by the character of the leaders. In a healthy group, the leader is outward-focused, concerned for the welfare of group members and supporting them in being able to carry out their mutually agreed-upon goals.[204] Deception is not used, and critical thinking and evaluation of progress are encouraged.[205] In a cult, by contrast, the leader is focused on having the group members serve his own interests, and any apparently good work done by the group is likely to be a mere by-product or even a front for the real reason for the group's existence—to satisfy the narcissistic needs of the leader (whether it be wealth, fame, admiration, or the sheer ability to exercise power). As Margaret Singer puts it succinctly, "Cult leaders center veneration on themselves"[206]—quite the opposite of Martin Luther's dictum regarding Christians' good deeds: "Soli Deo gloria" (glory to God alone).

In the case of Donald Trump, who for the moment seems to be the ultimate head and "ego ideal" for the vast majority of Christian nationalists, Lifton describes Trump's relationship with his band of followers as somewhat different from a more typical "sealed off cultic community": "Rather, his cultism is inseparable from his solipsistic reality. That solipsism emanates only from the self and what the self requires, which makes him the most bizarre and persistent would-be owner of reality. And in his way he has created a community of zealous believers who are geographically dispersed."[207] Not unlike the preaching style of evangelical church leaders, Trump's oratory uses the technique of chanting—"Lock her up!" "USA! USA!"—and a malignant form of call-and-response, as in "Build that wall!" . . . "Build that wall!" "And who will pay for it?" . . . "Mexico!" Like the gladiatorial games of ancient Rome, such spectacles lay bare "the lure of the arena,"[208] and many of Trump's remarks as early as his 2015 campaign rallies overtly encouraged violence. Lifton describes this in terms that could also describe many emotionally intense preachers' performances:

> The chants are rituals that generate "high states"—or what can even be called experiences of transcendence—in disciples. The back-and-forth brings them closer to the guru [*sic*] and enables them to share his claim to omnipotence and his sacred aura. Trump does not directly express an apocalyptic narrative, but his presence has an apocalyptic aura. He tells us that, as not only a genius but a "very stable genius," he alone can "fix" the terrible problems of our society. To be sure these are bizarre expressions of his extreme grandiosity, but also of a man who would be a savior to a disintegrating world. . . . The wall is a messianic promise, and there is deep confusion in both Trump and his followers between the physical entity (a barrier between Mexico and the United States that will never be built) and the metaphysical vision of safety and racial purity.[209]

Trump's oratory also uses other tricks of charismatic speakers—speaking very softly at times and making vague statements that could be filled in by his hearers' imaginations to mean any number of things that might best fulfill their own goals and desires. I was struck when listening to Trump's speech to the growing mob on January 6, which was the culmination of a TV and social media buildup to take the Capitol by force, that he really wasn't yelling very much. As in many of his speeches before large crowds, he often lapses into a singsong cadence that almost sounds like he is bored or asleep. On the contrary, in light of what we know about persuasive speech by manipulative leaders, this is actually one more technique of rhetorical influence in the Trumpian bag of tricks—even a form of group trance or hypnosis, as described in Singer's list of cult tactics earlier in this chapter.[210] Relevant to our study of Christian nationalism and evangelical

Christianity, Singer cites a student's research comparing taped speeches of cult leaders, televangelists, and mainline church leaders, which found that "the speeches by cult leaders and fundamentalist evangelists had more hypnotic qualities than those of the mainstream church leaders."[211]

The rest of us too, who are not Christian nationalists, are not immune to the impact of such persistent lies and distortions of reality. Even if we have not gone down the rabbit hole into the unreality of Christian nationalism, we become desensitized after so much repetition—what Lifton called "reality fatigue."[212] How many of us got tired of trying to fact-check every new pronouncement Trump tweeted overnight?

Psychologists differentiate between regular delusions and "bizarre delusions." Regular delusions are unshakably held beliefs that are not true but possibly could be—for example, "My neighbors are watching me all the time." Bizarre delusions, on the other hand, are unshakably held beliefs that are not true and could not possibly be—for example, "Aliens are watching me all the time and have implanted a chip in my body." As Trump's untruths have become more and more fantastic, they have moved from the plausible to the bizarre, but as his followers have become increasingly desensitized, he continues to be believed by millions in his base. Lifton writes, "With extreme forms of solipsism the external world and other minds cannot be known and may, in effect, have no existence."[213] This, in my view, is as good a definition as any of outright psychosis—being disconnected from reality.

Trump's insistence nearly one year and a half (as of this writing) after the 2020 presidential election that he actually won "by a landslide," and the continuing belief in this lie by millions of Americans—including church leaders and elected officials—becomes more obviously delusional by the day.[214] Lifton notes how even after a lie is generally recognized as false, the constant stirring up of debate by narcissistic leaders and their closest followers keeps the leader's *alternate reality* in circulation.[215] And as noted earlier, it is very difficult to prove the nonexistence of something (perhaps even when it is a bizarre delusion. There is always the possibility that aliens exist . . .).

Perhaps Trump's most delusional lie to date, alongside his continued insistence that he overwhelmingly won the election, is his refusal to recognize the insurrection on January 6 as a violent mob. In this statement, he manages to subtly praise all those who assaulted the Capitol on that day while telling a completely fictional version of the day's events: "There was such love at that rally. You had over a million people there. . . . They were there for one reason, the rigged election, they felt the election was rigged that's why they were there. They were peaceful people; these were great people. The crowd was unbelievable; I mentioned the word love, the love in the air. I've never seen anything like it."[216]

Trauma and Splitting

Finally, in addition to the narcissistic symbiosis of leaders and followers, there is the issue of trauma and its impact on individuals. While this factor is admittedly speculative because there are no studies (to my knowledge) on the percentage of Christian nationalists who have a history of trauma—although there is an increasing attention among therapists to the ways in which religion itself can cause trauma and how some people may need trauma-informed treatment after leaving a highly controlling church context[217]—perhaps some of the most vulnerable people who fall prey to extremist views and political agendas are those who (because of *prior* exposure to violence, abuse, or sexual assault) are prone to see the world in terms of absolute good versus evil.

One of the most difficult aspects of surviving trauma is that such extreme experience has the capacity to erase nuance from one's thinking. Witnessing or experiencing violence face-to-face has the shock effect of reframing many subsequent experiences in terms of all or nothing, totally pure and perfect versus utterly bad. Psychoanalysts identify this dynamic as psychological "splitting." This happens mostly below the level of our conscious awareness, especially because trauma is not established in memory in the same way as ordinary events—the unbearable and overwhelming nature of trauma causes the traumatized person most often to dissociate so that memories become "stored" separately, without creating a coherent story of what happened. Fragments of experience are kept in different parts of the brain, compartmentalized to be experienced as clouds or jolts of memory, not just in the mind, but also separately in the body, in emotions, and in behaviors that seem to just "happen" without our conscious intent.[218]

As Melanie Klein, one of the earliest psychoanalysts in the 20th century, described, such unconscious psychological splitting begins in all of us in infancy, as we try as best as we can as tiny nonverbal beings to manage our experiences of good (the milk is tasty and just the right temperature, I have a dry diaper and I'm comfortable, my parent is holding me and I feel safe) versus bad (nursing mom ate garlic for dinner or the bottle is too hot or too cold, I'm wet and scratchy, I'm crying but nobody is coming). Transient experiences of discomfort, if not too frequent, are fairly easily absorbed psychologically in the overall context of what early psychoanalyst and pediatrician D. W. Winnicott called "good enough" parenting.[219] No parent can (or should) be perfect (or a child would have no incentive to meet challenges and grow up). Reliable love and caregiving establish in the infant's psyche what attachment theorist John Bowlby called "a secure base"[220] and developmental psychologist Erik Erikson called "basic trust."[221] When bad experiences are too extreme or too frequent, however, as in traumatic situations of abuse and chronic neglect, mentally separating primal sensations of good and bad becomes a psychological necessity, a survival mechanism and defense against overwhelming terror or psychic disintegration.

In infancy, there is no capacity for what we would regard as rational thought or being able to think about a more nuanced reality over time. Experience is in the body, as here-and-now sensation, all good or all bad. We split off our awareness of badness in the parent because it intolerably threatens our primal attachment to the one on whom we are wholly dependent (and without such attachment, no one can survive intact[222]). We internalize it unconsciously, psychologically, so that we ourselves contain all the badness. But to feel that we are bad also then becomes intolerable, so then we switch to perceiving our parent as bad and ourselves as good. We are psychically restored to our original state of goodness within ourselves, but now the world *outside* ourselves (represented mainly by the parents) is bad, and that is terrifying. This is what leads to the destruction of "basic trust" and a state of paranoia.

The only way out of this unrelenting back-and-forth of projective splitting between all-good and all-bad states kept within ourselves or ejected psychically into our caretakers is, as Klein proposed, that as we mature (even as very young children), we begin to understand that sometimes we are *both* good *and* bad and the same is true for our parents. To learn that we are "good enough," and that our parents are also reliably "good enough" (if they are), is what enables healthy growth. This gradual recognition of the "good enough," rather than everything and everyone being either perfect or bad, can lead to reparation and a reduction of psychological splitting and projection—which Klein believed was the hallmark of mutual love and the goal of all mature relating.

Reaching this state of "good enough" is the sign of healthy infantile development. But of course, a good many children do not experience good enough parenting. Childhood abuse and neglect can set up a lifelong tendency toward splitting that can only be healed by a gradual experience of a new relationship (if one is lucky or resilient enough) that is good enough (a grandparent, a wise and caring partner, a good therapist). Under stress, we can all fall back into unconscious splitting, but when we experience real trauma—including well into adulthood—this unconscious dynamic can become the dominant way of perceiving the world. Especially after a sexual violation (as in sexual assault or childhood molestation) or up-close severe violence against oneself or other human beings (as in war or gang violence), or the experience of chronic and unrelenting pain or oppression, a common shared assumption of human goodness may be shattered. Appearances of goodness cannot be trusted.

It should not be assumed that all traumatic experiences lead to an official diagnosis of post-traumatic stress disorder (PTSD), with its particular symptoms such as flashbacks, nightmares, dissociation, uncontrollable panic, rage, or depressive anxiety.[223] But even in the best of circumstances, when the aftermath of trauma is well processed and cared for in the context of a strong support network, an encounter with extreme violence or suffering can still transform an individual's worldview from one of basic trust to a deep-seated and fundamental distrust, which is very hard to shake. Such experiences teach a tragic lesson that the world is no longer safe (if it ever was). Personal relationships can become laden with projections toward others that cast interactions in a binary victim-perpetrator dynamic, or, as contemporary relational psychoanalyst Jessica Benjamin has described in detail, a polarity of "doer and done-to."[224] The roles people find themselves unconsciously enacting in such relationships may switch back and forth as projections are triggered by different interactions. The psychic hot potato of the role of persecutor is tossed back and forth in the unconscious relationship between two people while both may seek to hold onto the position of innocence. In this post-traumatic type of unconscious splitting, there is very little room for one or the other partner to break out of the binary of perpetrator and victim into a different, less polarized mode of relating.

I am not suggesting that we should assume that all or even most individuals who have experienced trauma would be attracted to groups where fear and paranoia are major emotional features of the group's agenda.

Many trauma survivors, in fact, have well-attuned radar for the possibility of emotional retraumatization in such organizations or movements. Nor should we assume that all Christian nationalists are survivors of abuse or other trauma! But there are some—perhaps even many—in whom a tendency toward psychological splitting would make the extreme worldview of certain groups compelling, especially when a charismatic leader seems to present an all-good, idealizable protector. Simple (or simplistic) answers to big spiritual, existential, or political questions and unambiguous rules of right and wrong can appeal strongly to an all-or-nothing mindset.

A high-conformity group, with a highly manipulative leader, can exploit the victim-perpetrator thinking of a trauma survivor by framing everything in terms of good versus evil. Many survivors, having once seen or experienced evil directly, might not be put off as easily as nontraumatized people by the language of purity versus the demonic, and their own conscious or unconscious desire for justice might stimulate a desire to believe in an imminent cosmic day of reckoning.[225] As trauma survivors, they have already experienced the fire and the ice. Especially if such earlier life suffering is still deeply repressed and not available to conscious awareness, they may feel a resonance with apocalyptic rhetoric, and they may experience considerable emotional arousal when called to fight whatever or whoever has been named as the enemy.

This may help answer a question that many commentators posed immediately after the January 6 insurrection: How could so many former military and police participate in such a lawless rebellion? How could protesters be carrying distinctive Blue Live Matter flags one moment, mixing support for police and a strong "law and order" attitude, and the next moment be participating in or cheering on deadly acts of violence against the police who were there trying to maintain order? Countless military veterans and law enforcement officers have been exposed to horrible events, often many times over. Even a strong indoctrination into a military culture of masculinist bravado (which is expected of both male and female police and soldiers) may mask more raw and "unacceptable" feelings of fear and vulnerability.

Bulletproof vests and helmets and armored vehicles may (imperfectly) help protect soldiers' bodies, but there are no bulletproof vests for the psyche. An uncompromising "law and order" attitude, especially when amalgamated with white supremacy, is as much a symptom of psychological splitting as is a preference to use violence to solve problems (whether in public or private relationships[226]). There are good guys and bad guys, and when the fight is on (whether it is to "stop the steal," or to "take America back for God") there is no middle ground: *"If you don't fight like hell, you're not going to have a country anymore."*

Conclusion

In this chapter, I have attempted to present and summarize a broad array of perspectives drawn from personal training and experience as a psychotherapist, as well as the research and insights of many others. Of course, in the end, I am aware that every person who has ever lived is a unique individual and that "personality" is an unreproducible amalgamation of nature and nurture. While many of the dynamics, both conscious and unconscious, that lead people to become Christian nationalists of varying degrees can be identified, there are elements that defy all rational analysis.

In that knowledge, I encourage readers to use information presented here wisely. Nothing may raise another person's defenses faster than being "analyzed" or feeling "counseled" by an armchair psychologist! Nevertheless, if we are to be agents of change with hopes of bridging the chasms in our current polarized context, we need to move beyond analysis to finding ways to talk across the divide and recover healing moments of shared humanity. The following chapter will explore this possibility.

3

How to Talk Across the Divide

Creating Human Ties across (Extreme) Difference

> If you don't fight like hell, you're not going to have a country anymore.
>
> —Donald Trump on January 6, 2021

Divisiveness is hardly new in America. It has been with us since the founding of the country and is embedded in the very justifications and rationalizations for white settlers' arrival here. Fleeing persecution, they became the persecutors of others already living on this continent, also oppressing and fighting one another over both religious beliefs and political loyalties. In colonial and revolutionary times, Anglican royalists opposed Puritan patriots; Puritans condemned Quakers, Lutherans, and Anabaptists; and everybody hated the Catholics. Warring for independence from the English monarchy while fighting with Native Americans for their land (not to mention holding on to a still vivid belief in the continual threat of demonic torment) created a cauldron of terror, violence, and demonization of the other. Everyone was "doer" or "done to," to borrow Jessica Benjamin's words again, often occupying both positions depending on the immediate crisis, and there were few mediating forces to break the cycle of violence. In the musical *Hamilton*, the portrayal of the emerging nation as "young, scrappy and hungry" perpetuates the tired story of American grit and heroism against tyranny and evil.

The less told and most often repressed (and hence "forgotten") side of the story is that of the violence perpetrated by these same admired founders of the United States. The whole origin of the United States is steeped in blood and trauma. That trauma continued to roll down the generations, with another catastrophic outbreak in the form of the Civil War—the effects of which continued in Jim Crow and are still felt in mass incarceration[1] and in the myriad forms white supremacy takes today. As I have speculated elsewhere,[2] beneath the talk of freedom-loving American patriots lurks a mostly buried awareness that what whites most fear from other peoples and nations is precisely what our white colonial forebears perpetrated on the Native American and African peoples—theft, genocide, and slavery. This very dim but ever-present awareness of America's original sins continues to haunt us in the form of perpetual assertions of America's greatness and purity of ideals, and constant reminders that there are always multiple "enemies, both foreign and domestic."[3]

If we learn nothing else from psychoanalysis, we know that the repressed always returns. And if it does not return consciously, it will return in bodily suffering and the unconsciously driven repetition of original traumas, until something or someone helps it break through to awareness where it can be thought about and told at long last. It is only when the whole story of trauma—not just a whitewashed version that justifies a great wrong—is intentionally processed, talked about, evaluated, and understood that healing can begin and the unending cycle of reciprocal violence and hatred can be transcended to create a new way of being and relating.

This is not by any means to say that all points of view are equal when it comes to those who are fighting racism and sexism and fighting for justice versus those forces of conservative backlash who are fighting to maintain a white patriarchal—and Christian-dominated—society. The purpose of this chapter is by no means to suggest that efforts to talk across this increasingly toxic national divide are meant to create a false "unity" forged by once again trying to quiet movements for justice and social change. Calls for unity by forces of white supremacy most often are calls to suppress dissent in order to maintain the status quo.

New York Times columnist Charles Blow dealt a stinging rebuttal to the idea that unity is always the most important goal. He notes that "political polarization has increased as the percentage of nonwhite people in America has increased." Observing the election of a "white-power president after Democrats elected a Black one," he affirms the importance of resistance to such backlash, declaring, "I don't want to be unified with anyone who could openly cheer my oppression or sit silently while I endure it," and cautions that "the 'unity' of America is often conflated with the silence of the oppressed and the pacification of the oppressors."[4] The prophet Jeremiah knew this dynamic well when he scolded, "They have treated the wound of my people carelessly, saying, 'Peace, peace,' when there is no peace" (Jer 6:14).

From a psychological point of view, it is precisely the forces of conservative backlash that maintain the centripetal force of repression and suppression of the whole truth. White supremacy has been—and continues to be—the most repressed truth in American history. Sexism, heterosexism, and other forms of objectification are closely entwined with it in the twin processes of normalizing oppression and making it invisible. Movements for justice work to uncover the whole truth of such oppression and its impact on real people, while forces of backlash try desperately to keep the lid on in order to feel pure. But again, as psychoanalysis teaches, there is no such thing as purity. Purity is a fantasy born of splitting. Being human is better than being pure, which, in any case, is impossible. It means acknowledging the tragedy of our own impurity (both individual and corporate) in order to see more clearly how our humanity can be mobilized toward care. By letting go of the grandiose wish to be pure, we are also less prone to fall over into the other side of the split and to perpetrate evil. Freed from an endless cycling between neurotic guilt (and fear of guilt) and narcissistic self-inflation and claims of innocence, we can turn our energy toward healing ourselves and others—even our nation and the world.

By insisting on uncovering the whole truth, such developments as critical race theory and the #MeToo movement, contrary to their opponents, are contributing to the healing of violence—by bringing together the idealized story of America (including its genuine Enlightenment ideals) with its traumatic history. This is not, as the critics have been shouting, teaching our children to "hate America" but rather teaching them to see it for all that it is, both good and evil. And it brings to a broader, more public awareness what we have known for much longer within the movements for human rights—that, speaking in theological terms, hatred not only is a matter of individual sin (as the Southern Baptist Convention has perennially insisted) but has been baked into all our systems and institutions since the first white settler killed a Native American for her land and brought a kidnapped African to our shores to be enslaved. Only once we are fully able to face the shame of these truths—not only our personal but our corporate implication, our historical violence—can we more fully live into the ideals we like to claim as a nation, of "life, liberty, and the pursuit of happiness" for *all* people.

I believe that American divisiveness is at a crucial turning point. On the one hand, no president (at least in living memory) has incited as much divisiveness and outright hatred as Donald Trump (although the seeds were planted deep in previous decades by some of his predecessors). On the other hand, the eruption of hate speech and violence from under the cloak of civility where it had been festering for decades has aroused the conscience of a new generation of young adults, and reinvigorated those of us who lived through earlier fights for women's rights and racial justice. The #MeToo and Black Lives Matter movements have taken to the streets, the workplace, and the hallways of government to demand an end to long-embedded hatred and subjugation. Will backlash succeed in once again suppressing this truth-telling movement, or will we be able to enter a new era of sober introspection as a nation, toward the building of something more true, more decent, and more just?

Talking Across the Divide

The powers of backlash, of white supremacy and patriarchy, depend on lies in order to keep unjust systems in place. This goes to the heart of the question: How can I talk across the rift that has happened in my family, my church, my community because we have come to believe diametrically opposing ideas about faith, health, the economy, climate change, and politics? As noted in chapter 2, the combination of resentment, fear of losing the status of whiteness, and paranoia leading to a vulnerability to conspiracy thinking can induce many white Christians to live, for all intents and purposes, in an alternate reality where nationalistic rhetoric, lies, and disinformation look like a last best hope. Splitting between good and evil abounds in the thought world of Christian nationalists and is continually reinforced by a close atmosphere of Fox News, right-wing social media, and conservative religious preaching and evangelism. Is honest, open conversation even possible?

Psychologist Dolores Albarracin recently commented to an Associated Press reporter, "Once people buy into the lies, there can be no convincing them they aren't true."[5] Albarracin and her coauthors have done extensive empirical psychological work on the ways in which personal anxiety is fueled by right-wing media with its circumscribed, repetitive messaging. Similarly, psychologist Bandy X. Lee, who on professional ethics grounds spearheaded the movement among mental health experts during Trump's presidential term to break the so-called Goldwater rule (an American Psychiatric Association rule prohibiting psychologists from publishing diagnostic assessments of anyone they had not personally diagnosed and treated[6]), has written, "Mental health professionals are indeed frequently confronted with the question: 'How do we reason with a Trump supporter?' The quick answer to that query is: 'You don't.'"[7]

I disagree. As a therapist, I believe in talk—under the right conditions. I will adopt the emergency medical language of "triage" here[8] to suggest that the first step toward conversation is to determine whether fruitful conversation is possible. The first point of discernment is: *Am I the right person to have this conversation with this person?* Just as public health campaigns to convince people to receive the Covid-19 vaccine are relying more and more on respected figures from within the most impacted communities, such as primary care physicians, local clergy, and community leaders, we too might need to recognize that the best conversation partner is someone other than ourselves. "Trusted messengers" may be best positioned for dialogue—people who have (or once had) a foot inside the Christian nationalist or white evangelical worlds, "who sympathize with [their] shared values but are nevertheless willing to talk their comrades down from the brink."[9] In general, there will be more traction when evangelicals talk to evangelicals, Catholics to Catholics, and mainline Protestants to mainline Protestants, although this is not a hard-and-fast rule (other dimensions of common ground such as family or neighborhood may outweigh these considerations).

Triage involves not only assessing how hardened the potential dialogue partner is in their beliefs, and who is the right messenger, but also assessing the context—is this the right time, the right place, the right social context in which to have such a discussion? I offer three possible choices to make about whether to attempt a serious conversation across a wide religious and political divide, like a traffic light: (1) red light: STOP—talking will do no good—at least not here, not now, not by me; (2) yellow light: try but tread lightly; and (3) green light: go deeper, gently and wisely. Let's explore each of these options.

Red Light: STOP (at Least Here, at Least for Now)—
Talking with True Believers

It is not possible to have fruitful conversations with everyone who has taken a die-hard position, particularly if they have become embedded in a context where groupthink overcomes critical thinking and to disagree is to be excommunicated. *Direct argument will almost never work.* When conversing with a True Believer (or "ambassador," to use Whitehead and Perry's term described in chapter 1), it's well to remember that we're not just relating to this one person we know. We're talking to their favorite TV news network and the hundreds of tweets and Facebook posts they are consuming in an ever-self-reinforcing bubble of opinion fed to them through algorithms sifting through their clicks and "likes." When it comes to listening to a firmly entrenched Christian nationalist, we're also hearing the hundreds or even thousands of members of their church, where they just praised Jesus and asked him to save the "USA" while listening to heart-thumping rock music and indoctrinating sermons. We are hearing all the overlapping ideological groups to which this person is attuned, from Trump followers to adherents of QAnon and other conspiracy theories.

Arguing may simply reinforce the manipulative predictions of the demagogue and the group that we are not to be trusted. Even within the broad tent of Christianity, Singer writes, someone who has been thoroughly indoctrinated by propaganda "will have been taught that mainline clergy, the outside world, parents, relatives, and friends are evil, simply wrong about everything, and should be disbelieved."[10] Once someone becomes a hard-core True Believer, they are likely to seek out more "information" that aligns with their beliefs and disregard opposing evidence—a form of predisposition that psychologists call "confirmation bias."

Argumentation and debate will not work. Period. Nor, as some have suggested, will "godly admonition" or "chastisement"[11] from a religious perspective, or any sort of attempts at personal "deprogramming"[12] or "deradicalization."[13] "Deprogramming" or "deradicalization" smacks of coercive efforts at "reeducation," and if it succeeds, it may end up merely replacing one authoritarian dynamic for another—even in the interests of replacing lies with truth.

Lee advocates for a different, more societal level of reeducation, not in the form of coercive interventions with indoctrinated individuals, but rather in the much-needed movements for social change that will shift the very ground under the feet of authoritarian leaders and conspiracy mongers. Her steps include "reduction of exposure to 'the leader'" (i.e., first removing the pathogen)—in the case of Donald Trump, she means literally his removal from office; then "reduction of cultic programming" (i.e., finding ways to shut down or diminish the power of right-wing media outlets such as "Fox News, One America News Network, and other sites that promote right-wing conspiracy theories"); and finally, working for a "change of circumstances" that she believes "rendered them vulnerable to predators in the first place," such as poverty and lack of "access to education, health care, and social mobility."[14]

Here is another STOP moment: There are also simply times midconversation when we have to change the subject or walk away, because to continue a heated discussion about what is essentially a fusion of two taboo subjects—politics and religion—will either (a) violate our own sense of personal integrity by continuing to engage with what we consider to be hate speech or (b) cause harm to ourselves because we are being subjected to verbal violence, ad hominem attacks, and/or micro- or macroaggressions.[15] If one is convinced that an abrupt ending of a conversation may push someone over the edge into violence, measures of self-protection may need to be taken.

Does this mean throwing in the towel, and retreating from the important work of social justice? Is it copping out? I would say no. But recognizing that *my* having *this* conversation with *this* particular person at *this* time and place will not be fruitful does not mean that we altogether stop advocating for our core values around reasonableness, ethics, faith, and justice. Sometimes simply saying "I disagree" followed by walking (not storming) away preserves our integrity and avoids unintentionally conveying silent acquiescence. In fact, part of our self-care in such a situation is precisely the opposite of retreat—it is simply moving our ethical work and our energy for what we believe to be right where it will fall on more receptive ears, and working actively for justice and for social change in the long run.

Yellow Light: Tread Lightly Where We Sense Some Openness

The first point of discernment of whether conversation is possible is whether there are areas where the other person maintains some independent thinking about the issues—are they a "soft" nationalist-leaning "accommodator" (in Whitehead's and Perry's definition) who might be open to meaningful conversation? The longer we have known a person, and the more we already share some common interests apart from issues of politics and religion, the more likely it is that we may already have some sense of how committed they are to an extreme point of view, and how long they have believed it. The more civility—or, even better, mutual liking and trust—is already established in other areas (e.g., with a coworker, a neighbor, a skeptical family member, or a friendly acquaintance), the more possibility there may be for genuine dialogue.

If after some careful consideration we believe there is an opening for honest talk, the first step is probably *not to talk much at all*—at least not right away—but *to listen, and to show respect*. Respect is earned by not talking down, listening not in order to pounce on an error in their thinking, or to immediately "enlighten" or "heal" them, but to try to understand with as much empathy as one can muster what it must be like to be this person and to inhabit their life, with all its challenges and stresses. Note that empathy is not the same thing as sympathy. Empathy means being able to step into the other's shoes, at least to some meaningful degree, and understand why and how they are thinking and feeling as they do—it does not imply agreement. Sympathy might mean feeling sorry for the other person, but it also can subtly convey a patronizing attitude such as pity, or even contempt. Contempt is an immediate dialogue stopper. *Empathy—and genuine curiosity*—should be the guiding attitudes. The initial work is to try to understand, not to try to control the other person or to radically change their mind—especially all at once. It's not a one-time event but a process that requires considerable endurance. This is hard work.

As in the case of the red light STOP, after putting the toe in the water, there may still be moments when one's own integrity is too much at stake, and exercising empathy feels too much like signaling agreement and betraying one's own values. When this happens, it's time to calmly say, "I'm afraid I just can't agree with that." Then, depending on who the conversation partner is and the nature of the relationship, change the subject, call a time out, or simply walk away.

Green Light: Go Deeper, Gently and Wisely

When it appears that there is some real openness to reexamine convictions on a conversation partner's part, it may be the time to go deeper—with the recognition that a green light may turn yellow or even red at any moment! The following are some of the recommendations I can offer out of my own experience as a psychotherapist and teacher of pastoral and spiritual care. I imagine that many readers will recognize these as ways we naturally listen when we are at our best. But when conversation becomes conflictual, our sympathetic nervous systems can be aroused (more later on how we can momentarily lose the capacity to think rationally), and these practices of empathic listening can be easily forgotten in the heat of the moment. These are not magic formulas, and they will not always work. But sometimes they do.

1. *Building and maintaining relationship always comes first.* There are at least three important ways to do this (as marriage and family therapists know well!). First and always is respectful listening. Two additional factors stand out in building relationship: finding common ground, and kindness.

    a. *Find common ground.* Relationships can be hard, but when issues become points of ongoing tension, it's helpful to look for other areas where there is agreement, common interest—even common *self*-interest. Community organizers and union leaders have recognized that alliances can be formed with unlikely coalition partners around solving a problem that affects them all, even where there may be strong areas of disagreement, even opposition, on other issues.[16]

    Many years ago, a battered women's shelter where I worked had a board of trustees composed of a group of progressive social workers, lawyers, victim advocates, therapists, and antiviolence activists, with a mix of races, ethnicities, and sexual orientations—and one burly, straight, white male police officer. Likely leaning to the right of us on almost every political issue, he was invited onto the board because he had seen the devastation that intimate partner violence had wrought in families and in the community, and he was eager to support our work.

    This "public safety officer" became one of the best allies we had in the community! He could say things to conservative town council members and funders that would not have been heard coming directly from some of us. He could tell his fellow officers why domestic violence education was important. He supported a long-term partnership between our organization and the local police for training on appropriate and inappropriate actions when responding to "domestic" calls and how to ensure safety for victims. Over time, we all became much more than strategic partners—we became friends. Another way of thinking about this is that we stopped regarding each other as "Other" and came to know each other as complex persons with our own struggles, hopes, biases, and capacity for care.

Common ground cannot be faked or manufactured. It must be discovered. As the second-century African Roman playwright Terence wrote, "Nothing human is alien to me."[17] Finding places of genuine connection will provide the necessary first step in building genuine rapport and trust.[18]

b. *Kindness is an absolutely necessary ingredient.* As paradoxical as it may sound, it is even possible to have a heated debate and still be kind. Kindness means being attentive to the other's well-being. It does not mean trying to make the other person completely "comfortable"—a persistent dynamic that has impeded racial dialogue, in which "white fragility" (to use Robin DiAngelo's term[19]) trumps honest talk. In *Minor Feelings*, Cathy Park Hong describes walking with a white friend and her boyfriend and being subjected to a repeated anti-Asian racist verbal attack by a white man on the subway. When it was all over, her friend reacted by crying and saying, "That's never happened to me before!" Hong writes, "And just like that, I was shoved aside. I was about to comfort her and then I stopped myself from the absurdity of that impulse. All of my anger and hurt transferred to her, and even now, as I'm writing this, I'm more upset with her than that guy. We walked silently back to our apartment while she cried."[20]

The now infamous phrase "white women's tears"[21] (or "white tears") doesn't mean that white people shouldn't feel sorrow or a mix of painful emotions when learning about the suffering of people of color. And Hong notes that "of course, 'white tears' does not refer to all pain but to the particular emotional fragility a white person experiences when they find racial stress so intolerable they become hypersensitive and defensive, focusing the stress back into their own bruised ego."[22] As a therapist,

I will never tell someone not to feel their true feelings in the moment, or not to cry. But this does not mean that the person of color who is much *more* impacted by racism should have to shift focus and try to lessen the white person's pain just from witnessing or hearing about it.

I deliberately do not say, "Care for the white person," because—especially as a teacher and a therapist—I think that sometimes telling a truth that needs to be said *is in itself* a form of care: "I trust you enough to tell you this, and I want you to know." Even when truth telling causes discomfort and the pain of recognizing something horrible that was previously unknown, it is also bringing an opportunity for growth. Truth telling need not be combative, nor should it be a deliberate attempt to inflict harm on the other because of one's own pain, frustration, or anger. The truth itself is painful enough—for both the teller and the listener—and truth telling is not incompatible with kindness.

2. *Realize that old family dynamics will be stirred up by new conflicts.* Chaplains know that when family members come to the bedside of a hospital patient who is seriously ill or injured, and especially if that patient is near death, whatever chronic family conflicts and divisions were already there are likely to emerge with added intensity in this moment of crisis. In particular, habitual power struggles, resentments, and taking sides begin to come to the fore as family members may be asked to choose options around the patient's medical treatment, negotiate whose time and money may need to be spent in caring for the patient, and in the most painful instance, make end-of-life decisions. All families exist on a spectrum from "healthy" to "dysfunctional," and in times of stress, the pendulum tends to swing toward whatever dysfunction is the default. It is useful to *hold in awareness* that in times of stress, "Oh, yeah, well, Uncle John will start drinking and not show up when he says he will, Mom will start trying to control everything, Dad will sulk, my brother who tends not to be in touch with us very much will suddenly show up all concerned and lovey-dovey, my older and younger sisters will start bickering with each other, and I will . . . [*fill in the blank!*]." This holding in awareness can help us maintain realistic expectations, recognizing the mix of love and ambivalence

that exists in most families, and be emotionally prepared rather than falling into an idealizing fantasy of the family in anticipation of a totally happy gathering!

It takes perspective (and sometimes therapy) to disembed oneself enough from the family system to see the emotional and power dynamics for what they are—habitual responses to anxiety. So before the sniping even begins at the holiday table about religious and political convictions, it is helpful to keep in mind these habitual patterns, and to *make a plan* about how to respond. (Some family therapists might suggest: if you know you're likely to do *x* or *y*, try surprising everybody by doing *z*.) And have an escape hatch handy. To boil it down: recognize the pattern before it happens, don't get hooked, and if you do, disengage, distract, or go back to STOP as described earlier. Walk out calmly for as long as necessary—that is, "take a time out." Taking a time out is not storming out in a rage but saying, "I'm going to take a breather, I'll be back," then walking away to do self-care to *breathe*, calm down, and regain perspective.

3. *Breathe.* We have all had the experience in a conversation when someone says something unexpectedly that quite literally "blows our mind"—and not in a good way. We respond to speech that we perceive to be violent against ourselves or another person or group we care about as an attack. Our "ancient brain"—the amygdala and other parts of the brain down closest to the brain stem—perceives a threat faster than the parts of the brain responsible for mature, logical, and rational thought.[23] Our autonomic nervous system kicks into gear, our heart rate increases, our hands may sweat or shake, and our breath may become rapid and shallow. A chain reaction is set off in which we go into "fight, flight, or freeze" mode. Anger or fear (or often a mixture of the two) predominates in this state, and we are evolutionarily primed to stop thinking (which takes energy) and either run for the hills, retaliate aggressively, or just go silent (or maybe, as in shocking moments of harassment, to lapse into nervous laughter, which is another form of freezing, or dissociating). All these reactions are entirely natural. But they don't advance communication.

I am not advocating here for a passive, even seemingly accepting response to hate speech—not at all! But the type of reactive response that comes from our ancient brain will not be received well by the aggressor. On the contrary, it is likely to inflame defenses and create an even more combative situation. If it's a question of real safety, by all means, go back to the red light STOP section, and leave the scene. But if there is a chance for open dialogue and this moment is more of an aberration, the most important single thing that we can do to regain access to the thinking parts of our brain is *breathe*.

Remember when someone said, "Count to 10 before you react"? Ten seconds is a fairly long pause, in which we have to take a breath. Breathe, pause, slow down, and allow our rational minds to return and reflect: "What might have prompted that comment? Why now? What state is my conversation partner in right now?" Or even, "What might I have just said that got that reaction?" The goal is to shift from reacting to responding and, if we're staying in the conversation, to remain calm enough to keep engaging in a constructive way. Don't bite the bait! When it is possible to think clearly again, it may become possible to reenter productive conversation.

3. *Notice your feelings, especially defensiveness, and try to "bracket."* Set your feelings mentally to one side in order to listen. This may seem like a lot to pay attention to at the same time, but it is important to exercise what Freud himself called "evenly hovering attention"—in other words, listening carefully to the other person and what is being expressed, but also paying attention to what is going on at the same time in our bodies, our fleeting thoughts, and our emotions. If we don't notice—or try to ignore—when our heart is starting to beat faster, our palms are sweaty, we are breathing less deeply, and we are feeling angry or threatened, then it is much harder to remember to take a pause and breathe. Even before all those emotional and autonomic bodily signals fully kick in, we may find ourselves wanting to argue, or snap back, or defend ourselves in some way. It's important, and quite possible, to develop the habit of noticing when such impulses begin to come up—as well as any other strong feelings such as rage, overexcitement, overwhelming sadness that makes us want to cry, sexual desire, a personally painful memory, or hate for the other person—and let them pass through us without acting on them or saying something harmful to the other person. A regular practice of meditation or mindfulness can greatly help build this capacity for self-observation.

Having developed a practice of noticing one's own thoughts, feelings, and memory triggers—even bodily sensations—it becomes possible with practice to mentally "bracket" them, or put them in a kind of "basket" or another "room" in one's mind, and importantly, then to return to them later and tend to them with care. It never works to try to stamp out a feeling! It will always return, bidden or unbidden. But it is possible to tell oneself, "I need to set this reaction aside right now so that I can listen, but I promise myself that I will get back to it later and give it the attention and care that it, and I, deserve." Then it is possible in the moment to get back to being fully present and listening to the other person with undistracted attention.

4. *Learn to listen with intention, and listen more than you speak.* My first-year seminary students are sometimes surprised to realize that empathic listening is not an inborn talent or gift but a *skill* that can be *learned.* American culture tends to reward extroversion and value talk over reticence. Although very gabby people can be annoying, and interrupting is considered rude (harder to manage on Zoom with time delays!), it is generally the case that from school years to college to high-earning careers, being able to speak up with confidence, poise, and intelligent content is associated with greater success. (This is especially true for white men in a group. There is an entire literature around the gendered ways in which speech, body language, and power can intertwine, including research on who takes up more physical space, who is given credit for ideas, who interrupts, and whose ideas are validated while others' are ignored or put down.)[24] Introversion and speaking less in a group or even one-on-one is generally less valued in the dominant American culture. Even when we are not speaking, we are often listening just enough to be waiting for a moment to break in and formulating our response while our conversation partner is still talking.

Good listening, in contrast, is intentional listening—giving one's entire attention to what the other person is saying, without trying to formulate a comeback of any kind. A sign of good listening, in fact, is that there may be a pause between partners' moments of talking. The first exercise I ask students to do in my Pastoral Listening Practicum course is to get into dyads and take turns for two minutes each as "listener" and "sharer." The listener's job is simply to listen to a partner in complete silence (no "uh huh," no "mmm," no vocal cord action at all!). They are asked to silently listen with full, warm, empathic attention to their partner. Then we debrief and find out how it felt to be the listener, and how it felt to be listened to in that way.

Every year, many students express how strange it feels as a listener not to say anything back, or to be trying to formulate a response, although some (especially those who are familiar with meditation or otherwise are comfortable with silence) say it comes as a relief. Most students also express surprise and relief to be listened to in this way, to really have their say without fear of interruption or argumentation, and to have an experience of another person's warm and genuine attention, feeling truly heard—a rare oasis of being listened to in a sea of verbiage in everyday conversation.

Some also comment that they would like some kind of response—eventually—and the point of the exercise is not for a listener to refrain from speaking ever again. The *quality* of the silent listening is important here. Being open to eye contact (following the lead of the speaker, not staring them down), sitting in an open posture that conveys energy and interest (neither fidgeting too much nor sitting as stiff as a brick), allowing one's face to register genuine care and emotion (no faking!)—all of these are actually *by-products* of genuine, caring listening and not "techniques." These are among the well-known elements of "nondirective" care, pioneered by such gifted listeners as Carl Rogers, who coined the phrase "person-centered counseling."[25]

One of the simplest, but most powerful tools for empathic listening beyond listening in silence is a practice variously known in counseling psychology as "mirroring," "active listening," or "paraphrasing." I teach my students that mirroring is the baseline to which they should return if they are tilting in the direction of asking questions (which usually leads the conversation in some direction, even if the question is open-ended), giving advice, or debating. (Asking "why" almost always sounds judgmental even when judgment is not intended.) Mirroring is making a response that captures the essence—both content and feeling—of what the other person has said, without adding anything and without significantly leaving anything important out or, worse, distorting what was said, getting it wrong. It is usually worded as a tentative statement, like, "So if I'm hearing you correctly, you're saying that you felt really uplifted [*feeling*] by Rudy's sermon because it made you think about your parenting in a different way [*content*]." "So it sounds like you've been angry [*feeling*] about Marge's drinking for a long time now, but you've been afraid [*feeling*] to say anything because you don't want to create a big rift between you [*content*]."

Mirroring serves a further facilitative purpose beyond allowing the other person to feel heard and understood on their own terms. Sometimes it also allows the other person to really hear what they are saying, as opposed to only hearing it inside their own head. And when that happens, they may realize its importance, or how it sounds to someone else (which might require pausing to re-think something), or just get more clarity about something that happened. Mirroring is therefore an art as well as a skill—knowing when to reflect back, knowing what is most salient to pick up on (usually the most glossed over, unresolved, or emotionally charged element), or even knowing what was not said that reveals what might be an important gap.

I'm not suggesting that everyone now become a therapist and start rooting around in other peoples' psyches! But this kind of active listening extends from silent receiving to checking whether one heard the other person accurately (and being willing to have one's impressions corrected). It is a more active expression of empathy. Before interjecting our own thoughts and feelings, especially on a controversial subject, it helps to accurately and empathically come to some understanding of what the other person is really thinking and feeling.

Mirroring also helps because it puts the other person's thoughts and emotions at the center. By becoming attuned in this way, it is possible to have a better understanding of where they are coming from. Attentive listening in silence and mirroring actually draws people out and invites them to share more of the underlying reasons for thinking and believing as they do. It's true that silence can be an adversarial interviewing technique and is often used that way in interrogations. People, especially when nervous, tend to want to fill the void and say more than they intend. That is not what I am advocating here! But silence combined with care and nonjudgmental curiosity can be an invitation, can create a space for the conversation partner to say more.

This approach to listening is not only for professional counselors. Many couples therapists—for example, those practicing Imago Therapy, developed by family therapist Harville Hendrix and Helen LaKelly Hunt[26]—adapt such intentional listening practices into their work with couples in conflict. Nonprofit organizations that foster facilitated dialogue across differences—like Braver Angels, Beyond Civility, Living Room Conversations, Bridge the Divide, and Make America Dinner Again[27]—use many of the same principles for careful listening in their work. Braver Angels was cofounded by a family therapist and community organizer, Bill Doherty, who also directs the Minnesota Couples on the Brink project for the University of Minnesota[28] and now hosts workshops specifically designed to help family members who have become alienated over political disagreement.[29] They bring "red" and "blue" members from communities together to begin to break down barriers of mutual hostility and stereotyping, and to help them understand one another a bit more empathically even when it is impossible to agree.

5. *Avoid making assumptions.* Listening in silence and mirroring can create a helpful buffer against making assumptions about the other person's thoughts, feelings, and motivations. In everyday speech, we frequently make assumptions about other people before a conversation even begins. We lump people into overgeneralized categories and then assume we know everything they are going to say before they even have a chance to speak. Listening and mirroring allow the other person the space to express themselves in their own words and on their own terms, without being judged, interrupted, debated, or corrected. This, in turn, allows the possibility for more complexity to enter the dialogue.

Listening with empathy almost always brings an appreciation of the multiple ways in which the other person's ideas have been formed, why they feel as they do, and—sometimes—also shows that their actions reflect deep-seated fears and concerns beneath what initially we might have assumed was just ignorance or prejudice. Again, this is *not* to say that we simply listen and nod and appear to convey agreement with violence or hate. More will be said about that shortly. But even when ideas are expressed that we utterly oppose, it is important not to make assumptions about why the person feels as they do. When genuine curiosity replaces assumption making, we may even have the good fortune of cracking open a door that could allow some new light to enter.

6. *Make I statements.* When it is your turn to talk, avoid making universal-sounding truth claims. I no longer remember where I first encountered this good advice, but it is often used as a norm for constructive conversation in all kinds of group work, from 12-step programs to church youth groups; counseling support groups; antiracism and diversity, equity, and inclusion (DEI) trainings; and community organizing. One of the more problematic habits many of us have received from educational systems is that truth is a zero-sum game (either I have the truth or you do, but we can't both have differing truths). As students, we may have been taught to make pronouncements of "truth" that are meant to apply to all times, places, and persons in order to "win an argument" or sound authoritative. As I've written elsewhere, postmodern philosophy, quantum physics, and psychoanalysis have all challenged the modernist assumptions that truth is absolute, universal, and quantifiable.[30] Every person in a conversation (no matter how misguided—and in my clinical experience, I would say even psychotic) has some genuine piece of truth to share and contribute to a collective understanding that is greater than the sum of (our) parts.

I do not subscribe to the extreme version of postmodernism that ascribes everything we think we know entirely to social construction (i.e., we can only know reality insofar as we have arrived at some consensus as a society or a culture that something is real). In fact, more than ever since the onset of the Covid-19 pandemic, and the irrational politicization of vaccine science and epidemiological evidence, I have come to appreciate the scientific method. I do not want the pilots of my plane debating just before landing where the runway might be! Nevertheless, the white Western overconfidence in the truths "discovered" using European and North American methods since the 18th century has mistaken many interpretations for facts (a blatant example being the pseudoscience of race and racial hierarchy) and asserted Western mores and values as universal. There is no such thing as pure objectivity. Much of what we think we "know" can be challenged, even undone, by all that we don't. All knowledge—even the scientific—can be superseded by further learning, and everything we think we know is to some degree an interpretation. Postmodernists like to point out that wherever we stand, there is a horizon, beyond which we cannot see until we change our position.[31]

To bring this back to having fruitful conversations, it is therefore always useful to frame our assertions in terms of what *I* think and what has been true from my own experience (thus far). I often use the (fictional) example in teaching and group work of two women in a support group for recently divorced persons. The first woman to speak makes the pronouncement "Divorce is a sin!" A second woman, who would have liked to share a different perspective, feels shut down and ends up not speaking. The first woman made a universal truth claim that was a conversation stopper—and even potentially hurtful. But what if she had said this instead: "I feel very guilty for having an affair that ended up in my husband and me getting a divorce. To me, this divorce was sinful." The second woman might have then felt able to say, "I'm sorry how painful that is for you. In my situation, it's the opposite. I was being abused for years by my husband, and when I finally had the courage to take the kids and leave, I felt like the divorce was a blessing! It was a huge relief that we were finally safe."

By making *I* statements, we own responsibility for our own truths while leaving space for other truths to be expressed. In a group, this can expand comprehension and empathy for the complexity of varying perspectives. *I* statements are sometimes usefully preceded by saying "In my experience" or "Correct me if I'm wrong." (And mean it! Note that "In my humble opinion" more often than not comes across as sarcastic or argumentative and does not necessarily qualify as a genuine conversation opener! Similarly with the phrase "With all due respect." Both of these tend to convey the opposite!)

Tentativeness is often called for, when it's genuine—for example, prefacing a statement with "I've been wondering if . . ." or "It sometimes seems to me that . . ." The nonprofit group OpenMind calls this "intellectual humility."[32] My favorite caveat from several teachers in the Buddhist tradition is "Don't believe everything you think."[33]

In the view of social psychologist Jonathan Haidt, "to get along better, we should all be less self-righteous. We should recognize that nearly all of us are good people, and that our conflicts arise from our belonging to different cultural groups with different moral intuitions. We're very good at seeing through our opponents' moral rationalizations, but we need to get better at seeing our own. More specifically, liberals and conservatives should try to understand one another, be less hypocritical, and be more open to compromise."[34]

Haidt has posited that "liberals" and "conservatives" are often operating out of six good but separate, and therefore often competing, moral foundations: "care/harm, fairness/cheating, loyalty/betrayal, authority/subversion, sanctity/degradation, and liberty/oppression."[35] Conservatives lean more toward loyalty, authority, and sanctity (that which is to be held in reverence) as their primary foundations, while liberals tend more toward care and fairness. Both in their own way value liberty, and both share aspects of all six.[36] Politicians and other charismatic leaders can exploit these tendencies for their own ends. Identifying the underlying moral principles guiding a conversation partner's beliefs can be a stepping-stone toward common ground.[37]

7. *Avoid argumentation or debate.* This includes when you feel the need to correct your conversation partner, and when you feel you're being baited and want to bite back. When confronted with someone close to us who has been drawn in by an extremist web of lies carefully constructed by right-wing politicians and ultraconservative church leaders, it is tempting to want to just set them straight. It's natural to want to disprove lies and conspiracy theories, to try to combat mis- and disinformation about such life-or-death matters as the Covid-19 pandemic and vaccinations with scientific evidence—or even to quote scripture passages to counter the other person's understanding of "what the Bible says."

Argumentation all too often just raises defenses and causes our conversation partners to dig in their heels all the more. Bandy Lee advises to avoid such attempts to refute misinformation—acting as if by providing the right facts, we could simply flip a switch and convince the person to think differently:

First, they [die-hard Trump supporters] should not be confronted with facts, for it will only rouse resistance (subconsciously, they already know what is true, which is why they project onto others their own characteristics very accurately). . . . Second, persuasion should not be the goal, for that will only lead to exhaustion: the problem is in their granting an impaired individual power, not in their cognitive system or, most of the time, even their mental health. Third, people should continue to state facts, evidence, and science-based approaches elsewhere, repeatedly, and without apology, intimidation, or shame, so that a delusional narrative does not "bulldoze over" the truth through its sheer emotional force, upon which pathology depends.[38]

Argumentation tends to have the opposite effect from what we intend. It is usually heard as a threat before rational thought can be summoned. While the thinking parts of our conversation partner's brain are still rummaging around for better counterarguments, the ancient brain has activated the "fight, flight or freeze" reaction described earlier. Red-faced yelling (fight) or a storm of tears (flight) may ensue. Or the person may simply clam up (freeze). Many people hear argumentation as criticism not only of their beliefs but of themselves. Thinking again about much of American education as presenting a zero-sum game where there are winners and losers in the classroom and carried on into one's adult life, to be proven wrong is not only destabilizing intellectually—it is often experienced as shameful.[39]

As a final caveat regarding out-and-out conflict, political differences can meld together emotionally with a myriad of other painful conflicts, resulting in a rift that can be unrecoverable, especially with someone we are close to. When violence, physical or sexual abuse, untreated addiction, or continual psychological abuse and manipulation are present, then it is indeed time to go back to "triage," and safety *must* be the first priority for oneself (and children and other dependents). Full stop. Physical, sexual, and emotional violence is a painful reality among many couples and families.[40] Violence among family members is sadly all too common, and battering of women is reinforced by societal conventions regarding men's role as heads of households. Intimate partner violence cuts across all racial and class lines in America. In such instances, any kind of reasoned discussion about politics and religion can be dangerous because it can become weaponized against the victim of abuse.

8. *Don't allow political sparring to become the central feature of a relationship.* In families where dynamics are relatively healthy and stable, not laden with chronic severe dysfunction, there are sometimes people who just plain love to argue or play devil's advocate. Some people genuinely learn by arguing, and some others want to hear a well-articulated opposite point of view so they can consider it later (even if they don't want to admit it). Indulge this only to the extent that it doesn't cause you or your dialogue partner pain, and if it devolves into name-calling or ad hominem attacks, it's time to stop.

Between couples and family members, it is also not uncommon for there to be a chronic argument that is repeated so often that each "discussion" partner could write the script for the other. Partners in couples who bring somewhat different attitudes toward such things as money, child-rearing, or even the correct position of a toilet seat can begin to polarize until they are shouting "You always . . ." and "You never . . ." (an almost sure sign of overgeneralization). Polarization begins to happen until both partners may end up occupying much more extreme versions of their own point of view than they held originally. Family therapists call this "skew," and when it hardens into a perpetual fight, it becomes a "schism."

What is often at the root of such polarization is that the fight symbolizes more than the surface issue being argued about. "You never put down the toilet seat" may really mean "You don't pay attention to my needs," or even "You don't care about me / you don't love me." Fights about politics and religion can become symbolic fights as well. In almost every such instance, it is important to consider that by vehemently and repeatedly arguing about social and political issues, there is a value at stake for one or both conversation partners, and beneath that is the feeling that one is being attacked for *who they are*: "You don't respect me." "You don't love me for who I am." If a fight over politics or religion becomes intractable, it is worth considering seeing a couples therapist in order to get at the deeper issues underlying the chronic argumentation.

Family systems theorist Murray Bowen offered a good prescription for attempting to maintain relationship without sacrificing one's core values and principles: "Stay connected and stay differentiated."[41] Too much connection can lead to an unhealthy merger, dependency, or self-sacrifice; too much differentiation can lead to distance and alienation. Severing all ties, or "cutoffs," as they are called by family therapists, are most often necessary in situations of abuse or untreated addiction because, again, safety must always be the first priority. But in a healthy family or couple, although it is very hard to achieve all the time, staying close while maintaining one's own integrity and perspective is what builds honesty and trust for the long haul.

9. *Be willing to admit your own failings.* This goes back to intellectual humility—but also humility more generally. We are all flawed, and we may, in fact, not know everything we need to know about our conversation partner's reasons for believing as they do. Just as cult expert Margaret Singer rebutted the "Who me?" myth about cult induction,[42] anyone can be vulnerable, at least in certain times and circumstances, to being caught up in a false rumor or a politician's or church leader's charismatic lies. The more we try to portray our point of view as 100% correct, the more we are heard by others as self-righteous. The unconscious psychological dynamic is that we are likely projecting all our own inner doubts and "badness" onto the other person, where we can then try to correct what we fear is bad deep within ourselves. No one takes kindly to being the recipient of another person's unconscious projection of inner badness—even if they have no conscious awareness that it's happening. When one presumes to stand in the pure position, the "doer–done to" split once again comes to haunt the relationship and can eventually cause damage on both sides.

As an example, when trying to engage in a serious conversation across a political divide, accusing a dialogue partner of being a racist or a misogynist is an immediate conversation stopper. Ad hominem attacks ("You are a . . . !") are never helpful. As Ibram X. Kendi has advised,[43] being or not being racist *as a person* actually avoids the larger issue, which is that racism (and sexism) is embedded in our national history and pervade all our institutions and structures—including the church.[44] No one is immune to the toxic impact of racism, sexism, or other forms of oppression and supremacy. These poisons have infected us all in different, and unequal, but nevertheless destructive ways.

As a white person, for example, racism is in me. I cannot entirely exorcise it, or outrun it just by trying to be nice to everyone or pretending that "we're all really just the same" (i.e., trying to be "color blind"). What I can do is work on being antiracist in my words and my actions, and listen to my family, friends, and colleagues of color when I need correction.[45] As Robin DiAngelo wrote in her most recent book, progressives can, in fact, inflict some of the worst harm by speaking loudly of their good intentions and liberal "wokeness" (what some have called "virtue signaling"[46]) but acting in ways that perpetuate white privilege in every arena in which they live and refusing to examine the micro- and macro-aggressions they commit on a daily basis.[47] Correcting other white people on their racism, while doing little to actively work against systemic racism, is a form of deflection, designed consciously or unconsciously, to preserve a sense of personal righteousness and ward off the shame of being white. Activist Adrienne Maree Brown writes, "People mess up. We lie, exaggerate, betray, hurt, and abandon each other. When we hear that this has happened, it makes sense to feel anger, pain, confusion and sadness. But to move immediately to punishment means that we stay on the surface of what has happened."[48]

"Calling out," so vigorously critiqued and caricatured by conservatives, may sometimes be just plain ineffective. As noted earlier, criticism that is experienced as outright shaming will often just raise defenses and quickly shut down constructive conversation. Brown emphasizes that calling out, if it is to be part of a larger context of transformational justice making, must also invest in relationship: "I don't find it transformative to publicly call people out for instant consequences with no attempt at conversation, mediation, boundary setting, or community accountability."[49] She advocates, rather, for the kind of accountability and relationality that is more likely to occur "in a supported process with a limited number of known participants."[50]

Longtime antiracist, feminist activist, and professor Loretta Ross has countered "calling out" with what she has named "calling in." Ross sees aggressively calling someone else out on their mistakes in speaking or posting on social media as an overreaction that "assumes the worst" about the other person and perpetuates a cycle of outrage: "The antidote to that outrage cycle, Professor Ross believes, is 'calling in.' Calling in is like calling out, but done privately and with respect. 'It's a call out done with love,' she said. That may mean simply sending someone a private message, or even ringing them on the telephone (!) to discuss the matter, or simply taking a breath before commenting, screen-shotting or demanding one 'do better' without explaining how."[51]

Ross is not averse to having conversations that are uncomfortable. (Therapists know that real honesty often is the opposite of feeling cozy, which is a kind of emotional merger that keeps all tensions outside the circle of warmth and mutual liking.) Nor does she disagree with strategically calling out—or, as she puts it, "calling up"—the abuses of institutions and people wielding power to exploit others. She gives the example of NFL star Colin Kaepernick's publicly taking a knee during the playing of the national anthem as a form of resistance to racism in America now copied by athletes worldwide. What she asks for is a sense of proportionality—being able to differentiate between major and minor offenses, and not automatically making others into enemies.

Ross's message today is "I really, really want to build a culture and a world that invites people in instead of pushing them out. It's called a 'calling-in culture.'"[52] And echoing the words of many advocates of nonviolent resistance, she offers the warning that "when you treat potential allies like enemies, you're behaving like a cult, not the human rights movement." She clarifies, "When many different people think many different thoughts and they move in the same direction, that's a movement. But when many different people think one thought and they move in the same direction, that's a cult."[53]

She differentiates "calling in" from "calling out" in the following way:

> One of my students once said, "A call-out is not an invitation for growth. It's the expectation that you've already grown." This is the culture we're trapped in now. On the other hand, there is calling in. "Calling in" is a phrase invented by Loan Tran, and basically, a call-in is a call-out

done with love. So when you think somebody has done something wrong and you want to hold them accountable, you don't react with anger or hate. You just remain calm and look at them and say—and you can do this online and in person, too—you just look at them calmly, and you tell them, "That's an interesting viewpoint. Tell me more." With that, you've invited them into a conversation instead of a fight. And you don't have to agree with somebody to offer loving attention.[54]

Shortly after the January 6 Capitol riot, Rev. Dr. Serene Jones preached a sermon at the First Presbyterian Church of Cooperstown, New York, in which she said,

> The Christian voice of justice, righteousness, and accountability and the voice of forgiveness and love and healing the divide, are at war inside me, inside us, swirling around the collective psyche of our nation. . . . We are called to hold the tension. We cannot demonize or dismiss or refuse to love the quaking senator or the horned man. God loves them both as so should we. But . . . God's love is not a "get out of jail free" card when it comes to the world of human affairs. We must love them and in loving them, hold them accountable to the best standards of justice we can muster. Justice and mercy walk hand in hand.[55]

No one says this is easy. Nonviolent resistance isn't easy. Having the courage to have difficult conversations isn't easy. It requires just such holding in tension the impulses of care and outrage. Yet change is possible. And personal relationship is the place where it is most likely to begin.

Some General Recommendations

The suggestions in the previous section may be especially helpful when discussing fraught subjects of religion and politics, and even more critical when trying to understand and defuse what we see as another person's delusional or destructive thinking! In addition to these recommendations (which mainly apply to "green light" conversations, but are useful in all communications), I would like to offer several more suggestions that can be helpful more generally—in particular when we suspect a conversation might become tense—and especially when speaking with those whose viewpoints are most diametrically opposite to our own:

1. *Be attentive to power and social context.* There are few conversations that take place on a truly "level" playing field in terms of social hierarchies of relative status, authority, and access to power. The social location in which both partners stand, and the relative power dynamics those social locations represent, already establishes a foundation under their conversation, which can prime each participant's relative openness or defensiveness, depending on their relative social position.

   Most often these power differences are more subliminal than overt—in part because *social power is largely maintained by pretending it doesn't exist.* Groups who have traditionally held the most power often promote an idea or a semblance of egalitarianism in order to not actually share power but pretend not to have it—and thus be insulated from charges of authoritarianism. The language games that render power invisible undergird most forms of systemic oppression.

   A common example is the ways in which "white" people are not labeled racially, but people of color frequently are. The absence of a label is assumed to mean whiteness—which then becomes an unspoken norm, against which the "others" are differentiated. Try the experiment "the Race Game," recommended by Thandeka in her book *Learning to Be White*:[56] Every time in conversation you mention a white friend, colleague, acquaintance, and so on, add the adjective "white": "My white friend Linda said . . ." "I asked the white pharmacist . . ." "My white colleague Joe . . ." Thandeka assigned this exercise to her seminary students, and they reported being met with not only puzzlement but outright hostility. To "out" whiteness is to refuse the power of its invisibilization, and backlash often ensues.[57]

   I am not suggesting that it will be helpful or even possible to make every power difference explicit by bringing it into every conversation—although it might be interesting to see what would happen if we did this! But I am suggesting that if we want to have an honest conversation about such difficult topics as Christian nationalism, white supremacy, and gender oppression, we need to at the very least be conscious of where we and our partner stand in the current societal hierarchy, particularly in terms of racial and gender identities. Both in areas where we share a similar demographic and in areas where we are from very different social strata, we need to be cognizant of the ways in which this will shape our conversation partner's attitudes and our own.

This involves *intersectionality* as it was originally defined. Legal scholar Kimberlé Crenshaw coined the term not—as it is often now used—to mean that each of us is a complex amalgam of our racial, gender, class, and cultural upbringing and experience (although that is true) but rather to refer to the cumulative stress of multiple ways in which a person is targeted for oppression. Crenshaw originally introduced the idea of intersectionality in order to understand the complex burdens faced by African American women victims of intimate partner violence, who suffered not only from the violence itself but from both racism and sexism within the very systems set up to address their needs as survivors of violence—as well as possible poverty, job insecurity, housing discrimination, disability, and other circumstances added to their chronic experience of oppression.[58]

Where do we and our conversation partners fall on this spectrum of identities and life circumstances that cause us to be targeted for systemic oppression or to be beneficiaries of systemic privilege (whether we feel it or not, whether we want it or not)? What are the socially constructed assumptions we are bringing with us into the conversation, and in what ways might we be tempted to use what power we do have to impose our point of view rather than to fully hear the other person out? How does this influence how we talk to one another across racial, gender, economic, or other differences—as well as our political differences about Christian nationalism and conspiracy theories? How are we primed to come into such a conversation when we are the same gender identity but different races, or the same race but different gender identities? (And so forth.) Who is more likely to intimidate us or shut us down, and who are we more likely to intimidate or shut down (even without meaning to)? And who are the silent influencers in our minds whom we bring along with us into any encounter (CNN versus Fox News, a liberal church versus a conservative one, one social media bubble versus a very different one)?

Depending on the level of trust already created between us, will we have the courage to raise the power dynamics of the relationship itself as part of the conversation? When and how might that be generative, and when might it not? At least if we bear these dynamics in mind, we may be in a better position to choose consciously how to listen and respond in a more facilitative, open way than if we just ignored them or denied that they exist.

2. *Be attentive to conducive and unconducive times and places.* I often advise my students when we are talking about what level of confidentiality we should (and can) expect regarding what is shared in class to consider that what might feel safe to disclose in a small group or in a particular setting might not feel at all safe elsewhere. Even among the same conversation partners where what was shared previously is already known, I ask them to ask permission before assuming it's OK to continue a conversation from one context to another.[59] This is a good rule to observe with any sensitive conversation. Medical professionals are also trained not to discuss patients in a hallway or elevator for the sake of keeping patient information confidential, and teachers must observe similar protocols regarding the privacy of students.

There is no one right setting for a fruitful and honest conversation about political and/or religious differences. These will vary from person to person. For some, a crowded baseball stadium might be just the right place, where no one else is paying attention to the conversation; for others, a quiet and private spot might serve best. Some prefer to talk over a meal or a cup of tea or coffee. Some would prefer to be standing together looking at some project that physically needs doing, and just "getting around to" talking about more serious things.

Timing is also important. If you or the conversation partner are drunk, high, sick, exhausted, hungry, or some combination ("hangry"), it's not a good time for a heavy conversation. Similarly, if one or the other conversation partner has just had an emotionally intense experience such as a significant loss, a frightening diagnosis, or even a significant joy, it's not the time for a political discussion. Broaching the subject of one's political or religious views requires sensitivity and tact. People on both sides of a divide will be most able to think rather than react when stress is relatively low, physical needs are reasonably met, and there is sufficient time and space to relax.

3. *Choose your battles.* Christian nationalism and conspiracy theories abound, and it's tempting to jump into the fray whenever the subject comes up. But part of self-care—as well as caring for a conversation partner—is not to engage in every potential fight. In fact, if a fight has begun (say, among other people), it may not be the right time at all unless, again, you feel your integrity is at stake. What is the conversation that needs to happen right now, and what is the conversation that can wait? In 5 or 10 years, what encounters will you still remember as important, where you needed to make a contribution? How much energy do you have to give at any given moment—and when should you give it, even sacrificially, and when should you hold it in reserve? These are important matters of discernment, and it's not always easy to know in any given moment. Again, *breathe.* Take time to consider where your energy is best used for the sake of justice in the long run.

4. *Model civility; allow anger.* Using some of the practices described earlier, especially breathing and slowing down, it becomes possible not to fly off the handle. While the demand for "civility" can sometimes be used as a tool to suppress legitimate dissent or criticism—especially when a person with relative social power tells someone to "calm down" or "stop overreacting" (a not uncommon paternalistic move)—in general, maintaining a reasonable tone and showing interest and curiosity rather than irate judgment will help build rapport and encourage honest sharing. Note: fake calm and being a blank slate can be as infuriating as yelling and screaming—it is a display of superiority rather than an honest attempt at listening! Sarcasm, yelling, gesticulating, and threats or acts of violence are out of the question.

The goal is to be genuine, to remain open and caring, while entering truthfully into dialogue that can deepen as more is shared in an atmosphere of trust. If a conversation partner begins to become agitated and to become verbally aggressive, one possible response is to say, "I want to hear what you have to say, but I can't understand you when you're yelling at me" (or calling me names, etc.). If this doesn't work, or if at any point the other person becomes physically threatening or violent, it's time to go back to the red light STOP and disengage immediately. Walk away, and seek help if necessary.

This should not be taken to mean that anger should not be allowed into a constructive conversation. *Washington Post* columnist Julie Kohler has critiqued Braver Angels for idealizing what she calls "love politics"—a valorization of gentle communication for its own sake. She writes, "Love politics flattens anger. In their sincere belief that calmer conversations will heal our dysfunctional political system, advocates of a gentler approach to political disputation can end up framing all anger as equal—equally unjustifiable, equally counterproductive. But righteous anger in response to injustice is not the same as the oppressive anger that fuels it."[60]

Both she and Charles Blow note how Martin Luther King Jr. posthumously became a beloved American icon (while during his lifetime, "only a third of Americans had a favorable opinion of him"[61]) but that this was, as Kohler puts it, a "remaking" of King "into a placid icon."[62] She also asks, "Is it a coincidence that calls to lower the temperature of politics have arisen just as women's anger has begun to fuel progressive political victories?"[63] Beverly Harrison validated the importance of women's anger as an animating force for women's rights in church and society in her groundbreaking essay "The Power of Anger in the Work of Love."[64]

It is important to make the distinction between feelings and actions. To say "I am angry about x because y" is a self-disclosure that, if shared honestly, can further conversation. To suppress such feelings in the interests of maintaining peace at all costs actually introduces an element of untruthfulness. Feeling anger and communicating it honestly—without resorting to yelling, or violent speech or action—can actually deepen trust, especially when there is already a prior foundation of mutual care in the relationship. Breathing helps with this too!

5. *Practice self-care.* Conversations across a serious political and/or religious divide take considerable energy—mentally, physically, and emotionally. It's important to take time after such a conversation to do whatever works best for you, whether it is a time of quiet solitude or meditation or prayer, a highly confidential debrief

with a trusted partner or therapist, time for reading or watching a movie, taking a gentle walk or a warm bath, or engaging in vigorous physical activity. Be mindful that any addictive substances or behaviors are more likely to be tempting in the stress following an intense conversation—even if it went well—and be conscious of making a healthy choice. It is important not to rush into the next stressful thing if at all possible and to be intentional about caring for yourself—if not right away, then as soon as you can.

6. *Social activism* is *self-care*. What do we do with the leftover frustration from being unable to have a constructive conversation with someone "across the divide"? Again, in the interests of self-care as much as effectively continuing to promote the truth, Lee's suggestion to turn toward advocacy and activism provides us with an outlet for pent-up frustration regarding our inability to change the minds of people close to us. We should not just slink away and be quiet but rather continue to amplify messages that combat racism, health disparities, poverty, and heterosexism and—for those of us who are Christian—to insist that the overarching message of the Bible, both New Testament and Hebrew Bible, is a message of justice and mercy. The alt-right does not own social media, and studies have shown that even by "liking" someone else's post, one can prompt others to be more likely to take that message seriously.[65] One study showed, for example, that individuals are more likely to vote if they are made aware of friends and neighbors who have done so.[66] My extended family represents a fairly full range of political views from right to left, and we're all on Facebook at least occasionally. They are quite aware of where I stand on issues. It doesn't take face-to-face argumentation for me to make my values and beliefs known to people I know and love who have differing views.

Writing an op-ed[67] for a local newspaper has more impact than one might think. A recent study sponsored by Yale University and the Cato Institute found that people across the political spectrum were statistically significantly more likely to agree with a given op-ed piece after reading it than a control group of people who had not read the piece.[68] This effect lasted beyond the readers' immediate impressions (the authors measured again at 10 and 30 days). The impact may be even greater in smaller local newspapers because while readers of partisan political views may gravitate to large national papers they believe will reflect their views, local papers are read by everyone because they include news from the community, such as town and county council decisions about taxes, school board actions, and notices of local schools' and organizations' events and awards that everyone wants to know about.[69] Just as sending handwritten letters to political leaders may have more influence than signing online petitions (called *slacktivism* by some!), taking the time to write a local op-ed may satisfy our need to make an argument that might actually influence neighbors and members of our communities—even some who are close to us.

Direct action in the form of public protest can of course be a powerful tool—but even protest can be a two-edged sword, depending on when and how it is conducted. I know that some of my activist friends and colleagues will disagree with me here, but I do not believe that violent protest accomplishes its aims for social change. Nonviolent protest, on the other hand, humanizes both the protesters and—sometimes—those who would oppose them. In the worst-case scenario, even when nonviolence is met with violence, it can awaken the conscience of bystanders and still move the society in a direction for good. Violent protest and public rage may be cathartic, but they do not *in and of themselves* create constructive change—they need to be accompanied by the long-haul work of public education and political and legislative advocacy (including voting dangerous demagogues and purveyors of hate speech and disinformation out of office).

In his recently published memoir, Jim Forest describes a retreat of Christian peace activists years ago at Gethsemani Abbey, the home of the well-known monk and spiritual writer Thomas Merton. Forest recalls Merton reflecting with the group: "The grace to protest is a special gift of God requiring fidelity and purity of heart. The goal is not to humiliate an opponent but to assist him seeing the world in a new light. Far from seeing an adversary merely as an obstacle, one wishes for him or her [citing Merton] 'a better situation in which oppression no longer exists.' Ideally, protest aims at changes that benefit everyone one." Forest continues his recollections of that moment:

> Merton forced us to consider that protest, if it is to have any
> hope of constructive impact on others, has to be undertaken

not only for good reason but with great care for those who feel accused and judged by acts of protest. What is needed, Merton argued, was genuine sympathy and compassion for those who don't understand or who object to one's protest, who feel threatened and angered by it, who even regard the protester as a traitor. After all, what protest at its best aims at is not just to make a dissenting noise but to help others think freshly about our social order and the self-destructive direction in which we are going. The protestor needs to remember that no one is converted by anger, self-righteousness, contempt or hatred. Protest can backfire, hardening people in their opposition, bringing out the worst in the other. If it is to be transformative, protest needs to be animated by love, not love in the sentimental sense but in the sober biblical sense of the word.[70]

Bearing this perspective in mind, there are times when public protest is what is most needed—with the understanding that protest will have the greatest carrying power when done in a spirit of love and the care that justice requires. In this spirit, we should nevertheless not underestimate the power of being witnesses to truth and resist the desensitization to outrageous statements and actions as lies continue to metastasize, and demagogues continue to slowly turn up the heat under our feet. Robert J. Lifton describes this desensitization as "malignant normality": "a norm of destructive or violent behavior, so that such behavior is expected or required of people."[71] Lifton advocates that "as citizens, and especially as [those of us who are] professionals, we need to bear witness to malignant normality and expose it."[72]

And What If Someone's Mind Is Changed?

Finally, both Bandy Lee and Loretta Ross, coming from very different contexts, make the point that if one or more of our conversation partners end up changing their minds, we should not just dust off our hands and walk away, "mission accomplished." Renouncing or even critically questioning a deeply ingrained belief system can be profoundly destabilizing—especially if one's identity and sense of purpose were built on that foundation. Coming out from under the thrall of a charismatic leader often results in shame for having been taken in, doubt in one's own ability to perceive reality, or a shaken sense of personal morality. There are genuine losses—the loss of belonging to a mutually reinforcing group, the loss of the emotional highs, the loss of friendships, and pain that might feel akin to a divorce or a family schism. There may also be a kind of survivor guilt—worrying about those who were left back in the group, and even feeling that leaving was in some sense a betrayal of people once beloved (or at least bound together in a common cause).

Loretta Ross recounts how—while directing the Center for Democratic Renewal, an organization that monitored hate groups—she reluctantly attended Ku Klux Klan rallies "because it was my job. I monitored hate groups. But I really wanted to find out how people could hate strangers so much. Mostly I wanted to work for peace and justice. But fortunately for me, my mentor at the time was the legendary civil rights leader, Rev. C. T. Vivian who'd been an aide to Dr. Martin Luther King. And C. T. used to say, 'When you ask people to give up hate, you have to be there for them when they do.'"[73] She initially found this advice puzzling: "If the Klan hated Black folks, I was all right with hating them back. Sounded OK to me. But then something happened." She describes how her job began to include helping those who were exiting from such groups: "And once I got to know them, I couldn't hate them anymore." This eventually led her to reexamine her entire moral foundations, "to shift from hate to love."

In some situations, love—especially feeling loving emotions—may be too much to ask. But when something as powerful as a closed belief system with a charismatic leader and a tight-knit bond of True Believers is taken away, there needs to be something positive to fill the void and make up for the loss of intense belonging. As noted above in chapter 2, cult specialist Margaret Singer wrote, "Because of the powerful combination of belief, loyalty, dependency, guilt, fear, peer pressure, lack of information, and fatigue, all of which probably have equal psychological weight, members do not readily leave cults. Decent, honorable people do not easily give up on commitments, and the cult environment is such that it makes leaving practically impossible."[74] To the extent that Christian nationalism shares many common characteristics with a cult mentality—especially when melded together with apocalypticism and conspiracy theories—this is an important caveat regarding the emotional difficulty involved in such a radical change of mind.

Not only has Christian nationalism provided a firmly held set of beliefs—it has become an identity.[75] "Leaving a cult is for many one of the most difficult things they will ever do," Singer writes. "And it's especially difficult to do alone."[76] For that reason, support and information that counters the indoctrination of the Christian nationalist demagogues are crucial, both before and after leaving such a group.

It may have been months or years since the person we care about first became captivated by extremist views and has been bombarded daily by repetitive destructive messages from alt-right talk shows, cable TV, and social media, as well as in-person gatherings and rallies with like-minded individuals. Not unlike an addict in recovery, once having gone through physiological detoxification, it is important to move away from circles of friends who reinforced and encouraged drinking or drugs, both overtly and by example. Cultivating new circles where sobriety is valued is an important element in the prevention of relapse. So too an important part of "recovery" from Christian nationalist thinking requires a weaning away from the surround-sound right-wing evangelism and alt-right media that promote conspiracy theories, amplify and prey on fears, and promulgate paranoid lies.

We probably cannot accomplish this without what one pastoral care colleague of mine used to call "widening the circle of care."[77] Invitations to a new community, a new church, and a new circle of friends, and perhaps eventually replacing the excitement of right-wing rallies with the energy that comes from antiracism and gender justice activism—all of these need to be sustained over the long haul. Ongoing support is crucial in combating the political lies and biblical distortions that have so harmed both the church and society in recent decades.

Conclusion

None of this is easy, and it is important to remain mindful that the many ways in which Christian nationalists can become deeply entrenched and committed to their beliefs, particularly as a politics of fear and hate, have become fused with religious fervor. When such beliefs become virtually existential—tied to a person's very identity and sense of purpose and meaning—they are very difficult to dislodge.

Nothing in this chapter is meant to suggest that civil and compassionate conversation will be a panacea for a movement that is one more defensive eruption of white supremacy and heterosexist patriarchy. What distinguishes the approach in this chapter, I hope, is that the skills that promote constructive conversation are not merely an end in themselves. To quote Kohler's critique again, "of course, it is important that people try to connect, empathically, even across vast political disagreements. Personal relationships can be transformative. . . . But the notion that a larger dose of respectful conversations is all we need to close the deep cleavages in American politics is at best inadequate and at worst disingenuous. Love politics' proponents frame our nation's ills as interpersonal and, in so doing, gloss over structural inequities, fundamental clashes in values, and discrepancies in access to power. They also ignore conservative attacks on democratic institutions."[78] Genuinely talking "across the divide" requires honesty, and a commitment to truth—the whole truth, including both the ideals of America at its best and the shameful realities of the past and present. I agree with Kohler's conclusion: "For love politics to realize its healing potential, it must recognize sins of the past and present and work to build something greater. That's why the anger that fuels many of today's social movements, from Black Lives Matter to #MeToo, is itself such an important force for a broader, more encompassing version of love. That passion must not be suppressed to achieve the abstract goal of 'depolarization.' . . . Paeans to harmony alone won't help us harness the redemptive power of love."

Making a commitment to talk across the divide may be among the most challenging and arduous work of a lifetime—but it is holy work as well. And it is work for the long haul. Learning and practicing the skills of honest and difficult conversation across this kind of religious and political chasm do not happen overnight. To tolerate the sheer frustration and sometimes the feeling of hitting a brick wall, it's helpful to remember that whatever we hope to accomplish through dialogue—especially if our hope is to get the other person to see things differently—is not likely to happen in one brilliant flash of light or "aha!" moment after one conversation. Sharing our own point of view, with care, planting seeds of another way of thinking, takes time. Not only is cultivating patience good for the quality of our conversations—it is another practice of self-care.

Being willing to listen and speak about the whole truth of what is happening in America today is the opposite of psychological splitting, both at the larger national and structural/institutional level and also at the level of the interpersonal. Recognizing and resisting the initially unconscious temptation to split everything into a cosmic battle between good and evil (which is what conspiracy theorists thrive on) requires courage.

It takes courage to consciously take both the good and the bad of reality into one's hands and hold them together, regarding them with both mercy and justice. What it requires to begin, perhaps more than anything else, is to do our own inner work of healing the split between purity and evil within ourselves.[79] When we engage in such work—whether through our own therapy, spiritual direction, meditation, prayer, or other means of self-reflection—we are far more able, I believe, to withdraw the worst projections that we have placed on the other person and enter into genuine dialogue. This is tricky because some of the beliefs of Christian nationalists, white supremacists, and misogynists are truly reprehensible—and that is not merely our fantasy or neurotic projection. But if we can hold the badness of the belief together with a belief in the potential for basic human goodness in our conversation partner, then we not only have a chance to exercise the skill of listening. We may also be heard.

Further Reading and Resources

Suggestions for Further Reading

Butler, Anthea. *White Evangelical Racism: The Politics of Morality in America*. Chapel Hill: University of North Carolina Press, 2021.

Christians against Christian Nationalism. "Christians against Christian Nationalism." Statement, January 2021. Accessed January 29, 2021. https://www.christiansagainstchristiannationalism.org/statement.

Denker, Angela. *Red State Christians: Understanding the Voters Who Elected Donald Trump*. Minneapolis: Fortress, 2019.

Douglas, Kelly Brown. *Stand Your Ground: Black Bodies and the Justice of God*. Maryknoll, NY: Orbis, 2015.

Du Mez, Kristin Kobes. *Jesus and John Wayne: How White Evangelicals Corrupted a Faith and Fractured a Nation*. New York: Liveright, 2021.

Emerson, Michael, and Christian Smith. *Divided by Faith: Evangelical Religion and the Problem of Race in America*. Oxford: Oxford University Press, 2000.

Fitzgerald, Frances. *The Evangelicals: The Struggle to Shape America*. New York: Simon & Schuster, 2017.

Freud, Sigmund. *Group Psychology and the Analysis of the Ego*. Standard edition, translated by James Strachey. New York: W. W. Norton, 1990. First published 1921.

Goldberg, Michelle. *Kingdom Coming: The Rise of Christian Nationalism*. New York: W. W. Norton, 2007.

Gorski, Philip, and Samuel Perry. *The Flag and the Cross: White Christian Nationalism and the Threat to American Democracy*. Oxford: Oxford University Press, 2022.

Greene, Joshua. *Moral Tribes: Emotion, Reason, and the Gap between Us and Them*. New York: Penguin, 2013.

Haidt, Jonathan. *The Righteous Mind: Why Good People Are Divided by Politics and Religion*. New York: Vintage, 2013.

Hannah-Jones, Nicole. *The 1619 Project: A New Origin Story.* New York: One World/Random House, 2021.

Hendricks, Obery. *Christians against Christianity: How Right-Wing Evangelicals Are Destroying Our Nation and Our Faith.* Boston: Beacon, 2021.

Hofstader, Richard. "The Paranoid Style in American Politics." *Harper's Magazine,* November 1964. https://harpers.org/archive/1964/11/the-paranoid-style-in-american-politics/.

Jones, Robert P. *White Too Long: The Legacy of White Supremacy in American Christianity.* New York: Simon & Schuster, 2020.

Kendi, Ibram X. *How to Be an Anti-racist.* New York: One World, 2019.

Lee, Bandy X. *Profile of a Nation: Trump's Mind, America's Soul.* New York: World Mental Health Coalition, 2020.

Posner, Sarah. *Unholy: How White Christian Nationalists Powered the Trump Presidency, and the Devastating Legacy They Left Behind.* New York: Random House, 2020.

Putnam, Robert, and David Campbell. *American Grace: How Religion Unites and Divides Us.* New York: Simon & Schuster, 2010.

Say "No" to Christian Nationalism. "Evangelical Leaders Statement." Accessed December 7, 2021. https://saynotochristiannationalism.org/.

Stewart, Katherine. *The Power Worshippers: Inside the Dangerous Rise of Religious Nationalism.* New York: Bloomsbury, 2019.

West, Cornel. *Democracy Matters: Winning the Fight against Imperialism.* New York: Penguin, 2005.

Whitehead, Andrew, and Samuel Perry. *Taking American Back for God: Christian Nationalism in the United States.* New York: Oxford University Press, 2020.

Wilkerson, Isabel. *Caste: The Origins of Our Discontents.* New York: Random House, 2020.

Some Resources for Talking Across the Divide

Braver Angels (formerly "Better Angels"). https://braverangels.org/.

Bridge the Divide. https://www.bridge-the-divide.com/.

Day, Katie. *Difficult Conversations: Taking Risks, Acting with Integrity.* Herndon, VA: Alban, 2001.

Jubilee Media (https://www.jubileemedia.com/). "Liberal Christians vs. Conservative Christians | Middle Ground." YouTube, December 27, 2020. https://www.youtube.com/watch?v=6tYxnt3gCyI.

Living Room Conversations. https://livingroomconversations.org/.

Make America Dinner Again. http://www.makeamericadinneragain.com/.

OpenMind. https://openmindplatform.org/.

Parker, Priya. *The Art of Gathering: How We Meet and Why It Matters.* New York: Riverhead, 2018; see also https://www.priyaparker.com/.

The People's Supper. https://thepeoplessupper.org/.

Powers, Kirsten. *Saving Grace: Speak Your Truth, Stay Centered, and Learn to Coexist with People Who Drive You Nuts.* (New York: Convergent/Crown, 2021).

Ross, Loretta J. "What If Instead of Calling People Out, We Called Them In?" *New York Times*, November 19, 2020. https://www.nytimes.com/2020/11/19/style/loretta-ross-smith-college-cancel-culture.html.

Winthrop Rockefeller Institute. "Beyond Civility." https://rockefellerinstitute.org/workshops/beyond-civility-a-conflict-management-workshop/.

Notes

Introduction

1 Kelsie Smith and Travis Caldwell, "Disturbing Video Shows Officer Crushed against Door by Mob Storming the Capitol," CNN, January 9, 2021, https://www.cnn.com/2021/01/09/us/officer-crushed-capitol-riot-video/index.html. See also testimony to a congressional special committee on July 27, 2021, by several officers who had been attacked that day. "Watch: Full Statements from 4 Officers Who Defended Capitol from Jan. 6 Attack," *PBS NewsHour*, July 27, 2021, YouTube video, https://www.youtube.com/watch?v=a8WU8MRC2M8.

2 John Swaine, Dalton Bennett, Joyce Sohyun Lee, and Meg Kelly, "Video Shows Fatal Shooting of Ashli Babbitt in the Capitol," *Washington Post*, January 8, 2021, https://www.washingtonpost.com/investigations/2021/01/08/ashli-babbitt-shooting-video-capitol/. The officer who shot Babbitt was exonerated in an internal investigation on August 20, 2021. Ken Dilanian and Rich Schapiro, "Capitol Police Officer Who Shot Ashli Babbitt Exonerated in Internal Probe," NBC News, August 20, 2021, https://www.nbcnews.com/politics/politics-news/capitol-police-officer-who-shot-ashli-babbitt-exonerated-internal-probe-n1277336.

3 Paul Schwartzman and Josh Dawsey, "How Ashli Babbitt Went from Capitol Rioter to Trump-Embraced 'Martyr,'" *Washington Post*, July 30, 2021, https://www.washingtonpost.com/dc-md-va/2021/07/30/ashli-babbitt-trump-capitol-martyr/.

4 Chris Cameron, "These Are the People Who Died in Connection with the Capitol Riot," *New York Times*, January 5, 2022, https://www.nytimes.com/2022/01/05/us/politics/jan-6-capitol-deaths.html.

5 Calvin Woodward, "Trump's Call to Action Distorted in Debate," AP News, January 13, 2021, https://apnews.com/article/fact-check-trump-us-capitol-remarks-221518bc174f9bc3dd6e108e653ed08d.

6 "Public Supports Both Early Voting and Requiring Photo ID to Vote," Monmouth University Polling Institute, June 21, 2021, https://www.monmouth.edu/polling-institute/reports/monmouthpoll_us_062121/.

7 Andrew L. Whitehead and Samuel L. Perry, *Taking America Back for God: Christian Nationalism in the United States* (New York: Oxford University Press, 2020), 42. Statistics from Whitehead and Perry are used throughout this book, especially in chapter 1, by permission of the authors. Any errors or omissions are entirely my own.

8 Ibid., 28, 30, 42. This statistic is corroborated by my calculations from earlier statistics.

9 Ibid., 25. This percentage has actually declined slightly between 2007 and 2017, from approximately 59% to 52%, due to a general shift especially among younger generations away from organized religion altogether. Ibid., 46.

10 "When Mexico sends its people, they're not sending their best. They're not sending you. They're not sending you. They're sending people that have lots of problems, and they're bringing those problems with us. They're bringing drugs. They're bringing crime. They're rapists. And some, I assume, are good people." Quoted in Michelle Ye Hee Lee, "Donald Trump's False Comments Connecting Mexican Immigrants and Crime," *Washington Post*, July 8, 2015, https://www.washingtonpost.com/news/fact-checker/wp/2015/07/08/donald-trumps-false-comments-connecting-mexican-immigrants-and-crime/.

11 See, e.g., Pamela Cooper-White, *Many Voices: Pastoral Psychotherapy in Relational and Theological Perspective* (Minneapolis: Fortress, 2007); Pamela Cooper-White, *Braided Selves: Collected Essays on Multiplicity, God, and Persons* (Eugene, OR: Cascade, 2011).

12 Richard Hofstadter, "The Paranoid Style in American Politics," *Harper's Magazine*, November 1964, https://harpers.org/archive/1964/11/the-paranoid-style-in-american-politics/.

13 Loretta J. Ross, "Don't Call People Out, Call Them In," TEDMonterey, August 2021, https://www.ted.com/talks/loretta_j_ross_don_t_call_people_out_call_them_in?language=en.

14 "OpenMind: A Scalable, Evidence-Based Approach to Constructive Dialogue," OpenMind, accessed December 7, 2021. https://openmindplatform.org/.

Chapter 1

1 Brian Naylor, "Read Trump's Jan. 6 Speech, a Key Part of Impeachment Trial," NPR, last modified February 10, 2021, https://www.npr.org/2021/02/

10/966396848/read-trumps-jan-6-speech-a-key-part-of-impeachment-trial. Trump also stated, "All of us here today do not want to see our election victory stolen by emboldened radical-left Democrats, which is what they're doing. And stolen by the fake news media. That's what they've done and what they're doing. We will never give up, we will never concede. It doesn't happen. You don't concede when there's theft involved. Our country has had enough. We will not take it anymore and that's what this is all about. And to use a favorite term that all of you people really came up with: We will stop the steal."

2 John Wagner, "GOP Rep. Clyde Stands by Comparison of Jan. 6 Mob to 'Tourists' When Pressed by Democratic Rep. Raskin," *Washington Post*, July 28, 2021. https://www.washingtonpost.com/powerpost/capitol-attack-tourists -clyde-raskin/2021/07/28/e6087c04-ef9a-11eb-a452-4da5fe48582d_story .html. Comment made by Republican Congressman Andrew Clyde and reaffirmed when he was interviewed by Maryland Democratic Congressman Jamie Raskin on July 28, 2021, during the Congressional investigation into the January 6 insurrection. See also Alan Feuer, "Misunderstood Tourists? 'Political Hostages'? No. Debunking Riot Claims," *New York Times*, September 18, 2021, https://www.nytimes.com/2021/09/17/us/politics/capitol-riot -pro-trump-claims.html. For firsthand accounts of the terror and violence on that day, see also Emily Cochrane, Luke Broadwater, and Ellen Barry, "'It's Always Going to Haunt Me': The Capitol Riot Created a National Crisis. For Those Present, It Was Also a Personal Trauma," *New York Times*, September 18, 2021, A11, https://www.nytimes.com/interactive/2021/09/16/us/ politics/capitol-riot.html.

3 Joe Hiti, "Donald Trump: Jan. 6 Rally before Capitol Riot Had 'Love in the Air;' 'I've Never Seen Anything like It,'" MSN, last modified July 12, 2021, https://www.msn.com/en-us/news/politics/donald-trump-jan-6-rally -before-capitol-riot-had-love-in-the-air-ive-never-seen-anything-like-it/ar -AAM41ke.

4 Michael M. Grynbaum, Davey Alba, and Reid J. Epstein, "How Pro-Trump Forces Pushed a Lie about Antifa at the Capitol Riot," *New York Times*, March 1, 2021, https://www.nytimes.com/2021/03/01/us/politics/antifa -conspiracy-capitol-riot.html.

5 Siladitya Ray, "The Far-Right Is Flocking to These Alternate Social Media Apps—Not All of Them Are Thrilled," *Forbes*, January 14, 2021, https:// www.forbes.com/sites/siladityaray/2021/01/14/the-far-right-is-flocking-to -these-alternate-social-media-apps---not-all-of-them-are-thrilled/?sh=

268abd855a44. Consumers of right-wing social media migrate like flocks of starlings from one platform to another as access is blocked by parent companies over content issues (as was temporarily the case with Parler), creating an ever-changing series of internet locations for unfettered "free speech" where hate speech is not moderated. Popular sites have included Parler, Gettr, Gab, MeWe, and 4Chan. The mainstream media try to keep track of these movements but are often one step behind.

6 Dina Temple-Raston, "The 'Deep State': From Scholarly Critique to Toxic Conspiracy Theory," *Washington Post*, April 30, 2020, https://www.washingtonpost.com/outlook/the-deep-state-from-scholarly-critique-to-toxic-conspiracy-theory/2020/04/30/68960e2a-80a2-11ea-a3ee-13e1ae0a3571_story.html.

7 Gina Ciliberto and Stephanie Russell-Kraft, "They Invaded the Capitol Saying 'Jesus Is My Savior. Trump Is My President,'" *Sojourners*, January 7, 2021, https://sojo.net/articles/they-invaded-capitol-saying-jesus-my-savior-trump-my-president.

8 Carol Kuruvilla, "White Christian Radicalization Is a Violent Threat," Huff-Post, January 15, 2021, https://www.huffpost.com/entry/white-christian-nationalism-capitol-riot_n_5ff73916c5b612d958ea19db.

9 Ibid.

10 Win McNamee, photograph, in "A Christian Insurrection," by Emma Green, *Atlantic*, January 6, 2021, https://www.theatlantic.com/politics/archive/2021/01/evangelicals-catholics-jericho-march-capitol/617591/.

11 Ibid.

12 Green, "Christian Insurrection."

13 On January 8, 2021, the organization walked back its call to "take back America" and posted a brief statement declaring itself peaceful and suspending future marches for the sake of safety. The original post prior to January 6 called "patriots, people of faith and all those who want to take back America" to gather in Washington, DC. Bob Smietana, "Jericho March Returns to DC to Pray for a Trump Miracle," *Christianity Today*, January 5, 2021, https://www.christianitytoday.com/news/2021/january/jericho-march-dc-election-overturn-trump-biden-congress.html.

14 Ram's horn trumpet used since ancient times for Jewish ceremonial purposes and, especially in the context of January 6, associated with bringing down the walls of Jericho (Joshua 6). For more on fundamentalist Christians' appropriation of the shofar, see Kate Shellnutt, "Why So Many Christians Sound the Jewish Shofar in Israel," *Christianity Today*, May 24,

2018, https://www.christianitytoday.com/ct/2018/may-web-only/christians
-jewish-shofar-israel-huckabee.html.

15 Green, "Christian Insurrection."

16 Ibid.

17 Morgan Lee, "Christian Nationalism Is Worse Than You Think," *Christianity Today*, January 13, 2021, https://www.christianitytoday.com/ct/podcasts/
quick-to-listen/christian-nationalism-capitol-riots-trump-podcast.html.

18 Michael Luo, "The Wasting of the Evangelical Mind," *New Yorker*, March 4,
2021, https://www.newyorker.com/news/daily-comment/the-wasting-of-the
-evangelical-mind.

19 Jack Jenkins, "The Insurrectionists' Senate Floor Prayer Highlights a Curious Trumpian Ecumenism," *Religion News Service*, February 25, 2021,
https://religionnews.com/2021/02/25/the-insurrectionists-senate-floor
-prayer-highlights-a-curious-trumpian-ecumenism/.

20 Emily McFarlan, "How an Iconic Painting of Jesus as a White Man Was Distributed around the World," *Washington Post*, June 25, 2020, https://www
.washingtonpost.com/religion/2020/06/25/how-an-iconic-painting-jesus
-white-man-was-distributed-around-world/.

21 Reprinted in Trevor Hughes, "White Nationalists Are Once Again Using
Christian Symbols to Spread Hate," *USA Today*, February 28, 2021, https://
www.usatoday.com/story/news/nation/2021/02/28/white-nationalists-use
-christian-symbols-send-messages-racists/4457702001/.

22 Diana Butler Bass, "For Many Evangelicals, Jerusalem Is about Prophecy, Not
Politics," CNN, May 14, 2018, https://www.cnn.com/2017/12/08/opinions/
jerusalem-israel-evangelicals-end-times-butler-bass-opinion/index.html.
See also the documentary by Maya Zinshtein, *Til Kingdom Come: The Controversial Bond between Evangelicals and Jews in a Story of Faith, Power, and
Money* (2020); For more information see IMDb listing at https://www.imdb
.com/title/tt11405250/?ref_=ttexst_exst_tt.

23 Hughes, "White Nationalists," 1.

24 This "Gadsden flag" (named for its 1775 designer, Christopher Gadsden) was
flown by numerous militia groups in the 13 colonies during the American
Revolution, adopted by the Continental Congress in 1778 for the seal of the
War Office, and was reappropriated by libertarians in the 1970s, the conservative Tea Party movement as of 2009, and most recently right-wing extremist groups. Wikipedia, s.v. "Gadsden Flag," last modified December 5, 2021,
https://en.wikipedia.org/wiki/Gadsden_flag#cite_note-24. See also Matthew Rosenberg and Ainara Tiefenthäler, "Decoding the Far-Right Symbols

at the Capitol Riot," *New York Times*, January 13, 2021, https://www.nytimes
.com/2021/01/13/video/extremist-signs-symbols-capitol-riot.html.

25 Rosenberg and Tiefenthäler, "Decoding."

26 She at one time served as a chaplain with Marketplace Ministries at Martin's
Famous Potato Rolls and Bread in Chambersburg, PA. "Doug Mastriano for
State Senate," accessed December 7, 2021, https://fight4pa.com.

27 Kelly Weill, "Heir to Election Audit Freak Show Throne Has 'Army' behind Him," *Daily Beast*, July 19, 2021, https://www.thedailybeast.com/doug
-mastriano-heir-to-election-audit-freak-show-throne-in-pennsylvania-has
-army-behind-him?source=articles&via=rss.

28 Ibid.

29 Ibid.

30 Senate Majority Policy Committee, "Public Hearing on Election Issues," November 25, 2020, https://policy.pasenategop.com/112520/.

31 Eliza Griswold, "A Pennsylvania Lawmaker and the Resurgence of Christian
Nationalism," *New Yorker*, May 9, 2021, https://www.newyorker.com/news/
on-religion/a-pennsylvania-lawmaker-and-the-resurgence-of-christian
-nationalism.

32 As of February 13, 2021, Levine now serves as President Biden's Assistant
Secretary for Health.

33 Griswold, "Pennsylvania Lawmaker."

34 Candy Woodall, "Pa. Sen. Doug Mastriano Said the Fight Wasn't Over. Then
He Organized a Trip to the Capitol," *USA Today Network Pennsylvania
Capitol Bureau*, January 8, 2021, https://www.ydr.com/story/news/politics/
elections/2021/01/07/pa-democrats-call-for-doug-mastriano-resignation
-after-pro-trump-capitol-protests/6580807002/.

35 Griswold, "Pennsylvania Lawmaker."

36 Candy Woodall, "Perry, Mastriano Had Key Roles in Trump Effort to Overturn 2020 Election, Report Says," *York Daily Record*, October 8, 2021, https://
www.ydr.com/story/news/politics/elections/2021/10/08/perry-mastriano
-trump-overturn-election-report/6042787001/.

37 The study utilized data points from the 2017 Baylor Religion Survey (BRS)
and the 2016 General Social Survey (GSS) of the "nonpartisan and objective
research organization" (NORC) at the University of Chicago. Subsequent
waves of data collection can be examined directly at www.gss.norc.org. For
details of the authors' research methods, see Whitehead and Perry, *Taking
America Back*, 165–216.

38 Whitehead and Perry, *Taking America Back*, 10; emphasis added.

39 Ibid., 152.

40 Ibid., 169. This scale was tested to be both reliable and consistent across the data in both large-scale studies from 2007 to 2017.

41 Drawn from their large-scale data sets, the GSS and the NORC.

42 Whitehead and Perry, *Taking America Back*, 169.

43 Ibid., 30.

44 Ibid. This includes 80% of all Jews surveyed, 60% of those from other religious traditions, and 88% of "nones"—the largest group of non-Christians.

45 Ibid., 33–35.

46 Ibid., 34. Another quarter live in suburbs, and only 16% in cities.

47 Ibid. Versus 11% African American and 11% Hispanic.

48 Ibid. With 15% in rural areas.

49 Ibid., 37.

50 Ibid., 30.

51 Ibid.

52 Ibid., 30. Of those who oppose Christian nationalism, about 11% among the absolute "rejecters" and about 29% of those who mostly disagree with Christian nationalist ideas believe in the divine inspiration of the Bible. Virtually *all* of those who oppose Christian nationalist ideas agree that the "Bible is a book of legends"—71% among absolute rejecters and 29% among those who mostly resist Christian nationalism.

53 Ibid., 28, 30, 42; corroborated by my calculations from earlier statistics.

54 Ibid., 42.

55 Ibid.

56 A term referring to "the policy of protecting the interests of native-born or established inhabitants against those of immigrants." (Google online languages/ Oxford Languages). For more detail and history of the term, see Uri Friedman, "What Is a Nativist?," *Atlantic*, April 11, 2017, https://www.theatlantic.com/international/archive/2017/04/what-is-nativist-trump/521355/.

57 Whitehead and Perry, *Taking America Back*, 10.

58 E.g., "In God We Trust-Legacy Production," TBN, accessed December 9, 2021, https://www.tbn.org/programs/God-We-Trust-Legacy-Production; David Barton and Tim Barton, "America's Hidden History—Independence Day," TBN, accessed December 9, 2021, https://watch.tbn.org/videos/independence-day; David Barton, "Praise," TBN, https://watch.tbn.org/videos/praise-278, July 2, 2018; David Barton is the founder of the Texas-based Christian nationalist organization Wallbuilders (Wallbuilders, accessed December 7, 2021, https://wallbuilders.com/) (see Goldberg, *Kingdom Coming*, 44); Troy Brewer, Daystar,

December 1, 2021, https://daystar.tv/videos/imperfect-people-a-perfect-god -great-things-tim-barton; Rend Collective's (actually an Irish Christian band) "Build Your Kingdom Here" was on Billboard's Christian music chart for 29 weeks and became popular in American evangelical churches (Rend Collective, "Build Your Kingdom Here," September 20, 2012, YouTube video, https://www.youtube.com/watch?v=sbdJXKqVgtg); see also Michael Combs, "American Christian," YouTube, February 16, 2015, https://www.youtube .com/watch?v=dZ-jpVlMrWE, complete with video graphics bringing images of the flag together with images of a white Jesus, and numerous local church performances of the same song, e.g., McKenzie George, "American Christian," August 20, 2012, YouTube video, https://www.youtube.com/watch ?v=Qg_7BUTvvWc. "American Christian" is also available in Karaoke versions, e.g., Michael Combs, "American Christian," Ace Karaoke, https://www .acekaraoke.com/sday4227eg.html#.YVDmP2LMKUl; Gary Moore, "Make America Great Again," July 1, 2019, First Baptist Church, Dallas, Daystar TV Network / ABC News, https://abcnews.go.com/US/video/church-choir -sings-make-america-great-song-48438840; see also a suggested song list for the Fourth of July from *Christianity Today* (Kate Shellnutt, "Make Worship Patriotic Again? The Top 10 Songs for Fourth of July Services," *Christianity Today*, June 29, 2018, https://www.christianitytoday.com/ct/2018/june-web -only/make-worship-patriotic-again-top-10-songs-fourth-of-july.html). Perhaps best known is "God Bless the USA/Proud to Be an American" by Lee Greenwood, sung at the Republican National Convention in 1984 (during the Reagan administration) and on several Billboard charts in 1984, 2001, and again in 2020 (for digital song sales). It became the unofficial national anthem during Operation Desert Storm, again after 9/11, and at virtually every Fourth of July fireworks concert across the United States ever since. See, e.g., a post-9/11 video (Lee Greenwood, "God Bless the U.S.A.," July 10, 2007, YouTube video, https://www.youtube.com/watch?v=Q65KZIqay4E). A disturbing collection of antivaccination videos appears on Daystar TV Network under the heading "Vaccines: The Unauthorized Truth," Daystar, accessed December 7, 2021, https://vaccines.daystar.com/.

59 Whitehead and Perry, *Taking America Back*, 11.

60 Kristin Kobes Du Mez, *Jesus and John Wayne: How White Evangelicals Corrupted a Faith and Fractured a Nation* (New York: Liveright / W. W. Norton, 2020), 10, 12. See also Du Mez's description of Tim LaHaye's writings on "feminine surrender" and the theological rationale for subordination of

women—well before his best-selling Left Behind series hit American book-shelves. Ibid., 89–95.

61 Du Mez describes Dobson's rise in popularity from the 1970s to today in Du Mez, *Jesus and John Wayne*, 78–87.

62 E.g., Zachary Mettler, "Survey Finds Younger Americans No Longer Value Patriotism, Religion, and Having Children," Daily Citizen, August 28, 2019, https://dailycitizen.focusonthefamily.com/survey-finds-younger-americans -no-longer-value-patriotism-religion-and-having-children/; Timothy Goeglein, "Citizenship, Faith and Patriotism," Daily Citizen, January 4, 2017, https:// dailycitizen.focusonthefamily.com/citizenship-faith-and-patriotism/. For the latest postings, see https://dailycitizen.focusonthefamily.com/.

63 Kirstie Piper, "Pro-Life and Pro-Choice: What Does It Mean?," Focus on the Family, October 20, 2020, https://www.focusonthefamily.com/pro-life/ pro-life-pro-choice/.

64 Michelle Boorstein, "What It Means That Mike Pence Called Himself an 'Evangelical Catholic,'" *Washington Post*, July 18, 2016, https://www .washingtonpost.com/news/acts-of-faith/wp/2016/07/15/what-it-means-that -mike-pence-called-himself-an-evangelical-catholic/.

65 Is 45:1. Angela Denker, *Red State Christians: Understanding the Voters Who Elected Donald Trump* (Minneapolis: Fortress, 2019), 44–45.

66 For more detail on the strategy, see Katherine Stewart, *The Power Worship-pers: Inside the Dangerous Rise of Religious Nationalism* (New York: Blooms-bury, 2019), 209–34.

67 E.g., the 2021 Texas abortion law SB 8, which the US Supreme Court did not block, enabling the law to go into effect on September 1, 2021. For details, see Maggie Astor, "Here's What the Texas Abortion Law Says," *New York Times*, September 9, 2021, https://www.nytimes.com/article/abortion-law -texas.html.

68 Philip Gorski, *American Covenant: A History of Civil Religion from the Puri-tans to the Present* (Princeton, NJ: Princeton University Press, 2017), cited in Whitehead and Perry, *Taking America Back*, 11.

69 While it is true that religious liberty was a key motivation for the early colo-nists, especially the Puritans in the North, economic expansion and freedom from the monarchy in general were increasingly compelling factors as the 17th century progressed. It is not true that the framers of the Constitution were of one (Christian) mind either about establishing a Christian nation or about the separation of church and state. Contrary to overgeneralizations

on both conservative and liberal sides today, the framers and those who had their ear represented a range of viewpoints from Unitarian to Baptist, and many were overtly anti-Catholic. While the vast majority of colonists were Protestant (Puritan in the North, nominally Anglican in parts of the South), they mostly rejected the Calvinist emphasis on predestination and election in favor of individual responsibility and what Max Weber would eventually identify as the "Protestant work ethic" in *The Protestant Ethic and the Spirit of Capitalism, trans. Peter Baehr and Gordon C. Wells* (New York: Penguin, 2002; originally published in 1905). They viewed religious freedom in the context of the larger Enlightenment-inspired emphasis on individual liberties and rights and saw disestablishment and the public practice of religious tolerance as a means of both protecting religion from the state and protecting the state from religion. For a nuanced discussion of the religious differences and debates among the framers of the Constitution, see, e.g., Steven Waldman, *Founding Faith: How Our Founding Fathers Forged a Radical New Approach to Religious Liberty* (New York: Random House, 2009), 192–205.

70 Sarah Posner, *Unholy: How White Christian Nationalists Powered the Trump Presidency, and the Devastating Legacy They Left Behind* (New York: Random House, 2020), 246. See also Barron, 14.

71 Du Mez, *Jesus and John Wayne*, 89.

72 Michelle Goldberg, *Kingdom Coming: The Rise of Christian Nationalism* (New York: W. W. Norton, 2006), 39–40. See also Michelle Goldberg, "Kingdom Coming: The Rise of Christian Nationalism," Salon.com, May 12, 2006, https://www.salon.com/2006/05/12/goldberg_14/.

73 Goldberg, *Kingdom Coming*, 11. Goldberg notes that the John Birch Society began in 1958 as an anticommunist and "conspiracy-minded grassroots group." Ibid., 10.

74 Ibid., 11.

75 Anne Nelson, *Shadow Network: Media, Money, and the Secret Hub of the Radical Right* (New York: Bloomsbury, 2019), ix, 84–85. For more on the cynical strategic alliance of right-wing political operatives and right-wing evangelical leaders from the Reagan era onward, see especially 35–48, 77–99. Nelson documents how this secret organization within the right wing of the Republican party, the Council for National Policy, both courted and was created by conservative church leaders in league with extreme right-wing political ideologues. More recently, see also the degree to which Christian nationalists, especially attorney Michael P. Farris and the Alliance Defending Freedom (https://adflegal.org), were involved in clandestine activities to keep Donald

Trump in office after he lost the presidential election in November 2020. Eric Lipton and Mark Walker, "Christian Conservative Had Secretive Role in Bid to Overturn Election," *New York Times*, October 7, 2021, https://www.nytimes.com/2021/10/07/us/politics/religious-conservative-michael-farris-lawsuit-2020-election.html.

76 Goldberg, *Kingdom Coming*, 38; see also Whitehead and Perry, *Taking America*, 11–12.

77 Walter Olson, "Reasonable Doubts: Invitation to a Stoning," *Reason*, November 1998, https://reason.com/1998/11/01/invitation-to-a-stoning/.

78 George Grant and Mark Horne, *Legislating Immorality: The Homosexual Movement Comes Out of the Closet* (Chicago: Moody, 1993), 186–87.

79 George Grant and Gary North, *The Changing of the Guard: Biblical Principles for Political Action* (Fort Worth, TX: Dominion, 1987), 50–51, quoted in Goldberg, *Kingdom Coming*, 41.

80 Pat Robertson, *The New World Order* (Irving, TX: Word, 1991).

81 United States Holocaust Memorial Museum, "Protocols of the Elders of Zion," Holocaust Encyclopedia, accessed December 9, 2021, https://encyclopedia.ushmm.org/content/en/article/protocols-of-the-elders-of-zion.

82 Garry Wills, *Under God: Religion and American Politics* (New York: Simon & Schuster, 1990), 174, quoted in Goldberg, *Kingdom Coming*, 13. This interpretation of Genesis depends heavily on the theology of substitutionary atonement, which is considered a cornerstone of evangelical faith—that Jesus Christ was the "new Adam," who by his death on the cross satisfied God's need for the sake of justice to punish the first Adam for his sin and thereby save all believing Christians from their own sin.

83 Stewart, *Power Worshippers*, 123, also citing Frederick Clarkson, "Christian Reconstructionism: 'Theocratic Dominionism Gain Influence Part 3,'" *Public Eye* (Political Research Associates), May 19, 1994.

84 "About Liberty School of Law," Liberty University School of Law, accessed December 7, 2021, https://www.liberty.edu/law/about/. Regent University, founded by Pat Robertson Sr., states on its website,

> Regent University serves as a center of Christian thought and action to provide excellent education through a biblical perspective and global context, equipping Christian leaders to change the world. These values permeate the law school. Our mission is to provide an excellent legal education from a Christian perspective, to nurture and encourage our students toward spiritual maturity, and to engage the world through Christian legal

thought and practice. . . . The law school missions includes . . . a community of other law students, practicing lawyers, judges, legislators, government officials, educators, and others to recognize and seek the biblical foundations of law, legal institutions, and the processes of conflict resolution; to recognize questions of righteousness in the operation of the law; and to pursue true justice through professional legal service.

"Philosophy & Mission," Regent Law, accessed December 7, 2021, https://www.regent.edu/school-of-law/about-regent-law/philosophy-mission/. Smaller regional schools also exist, for example Oak Brook College of Law, https://www.obcl.edu/.

85 "Philosophy & Mission," Regent Law.

86 Rebecca Barrett-Fox makes this argument in relation to the vitriolic antigay hate speech of Fred Phelps and his Westboro church in Rebecca Barrett-Fox, *God Hates: Westboro Baptist Church, American Nationalism, and the Religious Right* (Lawrence: University of Kansas Press, 2016), 115, 135–37. See also Cynthia Burack, *Sin, Sex and Democracy: Antigay Rhetoric and the Christian Right* (Albany: SUNY Press, 2008): "Cynthia Burack argues that as the Christian Right has become a more sophisticated interest group, leaders have become adept at tailoring different messages for mainstream audiences and for the internal pedagogical processes of Christian conservatives. Understanding the rhetoric and the theological convictions that lie behind them, Burack claims, is essential to better understand how American politics work and how to effectively respond to exclusionary forms of political thought and practice" (Burack, back cover).

87 A good discussion of the various motivations and ramifications of this move is Stephen Farrell, "Why Is the U.S. Moving Its Embassy to Jerusalem?," Reuters, May 7, 2018, https://www.reuters.com/article/us-usa-israel-diplomacy-jerusalem-explai/why-is-the-u-s-moving-its-embassy-to-jerusalem-idUSKBN1I811N.

88 Butler Bass, "Prophecy, Not Politics."

89 Mary Boys, "Nationalisms and Their Effects on Jewish-Christian Relations," presented to the International Conference of the International Council of Christians and Jews (ICCJ), Lund, Sweden, July 1, 2019.

90 Goldberg, *Kingdom Coming*, 72–74. Goldberg notes that "the qualities the Nazis projected onto Jews are now ascribed to liberals and especially homosexuals." Both the Nazis and today's antigay preachers consider the LGBTQ community "degenerates."

91 When President Trump moved the U.S. Embassy to Jerusalem, many took it as a sign that the apocalypse was near. For more on this belief, see Butler Bass, "Prophecy, Not Politics."

92 Robert Jones, *The End of White Christian America* (New York: Simon & Schuster, 2016), 41, citing the US Census Bureau.

93 Ibid., 264–65nn73–76.

94 Robert P. Jones, *White Too Long: The Legacy of White Supremacy in American Christianity* (New York: Simon & Schuster, 2020), 94.

95 E.g., Congressional Prayer Caucus Foundation, "Report and Analysis on Religious Freedom Measures Impacting Prayer and Faith in America, 2018–19 Version," accessed December 7, 2021, https://rewirenewsgroup.com/wp-content/uploads/2018/12/Report-and-Analysis-on-Religious-Freedom-Measures-Impacting-Prayer-and-Faith_2018-2019.pdf. See also Frederick Clarkson, "Christian Right Bill Mill, Project Blitz, Hasn't Gone Away, It's Just Gotten More Secretive," *Religion Dispatches*, July 12, 2021, https://religiondispatches.org/exclusive-christian-right-bill-mill-project-blitz-hasnt-gone-away-its-just-gotten-more-secretive/; "Project Blitz," Religious Dispatches, https://religiondispatches.org/tag/project-blitz/ (a compilation of articles); Amanda Tyler, "Episode 4: Theological View of Christian Nationalism," August 21, 2019, *The Dangers of Christian Nationalism*, Christians against Christian Nationalism, podcast, SoundCloud, https://www.christiansagainstchristiannationalism.org/podcasts; Amanda Tyler, "Episode 6: Standing against Project Blitz in a State Legislature," September 4, 2019, *The Dangers of Christian Nationalism*, Christians against Christian Nationalism, podcast, SoundCloud, https://www.christiansagainstchristiannationalism.org/podcasts; and BlitzWatch, a project of the Coalition of National Civil Rights and Religious Freedom Organizations, accessed December 7, 2021, https://www.blitzwatch.org/.

96 Early examples of the current Christian resistance to Christian nationalism, from the time of George W. Bush's reelection to the US presidency, are described in Goldberg, *Kingdom Coming*, 212–14.

97 Ronald Sider, *The Spiritual Danger of Donald Trump: 30 Evangelical Christians on Justice, Truth, and Moral Integrity* (Eugene, OR: Cascade, 2020).

98 "Christians against Christian Nationalism," Christians against Christian Nationalism, statement, January 2021, accessed January 29, 2021, https://www.christiansagainstchristiannationalism.org/statement.

99 Jaziah Masters and Dan Hamil, "Responding to Christian Nationalism," Christians against Christian Nationalism, January 27, 2021, https://www .christiansagainstchristiannationalism.org/discussion-guides/responding -to-christian-nationalism-curriculum.

100 Ibid.

101 Governing Board of the National Council of Churches, "The Dangers of Christian Nationalism in the United States: A Policy Statement of the National Council of Churches," National Council of Churches, April 20, 2021, https://nationalcouncilofchurches.us/common-witness-ncc/the-dangers -of-christian-nationalism-in-the-united-states-a-policy-statement-of-the -national-council-of-churches/.

102 Evangelical Leaders Statement, "Say 'No' to Christian Nationalism: Condemning Christian Nationalism's Role in the January 6th Insurrection," February 17, 2021, https://saynotochristiannationalism.org/.

103 Whitehead and Perry, *Taking America Back*, 41.

104 Extrapolated from statistics in ibid., 28.

105 Ibid., 28.

106 Ibid., 19; emphasis added.

107 Du Mez, *Jesus and John Wayne*, 234.

108 Ibid., 6.

109 Obery Hendricks, "Toward Racial Justice: The Intersection of Race & Religion," interviewed by Charles D. Ellison, *WITF Public Media*, June 24, 2021, https://www.witf.org/2021/06/09/intersection-of-race-religion/.

110 W. Kamau Bell, "My Megachurch Adventure," CNN, April 19, 2019, https:// www.cnn.com/2019/04/27/opinions/kamau-bell-united-shades-of-america -looks-at-megachurches/index.html.

111 Baptist pastor and director of the nonprofit Repairers of the Breach, accessed December 7, 2019, https://www.breachrepairers.org/.

112 Director of the Kairos Center for Religions, Rights, and Social Justice, accessed December 7, 2019, https://kairoscenter.org/.

113 "About the Poor People's Campaign: A National Call for Moral Revival," Poor People's Campaign, accessed December 7, 2019, https://www.poorpeoples campaign.org/about/.

114 "Poor People's Moral Budget," Poor People's Campaign, June 15, 2020, https:// www.poorpeoplescampaign.org/resource/poor-peoples-moral-budget/.

115 Denker, *Red State Christians*, 163.

116 Stewart, *Power Worshippers*, 3.

117 Mia Brett, "America Was Not Founded as 'a Christian Country' Based on 'Judeo-Christian' Values," AlterNet, May 1, 2021, https://www.alternet.org/2021/05/is-america-a-christian-nation/. Brett writes,

> "Judeo-Christian values" is a dog whistle that erases Jewish values by subsuming Judaism into Christianity. It also excludes other religions, particularly Islam. When politicians claim "Judeo-Christian values" they're almost always describing Christian values but want to pretend they are being inclusive of Jews. Initially, in the 19th century the phrase referred to Jewish people who converted to Christianity. It wasn't intended to be inclusive of Jews at all. The current meaning of the term was an invention of American politics in the 1930s, as a phrase to show opposition to Hitler and communism. "Judeo-Christian values" is often used by politicians to proclaim common opposition to atheism, abortion and LGBT issues.

118 For some readers unfamiliar with the various mainline Christian denominations, the word *evangelical* in the name of the ELCA does not refer to what sociologists of religion and self-described "evangelical Christians" mean by evangelical. The use of the term seeks to reappropriate the original biblical meaning of the word *evangelion*—good news—and also echoes the use of the term *evangelisch* by German and Scandinavian Lutherans to mean simply "Protestant." The ELCA is a mainline denomination whose members espouse a wide range of social and political views from conservative to liberal to progressive.

119 Quoted in Elana Schor, "Christianity on Display at Capitol Riot Sparks New Debate," AP News, January 28, 2021, https://apnews.com/article/christianity-capitol-riot-6f13ef0030ad7b5a6f37a1e3b7b4c898.

120 Ibid.

121 Denker, *Red State Christians*, 17–18.

122 See Moore's resignation letter of May 31, 2021, at Russell D. Moore, Ethics & Religious Liberty of the Commission Southern Baptist Convention, May 31, 2021, https://baptistblog.files.wordpress.com/2021/06/rdm-final-letter.pdf. He had already publicly denounced Donald Trump, comparing him to a "Bronze Age warlord" and "an arrogant huckster," and stirred controversy within the denomination by calling out evangelical Trump supporters as "evangelicals-in-name-only." See Du Mez, *Jesus and John Wayne*, 259–60; and Bob Smietana, "Russell Moore Leaves Southern Baptist Leadership, but Denomination's Troubles Remain," *Religion News Service*, May 21, 2021,

https://religionnews.com/2021/05/21/russell-moore-is-leaving-southern
-baptist-leadership-the-denominations-troubles-remain/. For an account
of the controversy within the SBC, see Peter Wehner, "The Scandal Rocking
the Evangelical World," *Atlantic*, June 7, 2021, https://www.theatlantic.com/
ideas/archive/2021/06/russell-moore-sbc/619122/. As of May 2021, he now
directs the Public Theology Project at *Christianity Today* ("Russell Moore to
Join Christianity Today to Lead New Public Theology Project," *Christianity
Today*, May 18, 2021, https://www.christianitytoday.com/ct/2021/may-web
-only/russell-moore-to-join-christianity-today.html).

123 Quoted in Schor, "Christianity on Display"; emphasis added.

124 *Encyclopedia Britannica*, s.v. "Nationalism," by Hans Kohn, November 28,
2020, accessed July 7, 2021, https://www.britannica.com/topic/nationalism.

125 Philip Gorski, "Christianity and Democracy after Trump," *Political Theology* 19, no. 5 (2018): 361–62, https://www.tandfonline.com/doi/full/10.1080/
1462317X.2018.1476053, as summarized in Whitehead and Perry, *Taking
America Back*, 78. See also Gorski, *American Covenant*.

126 *Encyclopedia Britannica*, s.v. "Nationalism."

127 Isabel Wilkerson, *Caste: The Origins of Our Discontents* (New York: Random
House, 2020).

128 Whitehead and Perry, *Taking America Back*, 28. Twenty percent earned
below $20,000. In the last year of the survey as cited, 2017, the poverty line
was $24,600 for a family of four (add or subtract $4,180 for additional or
fewer persons). For exact federal poverty guidelines for each year, see https://
aspe.hhs.gov/topics/poverty-economic-mobility/poverty-guidelines/prior
-hhs-poverty-guidelines-federal-register-references. For a discussion of
more complex measures of poverty, see Rebecca M. Blank, "How to Im-
prove Poverty Measurement in the United States," Brookings, June 30, 2008,
https://aspe.hhs.gov/topics/poverty-economic-mobility/poverty-guidelines/
prior-hhs-poverty-guidelines-federal-register-references.

129 Whitehead and Perry, *Taking America Back*, 28. Twenty-three percent earn
less than $20,000.

130 Wilkerson, *Caste*, 159–64.

131 A. Renee Staton, William Evans, and Christopher Lucey, "Understanding
Social Class in the United States," in *Social Class and the Helping Professions*,
ed. Debbie C. Sturn and Donna M. Gibson (New York: Routledge, 2012), 28.

132 The Southern Poverty Law Center (SPLC) tracks hate groups in the United
States. Regarding white supremacists, see "White Nationalist," SPLC, https://
www.splcenter.org/fighting-hate/extremist-files/ideology/white-nationalist.

133 A definition by David Gillborn, quoted in Vann R. Newkirk II, "The Language of White Supremacy," *Atlantic*, October 6, 2017, https://www.theatlantic .com/politics/archive/2017/10/the-language-of-white-supremacy/542148/. Newkirk argues that those who would argue to keep the definition of "white supremacy" limited to extremist groups "actually help continue the work of the architects of the post-Jim Crow racial hierarchy."

134 Wilkerson, *Caste*, 49–50.

135 Jones, *End of White Christian America*, 61–66, 79. Regarding the whitening of Catholic immigrants, see also Jeannine Hill Fletcher, *The Sin of White Supremacy: Christianity, Racism, & Religious Diversity in America* (Maryknoll, NY: Orbis, 2017).

136 Chris Woolf, "A Brief History of America's Hostility to a Previous Generation of Mediterranean Migrants—Italians," *The World*, November 26, 2015, https://www.pri.org/stories/2015-11-26/brief-history-america-s-hostility -previous-generation-mediterranean-migrants.

137 Robert Besser, "During a Weekend of Racial Unrest, Greek Americans Recall Their Own Struggles with Racism," *Greek Reporter*, May 31, 2020, https:// greekreporter.com/2020/05/31/during-a-weekend-of-racial-unrest-greek -americans-recall-their-own-struggles-with-racism/.

138 For a discussion of Christian nationalism in particular and antisemitism, see Boys, "Nationalisms."

139 "Antisemitism in the US," Anti-Defamation League (ADL), accessed December 7, 2021, https://www.adl.org/what-we-do/anti-semitism/antisemitism-in -the-us. Antisemitic hate crimes are continuously tracked by the ADL, https://www.adl.org/education-and-resources/resource-knowledge-base/adl -tracker-of-antisemitic-incidents.

140 Melissa Eddy, "Amid the Rampage at the U.S. Capitol, a Sweatshirt Stirs Troubling Memories," *New York Times*, January 8, 2021, https://www.nytimes .com/2021/01/08/world/europe/us-capitol-rampage-camp-auschwitz.html ?searchResultPosition=2.

141 Du Mez details evangelicals' anti-Islam fear mongering and equation of Muslims with terrorists and evil. Du Mez, *Jesus and John Wayne*, 219–30.

142 Related to the creation of Indian boarding schools to force cultural assimilation in Native American children in the 19th century and continuing until the 1980s. Ward Churchill, *Kill the Indian, Save the Man: The Genocidal Impact of American Indian Residential Schools* (San Francisco: City Lights, 2004).

143 Anthea Butler, *White Evangelical Racism: The Politics of Morality in America* (Chapel Hill, NC: Ferris and Ferris, 2021), 23, citing Charles Reagan Wilson,

Baptized in Blood: The Religion of the Lost Cause, 1865–1920, 2nd ed. (Athens: University of Georgia Press, 2009).

144 Butler, *White Evangelical Racism*, 24.

145 W. Scott Poole, *Religion, Gender, and the Lost Cause* (Athens, GA: Southern Historical Association, 2002), cited in Butler, *White Evangelical Racism*, 24.

146 Reconstruction was the short-lived period begun immediately at the end of the Civil War in 1865 when Blacks were granted full citizenship and began to claim their rightful place in government and society but was cut short as whites in the South conspired to restore white supremacy in practice as well as belief and ushered in the long era of Jim Crow segregation and oppression. The Reconstruction era has generated its own academic field of both history and historiography, which is too large and complex to summarize here.

147 Michelle Alexander, *The New Jim Crow: Mass Incarceration in the Age of Colorblindness*, 10th anniversary ed. (New York: New Press, 2020).

148 Clint Smith, "The War on Nostalgia," *Atlantic*, June 2021, 54–55, https://www.theatlantic.com/magazine/archive/2021/06/confederate-lost-cause-myth/618711/. See also Jones, *End of White Christian America*, 82–84, 222, 230, 247; Jones, *White Too Long*, 89–92.

149 "Whose Heritage? Public Symbols of the Confederacy," SPLC, February 1, 2019, https://www.splcenter.org/20190201/whose-heritage-public-symbols-confederacy. See also Jones, *White Too Long*, 130–37.

150 "Whose Heritage?"

151 Jones, *White Too Long*, 140–42.

152 "Robert E. Lee Statue Is Removed in Richmond," *PBS NewsHour*, September 7, 2021, https://www.pbs.org/newshour/nation/virginia-is-set-to-remove-richmonds-lee-statue-on-wednesday.

153 Now United Lutheran Seminary.

154 Chris Cappella, "Historic Gettysburg Seminary Bans Confederate Flags," *Evening Sun*, June 29, 2015, https://www.eveningsun.com/story/news/local/2015/06/28/historic-gettysburg-seminary-bans-confederate-flags/32384169/.

155 Rev. John Spangler, former senior vice president, Gettysburg Lutheran Seminary, personal communication.

156 Butler, *White Evangelical Racism*, 93; Jones, *White Too Long*, 54–55.

157 Religious Landscape Study, "Members of the Southern Baptist Convention," Pew Research Center, https://www.pewforum.org/religious-landscape-study/religious-denomination/southern-baptist-convention/.

158 Gustav Niebuhr, "Baptist Group Votes to Repent Stand on Slaves," *New York Times*, June 21, 1995, https://www.nytimes.com/1995/06/21/us/baptist -group-votes-to-repent-stand-on-slaves.html.

159 Jones, *White Too Long*, 54.

160 Niebuhr, "Baptist Group." Partially quoted in Jones, *White Too Long*, 55.

161 Butler, *White Evangelical Racism*, 93.

162 Tisa Wenger, *Religious Freedom: The Contested History of an American Ideal* (Chapel Hill: University of North Carolina Press, 2020); also cited in Butler, *White Evangelical Racism*, 131.

163 Michael O. Emerson and Christian Smith, *Divided by Faith: Evangelical Religion and the Problem of Race in America* (Oxford: Oxford University Press, 2000), 76. Also cited in Jones, *White Too Long*, 97; see also Jones, 95–101. Jones notes that "all white Protestant affiliation generally is correlated with an individualist rather than structural cultural tool kit" and that "the cultural tool kits of white mainline Protestants increasingly contain the individualist tools of their white evangelical cousins" (99). On individualism, see also Philip Gorski and Samuel Perry, *The Flag and the Cross: White Christian Nationalism and the Threat to American Democracy* (Oxford: Oxford University Press, 2022); Jones, *End of White Christian America*, 175; and Ibram X. Kendi, *How to Be an Antiracist* (New York: One World, 2019), 19. The term *racial discrimination* similarly perpetuates racist policies because it puts the emphasis on individuals' actions rather than racist policies and policy makers.

164 Emerson and Smith, *Divided by Faith*, 76–77.

165 Jones, *White Too Long*, 97–98, 223–25, 234–36.

166 Butler, *White Evangelical Racism*, 11.

167 Wording from the final resolution as voted. "On Critical Race Theory and Intersectionality," SBC, June 1, 2019, https://www.sbc.net/resource-library/ resolutions/on-critical-race-theory-and-intersectionality/.

168 The 2019 convention as described by Rev. Marshal Ausberry Sr., president of the National African American Fellowship of the SBC, quoted in Adele M. Banks, "At Least Three Critical Race Theory Statements Proposed for Southern Baptist Meeting," *Religion News Service*, June 11, 2021, https:// religionnews.com/2021/06/11/at-least-three-critical-race-theory-statements -proposed-for-southern-baptist-meeting/. Ausberry further commented that he didn't see CRT as "the hill to die on."

169 Ibid.

170 Southern Baptist Convention 2019 Annual Meeting, "On Critical Race Theory and Intersectionality," SBC, June 1, 2019, https://www.sbc.net/resource

-library/resolutions/on-critical-race-theory-and-intersectionality/; emphasis added.

171 George Schroeder, "Seminary Presidents Reaffirm BFM, Declare CRT Incompatible," *Baptist Press*, November 30, 2020, https://www.baptistpress.com/resource-library/news/seminary-presidents-reaffirm-bfm-declare-crt-incompatible/; Yonat Shimron, "Southern Baptist Seminary Presidents Nix Critical Race Theory," *Religion News Service*, December 1, 2020, https://religionnews.com/2020/12/01/southern-baptist-seminary-presidents-nix-critical-race-theory/.

172 Just one month prior to the 2019 convention, Al Mohler, president of Southern Baptist Seminary, refused to entertain a petition from a group of Black and white Louisville clergy calling for the seminary to put action behind its recent words of apology for its origins as a slaveholding institution by tithing 10% of its $900 million endowment to a local historically Black Christian college. Mohler's reply was, "We agree with the policy of the Southern Baptist Convention in this regard, and we do not believe that financial reparations are the appropriate response." Adelle Banks, "Southern Baptist Seminary Denies Request for Reparations," *Religion News Service*, June 6, 2019, https://www.baptiststandard.com/news/baptists/southern-baptist-seminary-denies-request-for-reparations/; see also Jones, *White Too Long*, 61.

173 For more details on the SBC's fundamentalist turn and its impact on women, see Eileen Campbell-Reed, *Anatomy of a Schism: How Clergywomen's Narratives Reinterpret the Fracturing of the Southern Baptist Convention* (Knoxville: University of Tennessee Press, 2016).

174 One of the presidents soon backpedaled slightly, stating that CRT does "rightly decry racism and injustice," but "they reject the theory as a comprehensive way of understanding race-related problems." Sarah Pulliam Bailey and Michelle Boorstein, "Several Black Pastors Break with the Southern Baptist Convention over a Statement on Race," *Washington Post*, December 23, 2020, https://www.washingtonpost.com/religion/2020/12/23/black-pastors-break-southern-baptist-critical-race-theory/.

175 Ibid.

176 Ibid.

177 Ibid.

178 Ibid.

179 Robert P. Jones and PRRI, cited in Jennifer Rubin, "Why Are White Evangelicals Embracing an Anti-democratic Movement? Because They're Panicking,"

Washington Post, July 12, 2021, https://www.washingtonpost.com/opinions/2021/07/12/white-evangelicals-decline-spurs-an-anti-democratic-movement/.

180 Bob Smietana, "Southern Baptist Decline Continues," *Religion News Service*, May 21, 2021, https://religionnews.com/2021/05/21/southern-baptist-decline-continues-denomination-has-lost-more-than-2-million-members-since-2006/.

181 Southern Baptist Convention 2021 Annual Meeting, "On the Sufficiency of Scripture for Race and Racial Reconciliation," SBC, June 21, 2021, https://www.sbc.net/resource-library/resolutions/on-the-sufficiency-of-scripture-for-race-and-racial-reconciliation/.

182 Jones, *White Too Long*, 56.

183 Ibid.

184 Ibid., 63.

185 See Whitehead and Perry, *Taking America Back*, 12.

186 Ibid., 153.

187 Gorski, "Christianity and Democracy after Trump," 3, cited in Whitehead and Perry, *Taking America Back*, 21.

188 Charles Yu, *Interior Chinatown: A Novel* (New York: Vintage, 2020).

189 Charles Yu, "Reality," *Harper's Magazine*, February 2021, https://harpers.org/archive/2021/02/life-after-trump/#reality-charles-yu. See also Du Mez on evangelicals' support for Trump as "the culmination of evangelicals' embrace of militant masculinity, an ideology that enshrines patriarchal authority and condones the callous display of power, at home and abroad." Du Mez, *Jesus and John Wayne*, 3.

190 Nelson, *Shadow Network*.

191 *New York Times*, "The Guantánamo Docket," *New York Times*, September 1, 2021, https://www.nytimes.com/interactive/2021/us/guantanamo-bay-detainees.html.

192 Jones, *End of White Christian America*, 41, citing the US Census Bureau, 264–65nn73–76.

193 Du Mez, *Jesus and John Wayne*, 38.

194 Ibid., 38–39.

195 Butler, *White Evangelical Racism*, 117.

196 Du Mez, *Jesus and John Wayne*, 237.

197 Butler, *White Evangelical Racism*, 140.

198 Butler, *White Evangelical Racism*, 116–17.

199 Ibid., 124; see also Nelson, *Shadow Network*.

200 Butler, *White Evangelical Racism*, 125.

201 Ibid., 126.

Chapter 2

1 Andrew Whitehead and Samuel Perry, cited in chapter 1, also corroborated their quantitative research with interviewing and participant observation, providing a richer basis for their overall conclusions. Whitehead and Perry, *Taking America Back*, 172–76. Both Angela Denker (*Red State Christians*) and Kristin Kobes Du Mez (*Jesus and John Wayne*), cited in chapter 1, also used forms of qualitative research, from the disciplines of journalism and history, respectively.

2 Mary Moschella, *Ethnography as a Pastoral Practice* (Cleveland: Pilgrim, 2008).

3 Six thousand churches with an attendance of 1,000–1,999 (2% of all American churches) collectively represent *8 million weekly worshippers*; 1,170 churches with 2,000–9,999 attendees (0.4% of all American churches) collectively represent *4 million weekly worshippers*; and churches with 10,000+ members (only 40 in the United States, representing only 0.01% of congregations) represent *0.7 million weekly worshippers*—altogether totaling about 13 million worshippers or about 23% of all US church attendees. In comparison, 43 million Americans attend smaller churches, with 34 million in churches of less than 500 members (including 9 million in churches of fewer than 100). "Fast Facts about American Religion: What's the Average Size of U.S. Churches?," Hartford Institute for Religion Research, accessed December 8, 2021, http://hirr.hartsem.edu/research/fastfacts/fast_facts.html#sizecong. These figures are based on clergy interviews from 1998–2019 from the National Congregations Study, Duke University, accessed December 8, 2021, https://sites.duke.edu/ncsweb/.

4 Fifty-eight percent of megachurches report being "multiracial today, defined as having 20% or more minority presence," compared to 7% in 2005 and still just 16% in 2019. Warren Bird and Scott Thumma, "Megachurch 2020: The Changing Reality in America's Largest Churches," Hartford Institute for Religion Research, October 29, 2020, http://www.hartfordinstitute.org/megachurch/megachurches_research.html. This shows a significant increase just in one year between 2019 and 2020—yet it should be noted that a congregation with 20% "minority presence" (with no data to differentiate percentages in the range from 20 to over 50%) is still an overwhelmingly white church.

5 Ibid., 12.

6 "Size of Congregation," Association of Religion Data Archives, accessed December 8, 2021, https://www.thearda.com/ConQS/qs_6.asp. The raw

number of churches with 1,000+ members within this study is very small—32 churches of this size overall (just 3% of all churches of all sizes in the study). So the sample size is suggestive but not definitive.

7 Of the 1,000+ member churches, 18 were "more conservative" theologically, 12 "right in the middle," and only 2 "more liberal." The raw numbers across the political spectrum were 13 "more conservative," 12 "right in the middle," and 2 "more liberal." Ibid.

8 Goldberg, *Kingdom Coming*, 190.

9 Stewart, *Power Worshippers*, 6.

10 David Masci, "What Do Americans Look for in a Church, and How Do They Find One? It Depends in Part on Their Age," Pew Research Center, August 23, 2016, https://www.pewresearch.org/fact-tank/2016/08/23/what -do-americans-look-for-in-a-church-and-how-do-they-find-one-it-depends -in-part-on-their-age/.

11 For example, the Serendipity small-group book series was a much-emulated early resource (now owned by Lifeway/Small Group Life, accessed December 7, 2021, https://www.lifeway.com/en/shop/bible-studies/small -groups); https://www.smallgroups.com/; and http://smallgroupleadership .com/product-category/studies/; Augsburg Fortress Press developed its own small-group series, Intersections, in the mid-1990s in an effort to bring small-group ministry resources together with mainline church theology and Bible study, church growth, support group ministry, and discipleship. See, for example, George Johnson, *Starting Small Groups and Keeping Them Going* (Minneapolis: Augsburg Fortress, 1995) and more recent print and media resources for small groups at https://www.augsburgfortress.org/store/category/ 286917/Small-Group. In general, both conservative and mainline church resources for small groups have grown in sophistication from booklets with simple graphics to books and media with updated production values.

12 For example, "the preeminence of evangelism" is listed as the first "foundational value" in "Foundational Values," Focus on the Family, accessed December 8, 2021, https://www.focusonthefamily.com/about/foundational-values/.

13 A common divide exists in evangelizing strategy between evangelical Christians, whose evangelizing is often done through proselytizing, and many liberal and mainline Christians, who generally prefer to evangelize by showing a good example of Christian love for one another and the world.

14 For a detailed history of the development of denominationalism in the United States, a classic text is Sidney Ahlstrom, *A Religious History of the American People*, 2nd ed. (New Haven, CT: Yale University Press, 2004).

15 For a carefully researched description of the history of the two "Great Awakenings" in America, see Frances Fitzgerald, *The Evangelicals: The Struggle to Shape America* (New York: Simon & Schuster, 2017), 13–48.

16 Du Mez, *Jesus and John Wayne*, 7.

17 Ibid., 10.

18 Meagan Clark, "Exclusive: After Pushback HarperCollins Will Not Produce 'God Bless the USA' Bible," *Religion Unplugged*, May 25, 2021, https://religionunplugged.com/news/2021/5/25/after-pushback-harpercollins-will-not-produce-god-bless-the-usa-biblenbsp.

19 For more on the "God Bless America" Bible, see Peter W. Marty, "An American Bible?," *Christian Century*, June 30, 2021, 3; and Clark, "After Pushback."

20 Denker similarly describes the decor and attire of a megachurch where she also heard a sermon incorporating Christians wearing bulletproof vests and needing AR-15s. Denker, *Red State Christians*, 64–65.

21 For a more detailed description of the development of megachurches in the United States and their demographics, see Stephen Hunt, "The Megachurch Phenomenon," in *Handbook of Megachurches*, ed. Stephen Hunt (Leiden: Brill, 2020), https://doi.org/10.1163/9789004412927_002.

22 Du Mez, *Jesus and John Wayne*, 242. Metaxas's scholarship has been largely discredited by historians and theologians; for more on Metaxas and his support for Trump, see Du Mez, 242–44, 262–64; and Bob Smietana, "Eric Metaxas, Christian Radio Host, Tells Trump, 'Jesus Is with Us in This Fight,'" Religion News Service, November 30, 2020, https://religionnews.com/2020/11/30/eric-metaxas-christian-radio-host-offers-to-lay-down-his-life-for-trump-election-triumph/.

23 This is a very abbreviated summary of a chapter by Margaret Thaler Singer, "Recruiting New Members," in *Cults in Our Midst: The Continuing Fight against Their Hidden Menace* (San Francisco: Jossey-Bass, 2003), 105–24. She goes on to elaborate on physiological and psychological persuasion techniques in great detail.

24 A paraphrase and quote from Daniel Shaw, *Traumatic Narcissism: Relational Systems of Subjugation* (New York: Routledge, 2014), 49–50.

25 Ibid., 45–46.

26 Historically Black churches are also not homogeneous. E.g., see Eric L. McDaniel, Maraam A. Dwidar, and Hadill Calderon, "The Faith of Black Politics: The Relationship between Black Religious and Political Beliefs," *Journal of Black Studies* 49, no. 3 (2018): 256–83, https://journals.sagepub.com/doi/10.1177/0021934717753730: "This study examines the linkage between heterogeneity

in Black religious beliefs and heterogeneity in Black political attitudes. Offering measures of the social gospel, prosperity gospel, and Black theology, we demonstrate that each religious belief system is related to different aspects of Black public opinion. The social gospel is linked to continuing the legacy of the civil rights movement, while the prosperity gospel is associated with a departure from its legacy. Meanwhile, Black theology is linked to racial empowerment and extending the boundaries of Black politics." See also Eddie Glaude Jr.'s critique of the prosperity gospel: Eddie Glaude Jr., "Too Many Black Churches Preach the Gospel of Greed," *New York Times*, March 19, 2015, https://www.nytimes.com/roomfordebate/2014/06/25/has-capitalism -become-incompatible-with-christianity/too-many-black-churches-preach -the-gospel-of-greed.

27 Denker, *Red State Christians*, 19.

28 For more detail on the emotional disruption caused by leaving an authoritarian group, see Shaw, *Traumatic Narcissism*, 51, 89–115.

29 Singer, *Cults in Our Midst*, 170.

30 Ginny NiCarthy spells out the parallels to tactics of coercion used on prisoners of war in Ginny NiCarthy, *Getting Free: You Can End Abuse and Take Back Your Life* (Seattle: Seal, 2004), 285–92; see also Mary Romero, "A Comparison between Strategies Used on Prisoners of War and Battered Wives," *Sex Roles* 13 (1985): 537–47.

31 Pamela Cooper-White, *The Cry of Tamar*, 2nd ed. (Minneapolis: Fortress, 2012), 138–39, also citing Rebecca Emerson Dobash and Russell P. Dobash, *Women, Violence, and Social Change: A Case against the Patriarchy* (New York: Free Press, 1979), 223–31.

32 Singer, *Cults in Our Midst*, 274.

33 Robert Putnam, *Bowling Alone: The Collapse and Revival of American Community* (New York: Simon & Schuster, 2000); 2nd ed., 2020.

34 In Putnam's words, "The central premise of social capital is that social networks have value. Social capital refers to the collective value of all 'social networks' [who people know] and the inclinations that arise from these networks to do things for each other ['norms of reciprocity']. The term social capital emphasizes not just warm and cuddly feelings, but a wide variety of quite specific benefits that flow from the trust, reciprocity, information, and cooperation associated with social networks. Social capital creates value for the people who are connected and—at least sometimes—for bystanders as well." Robert D. Putnam, "Social Capital Primer," 2020, http://robertdputnam.com/bowling-alone/social-capital-primer/.

35 Putnam, *Bowling Alone*.

36 See chapter 1 for more detail on evangelicalism's emphasis on individual sin.

37 A hot topic in education that came to the fore in the 2000s with a series of court cases over eliminating evolution from public school curricula, e.g., the heavily publicized fight in the school district in Dover, Pennsylvania, in 2004 (Goldberg, *Kingdom Coming*, 80–105), which echoed the Scopes monkey trial in Dayton, Tennessee, in 1925. For more on this history, see Fitzgerald, *Evangelicals*, 133–42.

38 Goldberg, *Kingdom Coming*, 14.

39 Ibid., 1.

40 Ibid., 4.

41 Robert T. Palmer and Larry J. Walker, "Proposing a Concept of the Black Tax to Understand the Experiences of Blacks in America," *Diverse: Issues in Higher Education*, July 6, 2020, https://www.diverseeducation.com/ demographics/african-american/article/15107226/proposing-a-concept-of -the-black-tax-to-understand-the-experiences-of-blacks-in-america.

42 For an analysis of how taste is implicated in class difference, see Pierre Bourdieu, *Distinction: A Social Critique of the Judgment of Taste*, trans. Richard Nice (Oxford: Routledge Classics, 2010).

43 Robin DiAngelo, *Nice Racism: How Progressive White People Perpetuate Racial Harm* (Boston: Beacon, 2021); Chana Joffe-Walt, "Introducing: Nice White Parents," *New York Times*, July 23, 2020, https://www.nytimes.com/ 2020/07/23/podcasts/nice-white-parents-serial.html; see also Ligaya Mishan, "The March of the Karens," *New York Times Style Magazine*, August 12, 2021, 94–98, https://www.nytimes.com/2021/08/12/t-magazine/white-women -karen.html.

44 Ta-Nehisi Coates, "The First White President," *Atlantic*, October 2017, https://www.theatlantic.com/magazine/archive/2017/10/the-first-white -president-ta-nehisi-coates/537909/.

45 Dee Davis quoted in Helena Bottemiller Evich, "Revenge of the Rural Voter," *Politico*, November 13, 2016, https://www.politico.com/story/2016/11/hillary -clinton-rural-voters-trump-231266. Bottemiller Evich notes that "while Clinton released policy plans, Trump did campaign stops in small towns." See also Joan C. Williams on Trump's seemingly paradoxical appeal to working-class Americans in Joan C. Williams, "What So Many People Don't Get about the U.S. Working Class," *Harvard Business Review*, November 10, 2016, https://hbr.org/2016/11/what-so-many-people-dont-get-about-the-u-s -working-class.

46 Williams writes that of the culture gap between the working class and professional class is "that the white working class resents professionals but admires the rich." They view the rich as people who worked hard (as they do) and made it, while they view professionals as dishonest and exploiting them: "The dream is not to become upper-middle-class, with its different food, family, and friendship patterns; the dream is to live in your own class milieu, where you feel comfortable—just with more money. . . . The main thing is to be independent and give your own orders and not have to take them from anybody else." Williams, "So Many People." See also J. D. Vance, *Hillbilly Elegy: A Memoir of a Family and Culture in Crisis* (New York: HarperCollins, 2016).

47 E.g., see Jerrold M. Post with Stephanie Doucette, *Dangerous Charisma: The Political Psychology of Donald Trump and His Followers* (New York: Pegasus, 2019), 121–25.

48 In a 2016 *Washington Post* poll, only 42% of Republicans and 53% of Democrats thought Trump's father was "wealthy" when Trump was born; most of the others surveyed believed he was "middle class," "working class," or even "poor," "suggesting that they believe that Fred Trump's social class was essentially the same as the people in Queens who were buying his homes in the 1920s for about $4,000 (or roughly $56,000 in today's dollars)." John Sides, "Many Americans Do Not Think Donald Trump Was Born into Wealth," *Washington Post*, October 3, 2016, https://www.washingtonpost.com/news/monkey-cage/wp/2016/10/03/poll-many-americans-do-not-think-donald-trump-was-born-into-wealth/. See also Jared McDonald, David Karol, and Lilliana Mason, "Many Voters Think Trump's a Self-Made Man. What Happens When You Tell Them Otherwise?," *Politico*, January 17, 2019, https://www.politico.com/magazine/story/2019/01/17/many-voters-think-trumps-a-self-made-man-what-happens-when-you-tell-them-otherwise-224019/.

49 The Pew Research Center reported in 2020,

> The wealthiest families are also the only ones to have experienced gains in wealth in the years after the start of the Great Recession in 2007. From 2007 to 2016, the median net worth of the richest 20% increased 13%, to $1.2 million. For the top 5%, it increased by 4%, to $4.8 million. In contrast, the net worth of families in lower tiers of wealth decreased by at least 20% from 2007 to 2016. The greatest loss—39%—was experienced by the families in the second quintile of wealth, whose wealth fell from $32,100

in 2007 to \$19,500 in 2016. As a result, the wealth gap between America's richest and poorer families more than doubled from 1989 to 2016.

Juliana Menasce Horowitz, Ruth Igielnik, and Rakesh Kochhar, "Trends in Income and Wealth Inequality," Pew Research Center, January 9, 2020, https://www.pewresearch.org/social-trends/2020/01/09/trends-in-income -and-wealth-inequality/.

50 Bandy X. Lee, *Profile of a Nation: Trump's Mind, America's Soul* (New York: World Mental Health Coalition, 2020), 91, citing the US Census Bureau's report "Poverty in the United States."

51 Anne Case and Angus Deaton, *Deaths of Despair and the Future of Capitalism* (Princeton, NJ: Princeton University Press, 2020), cited in Lee, *Profile of a Nation*, 95.

52 Williams, "What So Many People"; see also Joe Bageant, *Deer Hunting with Jesus: Dispatches from America's Class War* (New York: Three Rivers, 2007).

53 "Historical Foundations of Race," National Museum of African American History and Culture, December 16, 2021, https://nmaahc.si.edu/learn/ talking-about-race/topics/historical-foundations-race.

54 As noted in chapter 1 and, e.g., in Wilkerson, *Caste*.

55 Jones, *End of White Christian America*, 41, citing the US Census Bureau (264–65nn73–76).

56 Mike Schneider, "Census Shows US Is Diversifying, White Population Shrinking," AP News, August 13, 2021, https://apnews.com/article/census -2020-house-elections-4ee80e72846c151aa41a808b06d975ea.

57 Ibid. Analysts caution that some of the statistical change from white to other groups is a factor of more whites identifying as "two or more races."

58 Natalie Musumeci and Madison Hoff, "A Striking US Census Map Shows How Much Rural America Has Shrunk in the Past Decade," *Business Insider*, August 12, 2021, https://www.businessinsider.com/us-census-map -widespread-population-declines-in-rural-areas-2021-8.

59 For more on this, see John Fea, *Believe Me: The Evangelical Road to Donald Trump* (Grand Rapids, MI: Eerdmans, 2018), esp. ch. 1, "The Evangelical Politics of Fear."

60 Robert Putnam and David Campbell, *American Grace: How Religion Unites and Divides Us* (New York: Simon & Schuster, 2010), 141.

61 Ibid., 139.

62 Ibid., 142.

63 Ibid., 142; see also 124–25 regarding decline of young adults in church.

64 Public Religion Research Institute (PRRI), "The American Religious Landscape in 2020," https://www.prri.org/research/2020-census-of-american-religion/.

65 Ibid. Mainline churches represented 17.8% of Americans in 2006, dropped to a low point of 12.8% in 2016, and rebounded to 16.4% in 2020.

66 Reaching a high point of 26% in 2018 and experiencing a slight decline to 23% as of 2020. PRRI staff, "The 2020 Census of American Religion," July 8, 2021, https://www.prri.org/research/2020-census-of-american-religion/, 2.

67 Ibid., 6. Catholics altogether still represent about one-fourth of the US population, mainly because as white Catholics decline in number, the percentage of Latinx Catholics is growing. Jones, *End of White Christian America*, 69.

68 Jones, *End of White Christian America*, 69.

69 Denker, *Red State Christians*, 35.

70 Ibid.

71 Ruth Ben-Ghiat, *Strongmen: Mussolini to the Present* (New York: W. W. Norton, 2020), 120–21. See entire chapter on "virility," 119–40.

72 Ibid., 251.

73 Du Mez, *Jesus and John Wayne*, 59.

74 Ibid., quoting Alan Bean, "Jesus and John Wayne: Must We Choose?," *Baptist News Global*, October 31, 2016, https://baptistnews.com/article/jesus-and-john-wayne-must-we-choose/#.YVNvcGLMKUk.

75 See Alan Bean "Friends of Justice" blog, https://friendsofjustice.blog/. Bean is a frequent contributor to Baptist Global News (https://baptistnews.com/).

76 Tessa Berenson, "John Wayne's Daughter Endorses Donald Trump," *Time*, January 19, 2016, https://time.com/4185378/donald-trump-john-wayne-iowa/.

77 Bean, "Jesus and John Wayne."

78 Du Mez, *Jesus and John Wayne*, book jacket flap, 233.

79 Ibid., 18.

80 The entire *New York Times* account can be accessed at "40,000 Cheer for War and Religion Mixed by Sunday," *New York Times*, April 9, 1917, https://timesmachine.nytimes.com/timesmachine/1917/04/09/102330865.html?pageNumber=1.

81 Du Mez, *Jesus and John Wayne*, [book jacket flap], 233.

82 "Foundational Values."

83 E.g., see John Piper and Wayne Grudem, *Recovering Biblical Manhood and Womanhood (Redesign): A Response to Evangelical Feminism* (Wheaton, IL: Crossway, 2012).

84 "Submission of Wives to Husbands," Focus on the Family, accessed December 7, 2021, https://www.focusonthefamily.com/family-qa/submission-of -wives-to-husbands/; emphasis original.

85 This has been a well-known insight of the battered women's movement for many decades. For more detail, see, e.g., Cooper-White, *Cry of Tamar*, 40–63.

86 Ibid.; emphasis original. See also "'Submission' May Not Mean What You Think It Means," Focus on the Family, August 20, 2018, https://www .focusonthefamily.com/marriage/submission-may-not-mean-what-you -think-it-means/, which softens the hierarchical emphasis on the husband's headship of the family by emphasizing the complementarity of roles within marriage—but reaffirms that "instead of sparking controversy and division between spouses, Ephesians 5:15–33 can unify couples as they conform to Christ's image."

87 For a concise handbook for victims of domestic violence in conservative Christian households, see Marie Fortune, *Keeping the Faith: A Guidebook for Christian Women Facing Abuse* (New York: HarperOne, 1995).

88 Terms first coined in Campbell-Reed, *Anatomy of a Schism*, 8.

89 Susan M. Shaw, "How Women in the Southern Baptist Convention Have Fought for Decades to Be Ordained," *Conversation*, June 1, 2021, https:// theconversation.com/how-women-in-the-southern-baptist-convention -have-fought-for-decades-to-be-ordained-161061.

90 Campbell-Reed, *Anatomy of a Schism*, 18.

91 "Resolution on Ordination and the Role of Women in Ministry," SBC, June 1, 1984, https://www.sbc.net/resource-library/resolutions/resolution -on-ordination-and-the-role-of-women-in-ministry/. See also Campbell-Reed, *Anatomy of a Schism*.

92 "Baptist Faith and Message 2000," SBC, accessed December 7, 2021, https:// bfm.sbc.net/bfm2000/#vi-the-church. See also Campbell-Reed, *Anatomy of a Schism*.

93 Shaw, "How Women"; Campbell-Reed, *Anatomy of a Schism*, 15.

94 Anthony Jordan et al., "Report of the Committee on Baptist Faith and Message: Final Version of the Report Presented and Approved at the 1998 SBC Convention," June 9, 1998, https://bfm.sbc.net/report-of-committee-on -baptist-faith-and-message/. The women signatories were Mary Mohler, wife of Al Mohler, identified in the document as "Homemaker and Director of the Seminary Wives Institute of The Southern Baptist Theological Seminary," and Dorothy Patterson, identified as "Homemaker and adjunct faculty member of Southeastern Baptist Theological Seminary."

95 Bob Smietana, "Saddleback Church Just Ordained Three Women as Pastors," *Washington Post*, May 11, 2021, https://www.washingtonpost.com/religion/ 2021/05/11/saddleback-ordain-women-sbc/.

96 Ibid.

97 Rick Warren, *The Purpose Driven Life: What on Earth Am I Here For?*, 2nd ed. (Grand Rapids, MI: Zondervan, 2002).

98 Smietana, "Saddleback Church."

99 Regarding Mohler, also see chapter 1.

100 R. Albert Mohler, "Women Pastors, Women Preachers, and the Looming Test of the Southern Baptist Convention," May 10, 2021, https://albertmohler .com/2021/05/10/women-pastors-women-preachers-and-the-looming-test -of-the-southern-baptist-convention; See also Smietana, "Moore Leaves Southern Baptist Leadership."

101 https://www.sbc.net/resource-library/resolutions/on-expanding-the-selective -service-to-include-women/. This reaffirmed the 2016 Southern Baptist Convention resolution "On Women Registering for the Draft," which made a further detailed statement about the complementarity of women and men. https://www.sbc.net/resource-library/resolutions/on-women-registering -for-the-draft/.

102 Founded by African American activist Tarana Burke, https://metoomvmt .org/get-to-know-us/tarana-burke-founder/, the movement went viral as celebrities and women leaders in business and politics adopted the hashtag #MeToo. See also Alix Langone, "#MeToo and Time's Up Founders Explain the Difference between the 2 Movements—and How They're Alike," *Time*, last modified March 22, 2018, https://time.com/5189945/whats-the -difference-between-the-metoo-and-times-up-movements/.

103 Southern Baptist Convention 2019 Annual Meeting, "On the Evil of Sexual Abuse," SBC, June 1, 2019, https://www.sbc.net/resource-library/resolutions/ on-the-evil-of-sexual-abuse/.

104 See chapter 1.

105 Paul O'Donnell and Bob Smietana, "Leaked Russell Moore Letter Blasts SBC Conservatives, Sheds Light on His Resignation," *Religion News Service*, June 2, 2021, https://religionnews.com/2021/06/02/leaked-russell-moore -letter-blasts-sbc-conservatives-sheds-light-on-his-resignation/; Adelle M. Banks, "Debates on Sex Abuse, Critical Race Theory Front and Center at First Day of SBC Meeting," *Religion News Service*, June 15, 2021, https:// religionnews.com/2021/06/15/southern-baptist-debates-on-sex-abuse -critical-race-theory-move-to-annual-meeting/.

106 Southern Baptist Convention 2019 Annual Meeting, "On Critical Race The-ory and Intersectionality," SBC, June 1, 2019, https://www.sbc.net/resource
-library/resolutions/on-critical-race-theory-and-intersectionality/. See also
Bob Smietana, "At Founders Event, Southern Baptists Urged to Choose
Bible over 'Paganism,' CRT," *Religion News Service*, June 15, 2021, https://
religionnews.com/2021/06/15/at-founders-event-southern-baptists-urged
-to-choose-the-bible-over-paganism-and-crt/.

107 Eileen Campbell-Reed, "The State of Clergywomen in the U.S.: A Statisti-cal Update," 2018, https://eileencampbellreed.org/state-of-clergy/download
-state-of-us-clergywomen/.

108 E.g., "What Percentage of Pastors Are Female?," Hartford Institute for Reli-gion Research, accessed December 6, 2021, http://hirr.hartsem.edu/research/
quick_question3.html. An overall percentage of evangelical churches must
include the SBC, which now has less than 1% women clergy, and other evan-gelical churches, such as the Reformed Church in America, which has 12%.
Campbell-Reed, "State of Clergywomen."

109 Eileen Campbell-Reed, personal communication, October 19, 2021.

110 Ibid.

111 Chanequa Walker-Barnes, *Too Heavy a Yoke: Black Women and the Burden
of Strength* (Eugene, OR: Cascade, 2014).

112 Originally built by Rev. Robert Schuller in Garden Grove, California, in
1980 as a flagship evangelical megachurch, the church building was bought
in 2019 to be consecrated as Christ Cathedral by the Catholic Diocese of
Orange.

113 Name changed for privacy.

114 Du Mez, *Jesus and John Wayne*, 237.

115 Women leaders are also now emerging among the far right in Europe, for
example, Marine Le Pen in France and Frauke Petry in Germany. See, e.g.,
Michaela Kottig, Renate Bitzan, and Andrea Petö, eds., *Gender and Far Right
Politics in Europe* (New York: Palgrave Macmillan, 2017), cited in Ben-Ghiat,
Strongmen, 251, 313n8; and Thomas Meaney, "The New Star of Germany's
Far Right," *New Yorker*, October 3, 2016, https://www.newyorker.com/
magazine/2016/10/03/the-new-star-of-germanys-far-right.

116 Petula Dvorak, "Why Are So Many Republican Women Holding Guns in Their
Campaign Ads?," *Washington Post*, May 10, 2021, https://www.washingtonpost
.com/local/why-are-so-many-republican-women-holding-guns-in-their
-campaign-ads/2021/05/10/656c387e-b1bf-11eb-ab43-bebddc5a0f65_story
.html.

117 Senator Kelly Loeffler compares herself to Attila the Hun in Kelly Loeffler, "Attila the Hun," September 21, 2020, YouTube video, https://www.youtube.com/watch?v=4pfvEFPvVGA.

118 Sudhin Thanawala, "Loeffler's Wealth, Trump Loyalty Face Scrutiny in Georgia," AP News, December 21, 2020, https://apnews.com/article/kelly-loeffler-georgia-senate-elections-7297622933c169ae093327e8b0e1ee75.

119 John Nichols, "Kelly Loeffler's Sacrilegious Campaign," *Nation*, December 29, 2020, https://www.thenation.com/article/politics/kelly-loeffler-lies/.

120 Marjorie Taylor Greene, "Marjorie Greene: Save America. Stop Socialism," April 6, 2020, Facebook video, https://www.facebook.com/watch/?v=357486375165667.

121 See also Dan Evon, "Did Marjorie Taylor Greene Pose with a Gun in Front of an Image of 'The Squad'?," Snopes fact check, September 4, 2020, https://www.snopes.com/fact-check/marjorie-taylor-greene-the-squad/.

122 Em Steck and Andrew Kaczynski, "Marjorie Taylor Greene Indicated Support for Executing Prominent Democrats . . . ," CNN, last modified January 26, 2021, https://www.cnn.com/2021/01/26/politics/marjorie-taylor-greene-democrats-violence/index.html.

123 PRRI Staff, "Understanding QAnon's Connection to American Politics, Religion, and Media," PRRI, May 27, 2021, https://www.prri.org/research/qanon-conspiracy-american-politics-report/.

124 These numbers do not add up to 100% because many gun owners cite multiple reasons. Kim Parker, Juliana Menasce Horowitz, Ruth Igielnik, J. Baxter Oliphant, and Anna Brown, "The Demographics of Gun Ownership," Pew Research Center, June 22, 2017, https://www.pewresearch.org/social-trends/2017/06/22/the-demographics-of-gun-ownership/.

125 Denker, *Red State Christians*, 75; emphasis added.

126 Ibid., 76.

127 Kim Parker, et al., "America's Complex Relationship With Guns," Pew Research Center, June 22, 2017, https://www.pewresearch.org/social-trends/2017/06/22/americas-complex-relationship-with-guns/, cited in Kate Shellnutt, "Packing in the Pews: The Connections between God and Guns," *Christianity Today*, November 8, 2017, https://www.christianitytoday.com/news/2017/november/god-gun-control-white-evangelicals-texas-church-shooting.html.

128 Robert Yamane, "Awash in a Sea of Faith and Firearms: Rediscovering the Connection between Religion and Gun Ownership in America," *Journal for the Scientific Study of Religion* 55 (2016): 622–36, https://www

.researchgate.net/publication/312410212_Awash_in_a_Sea_of_Faith_and
_Firearms_Rediscovering_the_Connection_Between_Religion_and_Gun
_Ownership_in_America_FAITH_AND_FIREARMS, based on the General Social Survey (GSS) data from 2006–14, cited in Stephen M. Merino, "God and Guns: Examining Religious Influences on Gun Control Attitudes in the United States," *Religions*, June 14, 2018, https://www.researchgate.net/publication/325776109_God_and_Guns_Examining_Religious_Influences_on_Gun_Control_Attitudes_in_the_United_States.

129 Merino, citing a 2012 PRRI study in "God and Guns," 7.

130 Merino, "God and Guns," 4.

131 Shane Claiborne and Michael Martin, *Beating Guns: Hope for People Who Are Weary of Violence* (Ada, MI: Brazos, 2019).

132 Eliza Griswold, "God, Guns, and Country: The Evangelical Fight over Firearms," *New Yorker*, April 19, 2019, https://www.newyorker.com/news/on-religion/god-guns-and-country-the-evangelical-fight-over-firearms.

133 Endorsed repeatedly by Donald Trump; e.g., see Post with Doucette, *Dangerous Charisma*, 117–19.

134 Jacob Paulsen, "Should I Conceal Carry in Church?," Concealedcarry.com, April 21, 2021, https://www.concealedcarry.com/law/concealed-carry-in-churches/.

135 Denker, *Red State Christians*, 60.

136 For more detail on the connection between evangelicals' "spiritual warfare" and right-wing conspiracy theories, see S. Jonathan O'Donnell, "Demons of the Deep State: How Evangelicals and Conspiracy Theories Combine in Trump's America," *Conversation*, September 14, 2020, https://theconversation.com/demons-of-the-deep-state-how-evangelicals-and-conspiracy-theories-combine-in-trumps-america-144898.

137 Goldberg, *Kingdom Coming*, 18; see also Du Mez, *Jesus and John Wayne*, 12–13.

138 Hofstadter, "Paranoid Style," 77.

139 Ibid., 86.

140 A delusion, clinically, is not just an irrational belief but one that is maintained unshakably in spite of all evidence to the contrary. The older psychoanalytic notion that schizophrenia is caused by poor parenting—the "schizophrenogenic mother"—has been largely discredited in favor of an understanding that schizophrenia and related mental illnesses, some forms of dementia, and delusional thinking caused by traumatic brain injury are disorders of the brain. However, an innate biological predisposition may

remain dormant until triggered by environmental factors such as abuse or other trauma. *Encyclopedia of Couple and Family Therapy*, ed. J. Lebow, A. Chambers, and D. Breunlin, s.v. "Schizophrenogenic Mother," by M. V. Seeman, December 28, 2016, https://doi.org/10.1007/978-3-319-15877-8_482-1.

141 Goldberg, *Kingdom Coming*, 22.

142 Hannah Arendt quoted in ibid.

143 E.g., David Brooks, "One Nation, Slightly Divisible," *Atlantic*, December 2001, https://www.theatlantic.com/magazine/archive/2001/12/one-nation-slightly-divisible/376441/; James E. Campbell, *Polarized: Making Sense of a Divided America* (Princeton, NJ: Princeton University Press, 2018); George Packer, "How America Fractured into Four Parts," *Atlantic*, July/August 2021, https://www.theatlantic.com/magazine/archive/2021/07/george-packer-four-americas/619012/; George Packer, *Last Best Hope: America in Crisis and Renewal* (New York: Farrar, Straus & Giroux, 2021); and Seth David Radwell, *American Schism* (Austin, TX: Greenleaf, 2021).

144 Michael Sherer, "President Trump Struggles to Play Role of National Healer after Charlottesville," *Time*, August 12, 2017, https://time.com/4898422/charlottesville-white-nationalist-donald-trump/.

145 "Two Years Ago, They Marched in Charlottesville. Where Are They Now?," August 8, 2019, ADL, https://www.adl.org/blog/two-years-ago-they-marched-in-charlottesville-where-are-they-now. See also "The New Hate and the Old: The Changing Face of American White Supremacy," ADL, September 2018, https://www.adl.org/new-hate-and-old-the-changing-face-of-american-white-supremacy-report.

146 "FBI Reports an Increase in Hate Crimes in 2019: Hate-Based Murders More than Doubled," Southern Poverty Law Center, November 16, 2020, https://www.splcenter.org/news/2020/11/16/fbi-reports-increase-hate-crimes-2019-hate-based-murders-more-doubled.

147 Kaleigh Rogers, "Why QAnon Has Attracted So Many White Evangelicals," FiveThirtyEight/ABC News, March 4, 2021, https://fivethirtyeight.com/features/why-qanon-has-attracted-so-many-white-evangelicals/.

148 Ibid.

149 Ibid. See also Jaweed Kaleem, "QAnon and Other Conspiracy Theories Are Taking Hold in Churches. Pastors Are Fighting Back," *LA Times*, March 3, 2021, https://www.latimes.com/world-nation/story/2021-03-03/la-na-church-qanon-conspiracy-theories.

150 PRRI Staff, "Understanding QAnon."

151 Anna North, "White Women's Role in White Supremacy, Explained," *Vox*, January 15, 2021, https://www.vox.com/2021/1/15/22231079/capitol-riot -women-qanon-white-supremacy.

152 Marjorie Greene, "MUST READ—Democratic Party Involved with Child Sex, Satanism, and the Occult," American Truth Seekers, September 15, 2017, https://web.archive.org/web/20170924120108/http://americantruthseekers .com/must-read-democratic-party-involved-with-child-sex-satanism-and -the-occult. "MSM" refers to the "mainstream media."

153 "Marjorie Taylor Greene," Ballotpedia, accessed December 7, 2021, https:// ballotpedia.org/Marjorie_Taylor_Greene. The 14th District in the far north-west of Georgia is a Republican stronghold, with roughly three-quarters of voters reliably supporting Republican candidates. "Congressional District 14, GA," Data USA, accessed December 7, 2021, https://datausa.io/profile/ geo/congressional-district-14-ga. See also Michael Kranish, Reis Thebault, and Stephanie McCrummen, "How Marjorie Taylor Greene, Promoter of QAnon's Baseless Theories, Rose with Support from Key Republications," *Washington Post*, January 30, 2021, https://www.washingtonpost.com/ politics/greene-qanon-house-trump-republicans/2021/01/30/321b4258 -623c-11eb-ac8f-4ae05557196e_story.html.

154 Luo, "Wasting of the Evangelical Mind."

155 E.g., Fortune, *Keeping the Faith*; Cooper-White, *Cry of Tamar*; Cooper-White, *Gender, Violence, and Justice: Collected Essays on Violence against Women* (Eugene, OR: Cascade, 2019); and Catherine Clark Kroeger and Nancy Nason-Clark, *No Place for Abuse: Biblical Practical Resources to Counteract Domestic Violence* (Westmont, IL: IVP, 2010).

156 United Nations Office on Drugs and Crime, *Fifth Global Report on Trafficking in Persons* (Vienna: UNODC Research, 2020), https://www.unodc.org/ unodc/data-and-analysis/glotip.html; full report at https://www.unodc .org/documents/data-and-analysis/tip/2021/GLOTiP_2020_15jan_web.pdf.

157 United Nations Office on Drugs and Crime, "2020: A Year in Review: Human Trafficking and Migrant Smuggling Section," press release, Vienna, Austria, April 13, 2021, https://www.unodc.org/unodc/en/human -trafficking/Webstories2021/2020-annual-report-human-trafficking-and -migrant-smuggling-section.html. About 50,000 victims of smuggling were reported in the year 2018, and many more go unreported each year. About 50% are women trafficked mainly for sex (including forced marriage, and some also for domestic work), and another 20% are girls; the other 30% of trafficking victims are men and boys sold mainly into forced labor but also

for sex slavery. A small percentage of both women and men are trafficked for other purposes, including organ removal, child soldiers, debt bondage, and forced begging.

158 "New UN Report Reveals Impact of COVID on Human Trafficking," UN News, July 8, 2021, https://news.un.org/en/story/2021/07/1095472.

159 Seyward Darby, *Sisters in Hate: American Women and White Extremism* (New York: Little, Brown, 2020), quoted in Susan Shaw, "The Women of the Insurrection," *Ms. Magazine*, February 9, 2021, https://msmagazine .com/2021/02/09/trump-women-capitol-insurrection-riot-funding; see also North, "White Women's Role."

160 Darby quoted in Shaw, "Women of the Insurrection."

161 Ibid.

162 Kathleen M. Blee, *Inside Organized Racism: Women in the Hate Movement* (Berkeley: University of California Press, 2002).

163 This tendency to shut down opposing viewpoints, it should be noted, reflects a larger "illiberalism" and divisiveness across the entire US political spectrum, as described in Anne Applebaum, "The New Puritans," *Atlantic*, August 31, 2021, 60–70, https://www.theatlantic.com/magazine/archive/2021/ 10/new-puritans-mob-justice-canceled/619818/.

164 Shaw, "Women of the Insurrection."

165 See also Bandy X. Lee on the role of Fox News and right-wing media as mind control. Lee, *Profile of a Nation*, 102–7.

166 See, e.g., Post with Doucette, *Dangerous Charisma*, 135–64. Post gives examples of numerous tweets, retweets, and public statements by Donald Trump that endorsed hate speech against people of color, LGBTQ persons, Muslims, immigrants, and Jews. For statistical corroboration, see Daniel Villarreal, "Hate Crimes under Trump Surged Nearly 20 Percent Says FBI Report," *Newsweek*, November 16, 2020, https://www.newsweek.com/hate-crimes -under-trump-surged-nearly-20-percent-says-fbi-report-1547870.

167 Villarreal, "Hate Crimes."

168 For more about elements of Freud's theories that have continuing relevance, see Pamela Cooper-White, "A Critical Tradition: Psychoanalysis," in *Pastoral Psychology and Psychology of Religion in Dialogue: Implications*, ed. Isabelle Noth, Christoph Morgenthaler, and Kathleen J. Greider (Stuttgart, Germany: Kohlhammer Verlag, 2011), 41–68.

169 Sigmund Freud, *Group Psychology and the Analysis of the Ego*, in *The Standard Edition of the Complete Psychological Works of Sigmund Freud*, vol. 18, ed. and trans. James Strachey (London: Hogarth, 1955), 65–144.

170 Pamela Cooper-White, *Old and Dirty Gods: Religion, Antisemitism, and the Origins of Psychoanalysis* (London: Routledge, 2018), esp. 1–17, 215–74.

171 Gustave Le Bon, *The Crowd: A Study of the Popular Mind* (Mineola, NY: Dover, 2001).

172 Ibid., quoted in Freud, *Group Psychology*, 72–73.

173 C. G. Jung, *Archetypes and the Collective Unconscious*, Collected Works of C. G. Jung, vol. 9, no. 1, trans. R. F. C. Hull (Princeton, NJ: Princeton University Press, 1981).

174 Freud, *Group Psychology*, 74.

175 Ibid., 77n1.

176 Ibid., 78.

177 For those who are familiar with Freud's tripartite or so-called structural model of mind—ego, id, and superego—the superego together with the ego ideal create a "conscience" in the ego. The superego, however, is often harsher, trying to stop the id—the repository of the drives of sex and aggression—from wreaking havoc. The superego is an internalization of the parental "no," whereas the ego ideal, it might be said, is more an internalization of the parental "yes." When the superego is too dominant, the result is neurotic guilt, whereas a sense of oneness with one's inner ego ideal gives a feeling of fulfillment, even a temporary state of ecstasy.

178 See Freud's graphic representation of this in Freud, *Group Psychology*, 116.

179 The first two phrases are from Post with Doucette, *Dangerous Charisma*, xxii, 81. Shaw elaborates on this pathological symbiosis in Shaw, *Traumatic Narcissism*. "The spell cast by persons" is from Ernest Becker, *The Denial of Death* (New York: Free Press, 1973), ch. 7, cited in Shaw, *Traumatic Narcissism*, 47.

180 Freud, *Group Psychology*, 123.

181 Ibid., 124.

182 E.g., Heinz Kohut, "Forms and Transformations of Narcissism," *Journal of the American Psychoanalytic Association* 14 (1966): 243–72; Heinz Kohut, *The Analysis of the Self* (New York: International Universities Press, 1971); and Heinz Kohut, *The Restoration of the Self* (New York: International Universities Press, 1977).

183 Post with Doucette, *Dangerous Charisma*, xix.

184 Ibid., xx–xxi.

185 Kohut, *Restoration of the Self*.

186 Ibid. Kohut also identified a third "selfobject" need beyond mirroring and idealizing, which he identified as the "alter-ego" or "twinship" need—to find

someone like oneself. This need is another way of accounting for the need for belonging discussed earlier in this chapter. Kohut, *Analysis of the Self*, 115.

187 Post with Doucette, *Dangerous Charisma*, 80; see also 107–8.

188 Singer, *Cults in Our Midst*, 25–27.

189 Post with Doucette, *Dangerous Charisma*, xxiii.

190 Singer, *Cults in Our Midst*, 15.

191 Ibid., 17.

192 Ibid., 15–20.

193 Ibid., 25.

194 Ibid., 27.

195 Ben-Ghiat, *Strongmen*, 70.

196 Michelle Boorstein, "For Some Christians, the Capitol Riot Doesn't Change the Prophecy: Trump Will Be President," *Washington Post*, January 14, 2021, https://www.washingtonpost.com/religion/2021/01/14/prophets-apostles -christian-prophesy-trump-won-biden-capitol/.

197 Jack Beresford, "Billboard Hailing Donald Trump as Second Coming of Jesus Appears in Georgia," *Newsweek*, September 14, 2021, https://www .msn.com/en-us/news/politics/billboard-hailing-donald-trump-as-second -coming-of-jesus-appears-in-georgia/ar-AAOqxEH?ocid=msedgdhp&pc= U531; To view the original billboard image posted on Twitter, see Relevant, @Relevant, September 17, 2021, https://www.relevantmagazine.com/current/ a-billboard-featuring-donald-trump-as-the-second-coming-of-jesus-has -been-taken-down/.

198 Goldberg, *Kingdom Coming*, 59.

199 The term *guru* is used here pejoratively, but it is a legitimate title of respect for a spiritual teacher in Hinduism and Buddhism, and should not automat- ically be equated with a cult leader.

200 Robert Jay Lifton, *Losing Reality: On Cults, Cultism, and the Mindset of Political and Religious Zealotry* (New York: New Press, 2019), 4.

201 Ibid., 5.

202 Peter L. Berger and Thomas Luckmann, *The Social Construction of Reality: A Treatise in the Sociology of Knowledge* (New York: Anchor, 1967).

203 Lifton, *Losing Reality*, 1.

204 Wilfred Bion, a founder of unconscious group theory, describes healthy "work groups" versus pathological "basic assumption groups" in Wilfred Bion, *Experiences in Groups* (London: Tavistock, 1951). Post also cites psy- choanalyst Vamik D. Volkan and historian Norman Itzkowitz, who have identified a form of "reparative charismatic leadership" in which the leader

heals his own narcissistic wounding by "resolving splits in a wounded society," in Vamik D. Volkan, Norman Itzkowitz, and Andrew W. Dod, *Richard Nixon: A Psychobiography* (New York: Columbia University Press, 1999), 133, quoted in Post with Doucette, *Dangerous Charisma*, 83. See also Volkan, "Narcissistic Personality Organization and 'Reparative' Leadership," *International Journal of Group Psychology* 30 (1980): 131–52, https://doi.org/10.1080/00207284.1980.11491677.

205 E.g., Thaler outlines five stages, from education to thought reform in Singer, *Cults in Our Midst*, 58–59.

206 Ibid., 8.

207 Lifton prefers this term to "narcissism" because he wants to highlight the element of cognitive distortion over and above the libidinal attachment to oneself as in classical psychoanalytic definitions of narcissism. Lifton, *Losing Reality*, 156.

208 Post with Doucette, *Dangerous Charisma*, 81, citing Garrett Fagan, *The Lure of the Arena: Social Psychology and the Crowd at the Roman Games* (Cambridge: Cambridge University Press, 2011).

209 Lifton, *Losing Reality*, 153, 154.

210 Singer, *Cults in Our Midst*, 153–56; see also Ben-Ghiat, *Strongmen*, 102–6, on authoritarian leaders' use of voice and political theater to spread propaganda and influence crowds.

211 Singer, *Cults in Our Midst*, 155.

212 Lifton, *Losing Reality*, 161.

213 Ibid., 156.

214 For a detailed account of Trump's increasingly erratic behavior while in office, see Carol Leonnig and Philip Rucker, *I Alone Can Fix It: Donald J. Trump's Catastrophic Final Year* (New York: Penguin, 2021); see also Robert Woodward, *Rage* (New York: Simon & Schuster, 2020).

215 See also Ben-Ghiat, *Strongmen*, 116.

216 https://www.msn.com/en-us/news/politics/donald-trump-jan-6-rally-before-capitol-riot-had-love-in-the-air-ive-never-seen-anything-like-it/ar-AAM41ke. As of this writing, Trump is still publicly defending the January 6 insurrectionists, and his most ardent supporters have organized protests against the arrests of those who participated on that day. Alan Feuer, "Debunking the Pro-Trump Right's Claims about Jan. 6 Riot," *New York Times*, September 18, 2021, https://www.nytimes.com/2021/09/17/us/politics/capitol-riot-pro-trump-claims.html.

217 Stephanie Russell-Kraft, "Can Religion Give You PTSD? Meet the 'Exvangelicals' Seeking Therapy for Religious Trauma," *New Republic*, March 23,

2021. See also Marjorie Winell, "Religious Trauma Syndrome," Journey Free, accessed December 7, 2021, https://journeyfree.org/rts/.

218 There is a large and growing clinical literature on the nature of trauma. For a foundational text, see Bessel Van der Kolk, *The Body Keeps the Score: Brain, Mind, and Body in the Healing of Trauma* (New York: Penguin, 2014).

219 D. W. Winnicott, "The Theory of the Parent-Infant Relationship (1960)," in *The Maturational Processes and the Facilitating Environment*, ed. D. W. Winnicott (London: Routledge, 2018).

220 John Bowlby, *A Secure Base: Parent-Child Attachment and Healthy Human Development* (London: Routledge, 1988).

221 Erik Erikson, *Childhood and Society* (New York: W. W. Norton, 1950), 247–50.

222 Harry Harlow, "The Nature of Love," *American Psychologist* 13, no. 1 (1958): 673–85.

223 E.g., Richard McNally, *Remembering Trauma* (Cambridge, MA: Harvard University Press, 2003); see also Shaw, *Traumatic Narcissism*.

224 Shaw elaborates on this pathological symbiosis in Shaw, *Traumatic Narcissism*, throughout.

225 Biblical scholars have interpreted the apocalyptic genre in both the Hebrew Bible and the New Testament as the expression of hope of an oppressed people—we could even say, as the product of collective trauma, as explored in e.g., Kathleen O'Connor, *Jeremiah: Pain and Promise* (Minneapolis: Fortress, 2012); David Carr, *Holy Resilience: The Bible's Traumatic Origins* (New Haven, CT: Yale University Press, 2014); Wil Gafney, "Crucifixion and Sexual Violence," HuffPost, March 28, 2013, https://www.huffpost.com/entry/crucifixion-and-sexual-violence_b_2965369; and Jayme R. Reaves, David Tombs, and Rocio Figueroa, *When Did We See You Naked? Jesus as a Victim of Sexual Abuse* (London: SCM, 2021).

226 On gender-based violence and power dynamics, see Cooper-White, *Cry of Tamar*, 40–63.

Chapter 3

1 Alexander, *New Jim Crow*.

2 Pamela Cooper-White, "Epilogue: Reflections on Irony and Eschatological Hope," in *Postcolonial Images of Spiritual Care*, ed. Hellena Moon and Emmanuel Lartey, vol. 2 (New York: Routledge, 2021).

3 A phrase from the oath of office required of all federal employees, including the military. https://www.law.cornell.edu/uscode/text/5/3331.

4 Charles Blow, "What Unity?," *New York Times*, January 13, 2021, https://www.nytimes.com/2021/01/13/opinion/trump-impeachment-unity.html.

5 https://apnews.com/article/capitol-siege-trump-misinformation-aa051fa751d718407638dbe308647a7a. Dolores Albarracin is co-author, with Julia Albarracin, Man-Pui Sally Chan, and Kathleen Hall Jamieson, of *Creating Conspiracy Beliefs: How Our Thoughts Are Shaped* (Cambridge: Cambridge University Press, 2021).

6 Bandy X. Lee, ed. *The Dangerous Case of Donald Trump: 37 Psychiatrists and Mental Health Experts Assess a President*, 2nd ed. (New York: Macmillan, 2019); see also Lee, *Profile of a Nation*, 1–11, 109–10, 149–51.

7 Lee, *Profile of a Nation*, 1–11, 109–10, 142, 149–51.

8 Lee also uses this metaphor, but for a somewhat different goal—she is speaking of triage in terms of reducing the influence of Donald Trump and the "cultic programming" of the right wing.

9 Anne Applebaum, "Coexistence Is the Only Option," *Atlantic*, January 20, 2021, https://www.theatlantic.com/ideas/archive/2021/01/seditionists-need-path-back-society/617746/.

10 Singer, *Cults in Our Midst*, 290.

11 Andrew Gardner, "Why Are Christians So Susceptible to Conspiracy?," *Baptist News Global*, August 31, 2021, https://baptistnews.com/article/why-are-christians-so-susceptible-to-conspiracy/#.YWCBWtrMI2z.

12 Brian Klaas, "Why Is It So Hard to Deprogram Trumpian Conspiracy Theorists?," *Washington Post*, January 25, 2021, https://www.washingtonpost.com/opinions/2021/01/25/why-is-it-so-hard-deprogram-trumpian-conspiracy-theorists/.

13 Melissa Graves, "The U.S. Needs Deradicalization—for Christian Extremists," *Foreign Policy*, March 3, 2021, https://foreignpolicy.com/2021/03/23/usa-needs-qanon-deradicalization-christian-extremists/.

14 Lee, *Profile of a Nation*, 143. She also elaborates on "intervention at the level of society" (144–48). Applebaum, "Coexistence," also notes the need for there to be meaningful solutions to unemployment or underemployment, and longer-term training and counseling "offering former outcasts the hope of a positive future, and . . . help to [re-]assimilate."

15 See also Lauren Alpert Maurer, "Welcome Diverse Perspectives," Open-Mind Lesson #4, November 11, 2020, https://openmindplatform.org/library/welcome-diverse-perspectives/. Some helpful signs for recognizing when

conversation could be unproductive or even harmful include when the other is acting in bad faith just to provoke or harass you; when the other is purposely creating misinformation (as opposed to simply having fallen prey to it); when the other has power or authority over you so it isn't a level playing field; or when you might be risking your safety.

16 E.g., Tom Wolff, introduction to "Community Coalition Building—Contemporary Practice and Research," *American Journal of Community Psychology* 2 (2001): 165–72, 205–11. Earlier organizing models, such as in Saul Alinsky, *Rules for Radicals* (New York: Random House, 1971), emphasized coalition building through identifying a common enemy; some contemporary models continue to follow this strategy, while some others tend to lean more toward common interests.

17 Publius Terentius Afer, *The Self-Tormentor (Heautontimorumenos)*, trans. Frederick W. Ricord (New York: Charles Scribner's Sons, 1885), act 1, scene 1, p. 25, https://archive.org/details/selftormentorhea00rico?view=theater #page/24/mode/2up. "*Homo sum: humani nihil a me alienum puto.*"

18 For this reason, I do not entirely agree with Charles Yu's recommendation of engaging in "tradecraft," although I agree with him that "frontal assaults" will not work. He writes, "Get behind their lines, live among them, learn the language. Gain an understanding of their world, not as a citizen but as an informed visitor. Differentiate between those controlling the narrative and those consuming it. Remember that the consumers include our neighbors, co-workers, friends, and family. Understand that the goal is not destruction but reunification, that engagement does not have to be about politics or religion. We don't have to agree on everything, or even on most things. Just that we are one country, not two. And that our country exists in the real world." Becoming a participant observer, as anthropologists would call it—or, more concerning, an infiltrator and "asset developer"—will only be helpful to the extent that the desire to understand, and to form real relationships, is genuine and not merely strategic. See Yu, "Reality."

19 Robin J. DiAngelo, *White Fragility: Why It's So Hard for White People to Talk about Racism* (Boston: Beacon, 2018).

20 Cathy Park Hong, *Minor Feelings: An Asian American Reckoning* (New York: One World, 2020), 82–83.

21 DiAngelo, *White Fragility*, 131; see also Ruby Hamad, *White Tears/Brown Scars, How White Feminism Betrays Women of Color* (New York: Catapult, 2020).

22 Hong, *Minor Feelings*, 83.

23 For some helpful and accessible ways of understanding more about this re-
    action, see, e.g., Lauren Alpert Maurer, "Explore the Inner Workings of the
    Mind," OpenMind Lesson #1, November 2, 2020, https://openmindplatform
    .org/library/explore-the-inner-workings-of-the-mind/. OpenMind uses a help-
    ful (and easily remembered) metaphor of a rider and an elephant (a model
    first developed by social psychologist and OpenMind cofounder Jonathan
    Haidt in *The Righteous Mind: Why Good People Are Divided by Politics and
    Religion* [New York: Pantheon, 2012]). The rider is the part of ourselves that
    is guided by our rational thinking function, and the elephant is the part
    of ourselves that is controlled by our emotions, intuitions, and autonomic
    physical reactions. OpenMind offers some helpful tools for helping the rider
    regain control of the reins. The neuroscience behind their recommendations
    also supports the earlier psychoanalytic insight that the ego thinks it is con-
    trol but is often influenced by the unconscious "Id" drives of sex and ag-
    gression (survival instincts) as well as repressed traumatic experiences, or,
    in other branches of psychoanalysis, by unconscious needs for attachment,
    power, recognition, and so on. Later lessons in the online training involve
    insights from cognitive behavioral therapy and guidance on replacing auto-
    matic or irrational beliefs with more realistic assessments of situations.

24 E.g., Nancy Henley, *Body Politics: Power, Sex, and Nonverbal Communica-
    tion* (New York: Prentice-Hall, 1977); Robin Tolmach Lakoff, *Language and
    Woman's Place* (New York: Oxford University Press, 2004); Deborah Tan-
    nen, "The Power of Talk: Who Gets Heard and Why," *Harvard Business Re-
    view*, September–October 1995, https://hbr.org/1995/09/the-power-of-talk
    -who-gets-heard-and-why.

25 Carl R. Rogers, *Becoming a Person: A Therapist's View of Psychotherapy* (Bos-
    ton: Houghton Mifflin, 1995).

26 https://imagorelationships.org/; see also Harville Hendrix and Helen La-
    Kelly Hunt, *Getting the Love You Want: A Guide for Couples*, 3rd ed. (New
    York: St. Martin's, 2019).

27 Described in Nellie Bowles, "How to Get Trump Voters and Liberals to Talk:
    Don't Make Anyone Sit in a Circle," *New York Times*, November 3, 2019,
    https://www.nytimes.com/2019/11/03/us/trump-voters-liberals.html; and An-
    drew Ferguson, "Can Marriage Counseling Save America?," *Atlantic*, De-
    cember 2019, https://www.theatlantic.com/magazine/archive/2019/12/better
    -angels-can-this-union-be-saved/600775/. Regarding an approach to serious
    group conversation, see also Priya Parker, *The Art of Gathering: How We
    Meet and Why It Matters* (New York: Riverhead, 2018). Thanks to Laine C.

Walters Young for introducing me to Parker's work at the Society for Pastoral Theology annual meeting on June 18, 2021.

28 "Our Leadership," Braver Angels, accessed December 7, 2021, https://braver angels.org/our-story/#leadership. See also Ferguson, "Marriage Counseling."

29 "Helping Loved Ones Divided by Politics," Braver Angels, accessed December 7, 2021, https://braverangels.org/calling-family-members-divided-by-politics/.

30 Pamela Cooper-White, *Shared Wisdom: Use of the Self in Pastoral Care and Counseling* (Minneapolis: Fortress, 2004), 35–60. See also Berger and Luckmann, *Social Construction of Reality*; Kenneth Gergen, *An Invitation to Social Construction*, 3rd ed. (Los Angeles: Sage, 2015). For more detail on positivism, postpositivism, and social constructivism as models of knowledge, see Egon Guba, ed., *The Paradigm Dialog* (Newbury Park, CA: Sage, 1990).

31 E.g., Hans-Georg Gadamer, *Truth and Method*, 2nd ed., trans. Joel Weinsheimer and Donald G. Marshall (London: Bloomsbury Academic, 2013), 313–17.

32 Lauren Alpert Maurer, "Cultivate Intellectual Humility," OpenMind Lesson #3, November 9, 2020, https://openmindplatform.org.

33 I originally thought this saying came from the Buddhist teacher Pema Chödrön, but I now find that it is repeated by numerous Buddhist and other spiritual writers, e.g., Bhikshuni Thubten Chodron, *Don't Believe Everything You Think: Living Wisdom and Compassion* (Ithaca, NY: Snow Lion, 2013); and even quoted from a bumper sticker in Robert Fulghum, *Everything I Needed to Know I Learned in Kindergarten*, 15th anniversary ed. (New York: Ballantine, 2003), iii.

34 Joshua Greene, *Moral Tribes: Emotion, Reason, and the Gap Between Us and Them* (New York: Penguin, 2013), 335, citing Haidt, *Righteous Mind*.

35 Haidt, *Righteous Mind*, 109–216.

36 Ibid., 214.

37 Steps toward understanding another's moral foundations are outlined in Lauren Alpert Maurer, "Explore Other Worldviews," OpenMind Lesson #5, November 11, 2020, https://openmindplatform.org/.

38 Lee, *Profile of a Nation*, 142–43.

39 Lauren Alpert Maurer, "Uncover the Roots of Our Differences," OpenMind Lesson #2, November 3, 2020, https://openmindplatform.org/.

40 For statistics on prevalence and appropriate forms of prevention and intervention, see, e.g., Cooper-White, *Cry of Tamar*; and Cooper-White, *Gender, Violence, and Justice*.

41 Murray Bowen, *Family Therapy in Clinical Practice* (Lanham, MD: Rowman & Littlefield, 2004), 109.

42 Singer, *Cults in Our Midst*, 15–20.

43 Kendi, *How to Be an Antiracist*.

44 I do not agree with Kendi that persons of color can be racist if racism is more than skin-color prejudice but is, in fact, prejudice wedded to power and privilege. Racism, I have been taught, is prejudice *plus power*, for example in Crossroads, accessed December 7, 2021, https://crossroadsantiracism .org/.

45 Ross, "Don't Call People Out." Ross is currently writing a book entitled *Calling In the Calling Out Culture: Detoxing Our Movement* (New York: Simon & Schuster, forthcoming, 2022).

46 Jessica Bennett, "What If Instead of Calling People Out, We Called Them In?," interview with Loretta Ross, *New York Times*, November 19, 2020, last modified February 24, 2021, https://www.nytimes.com/2020/11/19/style/loretta -ross-smith-college-cancel-culture.html. Unfortunately, this term—like "political correctness," "cancel culture," and so many others—has become a pejorative used so frequently in conservative circles that the original usefulness of the term is often obscured. Kishundra D. King has also noted that "calling out" is more harshly criticized when it is done by people of color in a discussion during Laine Walters Young, "Dinner Conversation and the Art of Calling In as Pastoral Care," Society for Pastoral Theology Annual Study Conference (online), June 18, 2021, livestream.

47 DiAngelo, *Nice Racism*.

48 Adrienne Maree Brown, "What Is/Isn't Transformative Justice?," Wordpress blog post, July 9, 2015, http://adriennemareebrown.net/2015/07/09/what -isisnt-transformative-justice/. See also Adrienne Maree Brown, *We Will Not Cancel Us: And Other Dreams of Transformative Justice* (Chico, CA: AK, 2020), cited in Young, "Dinner Conversation."

49 Brown, *We Will Not Cancel Us*, cited in Young, "Dinner Conversation."

50 Ibid.

51 Bennett, "What If Instead."

52 Ibid.; Ross, "Don't Call People Out."

53 Ross, "Don't Call People Out," 02:02.

54 Ibid., 05:23.

55 Serene Jones, "Both Love, Justice Required in Dealing with Capitol Mob," Allotsego.com, January 14, 2021, https://www.allotsego.com/both-love-justice -required-in-dealing-with-capitol-mob/.

56 Thandeka, *Learning to Be White: Money, Race and God in America* (New York: Continuum, 2000), 14.

57 Ibid.

58 Cooper-White, *Gender, Violence, and Justice.*

59 Parker Palmer, "Circle of Trust Approach," Center for Courage and Renewal, http://couragerenewal.org/approach/.

60 Julie Kohler, "How Calls to 'Love Your Enemies' Enforce the Status Quo," *Washington Post*, June 6, 2019, https://www.washingtonpost.com/outlook/2019/06/06/how-calls-love-your-enemies-enforce-status-quo/.

61 Blow, "What Unity?"

62 Kohler, "How Calls."

63 Ibid.

64 Beverly W. Harrison, "The Power of Anger in the Work of Love," *Union Seminary Quarterly Review* 36 (1981): 41–57; reprinted in Harrison, *Making the Connections: Essays in Feminist Social Ethics* (Boston: Beacon, 1986).

65 E.g., Andrew Perrin, "23% of Users in U.S. Say Social Media Led Them to Change Views on an Issue; Some Cite Black Lives Matter," Pew Research Center, October 15, 2020, https://www.pewresearch.org/fact-tank/2020/10/15/23-of-users-in-us-say-social-media-led-them-to-change-views-on-issue-some-cite-black-lives-matter/. In the same article, 76% of Americans said their views did not change because of social media, but this was down from 84% just two years before. And of course, change can be either positive or negative.

66 Nicholas Portuondo, "Family and Friends May Decide Whether You Vote or Not, According to New Nonvoter Survey," Medill News Service, December 15, 2020, https://dc.medill.northwestern.edu/blog/2020/12/15/family-and-friends-may-decide-whether-you-vote-or-not-according-to-new-nonvoter-survey/#sthash.CcEX9jvG.dpbs.

67 The term *op-ed* comes from the first such column, published in the New York Times in 1970, where local citizens could submit essays on the page opposite the editorial page (featuring editorials by professional journalists). Mike Cummings, "Study Shows Newspaper Op-Eds Change Minds," *Yale News*, April 24, 2018, https://news.yale.edu/2018/04/24/study-shows-newspaper-op-eds-change-minds.

68 Ibid. For the full study, see Alexander Coppock, Emily Ekins, and David Kirby, "The Long-Lasting Effects of Op-Eds on Public Opinion," *Quarterly Journal of Political Science* 13, no. 1 (March 29, 2018): 59–87, https://www.nowpublishers.com/article/Details/QJPS-16112.

69 Michael Cooper-White, "Do We Make Any Difference?," *Gettysburg Times*, August 2, 2021, A4, https://www.gettysburgtimes.com/opinion/staff _columns/article_49a85428-859c-5faf-bfdd-7b2f7a776586.html.

70 Jim Forest, *Writing Straight with Crooked Lines: A Memoir* (New York: Orbis, 2020), 148–49.

71 Lifton, *Losing Reality*, 189.

72 Ibid., 190.

73 Bennett, "What If Instead"; Ross, "Don't Call People Out."

74 Singer, *Cults in Our Midst*, 274.

75 Ibid., 77–79.

76 Ibid., 276.

77 Rev. Skip Johnson, personal communication, Columbia Theological Seminary, Decatur, GA, 2014.

78 Kohler, "How Calls."

79 Pamela Cooper-White, "The 'Other' Within: Multiple Selves Making a World of Difference," ch. 7 in Cooper-White, *Braided Selves*, 156–70.